EX LIBRIS

VINTAGE CLASSICS

D1586322

EX LIBRIS

REFLECTIONS

Graham Greene was born in 1904. On coming down from Balliol College, Oxford, he worked for four years as sub-editor on *The Times*. He established his reputation with his fourth novel, *Stamboul Train*. In 1935 he made a journey across Liberia, described in *Journey Without Maps*, and on his return was appointed film critic of the *Spectator*. In 1926 he had been received into the Roman Catholic Church and visited Mexico in 1938 to report on the religious persecution there. As a result he wrote *The Lawless Roads* and, later, his famous novel *The Power and the Glory*. *Brighton Rock* was published in 1938 and in 1940 he became literary editor of the *Spectator*. The next year he undertook work for the Foreign Office and was stationed in Sierra Leone from 1941 to 1943. This later produced the novel *The Heart of the Matter*, set in West Africa.

As well as his many novels, Graham Greene wrote several collections of short stories, four travel books, six plays, two books of autobiography – *A Sort of Life* and *Ways of Escape* – two of biography and four books for children. He also contributed hundreds of essays, and film and book reviews, some of which appear in the collections *Reflections* and *Mornings in the Dark*. Many of his novels and short stories have been filmed and *The Third Man* was written as a film treatment. Graham Greene was a member of the Order of Merit and a Companion of Honour. He died in April 1991.

ALSO BY GRAHAM GREENE

Novels
The Man Within
Stamboul Train
It's a Battlefield
England Made Me
A Gun for Sale
Brighton Rock
The Confidential Agent
The Power and the Glory
The Ministry of Fear
The Heart of the Matter
The Third Man
The End of the Affair
Loser Takes All
The Quiet American
Our Man in Havana
A Burnt-Out Case
The Comedians
Travels with My Aunt
The Honorary Consul
The Human Factor
Doctor Fischer of Geneva or The Bomb Party
Monsignor Quixote
The Tenth Man
The Captain and the Enemy

Short stories
Collected Stories
Twenty-One Stories
A Sense of Reality
May We Borrow Your Husband?
The Last Word and Other Stories

Travel
Journey Without Maps
The Lawless Roads
In Search of a Character
Getting to Know the General

Essays
Collected Essays
The Pleasure Dome
British Dramatists
J'accuse
Yours etc

Plays
The Living Room
The Potting Shed
The Complaisant Lover
Carving a Statue
The Return of A. J. Raffles
The Great Jowett
Yes and No
For Whom the Bell Chimes

Autobiography
A Sort of Life
Ways of Escape
A World of My Own

Biography
Lord Rochester's Monkey
An Impossible Woman

Children's Books
The Little Train
The Little Horse-Bus
The Little Steamroller
The Little Fire Engine

GRAHAM GREENE

REFLECTIONS

SELECTED AND INTRODUCED BY
JUDITH ADAMSON

VINTAGE BOOKS
London

Published by Vintage 2014

2 4 6 8 10 9 7 5 3 1

Selection and introduction © Judith Adamson, 1990, 2014
Graham Greene's essays, reviews, poems and
diary extracts © Graham Greene, 1990, 2014

This book is sold subject to the condition that it shall not,
by way of trade or otherwise, be lent, resold, hired out,
or otherwise circulated without the publisher's prior
consent in any form of binding or cover other than that
in which it is published and without a similar condition,
including this condition, being imposed
on the subsequent purchaser

First published by Reinhardt Books in 1990

Vintage
Random House, 20 Vauxhall Bridge Road,
London SW1V 2SA

www.vintage-classics.info

Addresses for companies within The Random House Group Limited
can be
found at: www.randomhouse.co.uk/offices.htm

The Random House Group Limited Reg. No. 954009

A CIP catalogue record for this book
is available from the British Library

ISBN 9780099582878

The Random House Group Limited supports the Forest Stewardship
Council® (FSC®), the leading international forest-certification
organisation. Our books carrying the FSC label are printed on
FSC®-certified paper. FSC is the only forest-certification scheme
supported by the leading environmental organisations, including
Greenpeace. Our paper procurement policy can be found at:
www.randomhouse.co.uk/environment

Printed and bound in Great Britain by
CPI Group (UK) Ltd, Croydon, CR0 4YY

Contents

Principal Dates, Travels, Books

1904	Born at Berkhamsted (2 October)	
1912–1922	Berkhamsted School	
1922–1925	Balliol College, Oxford; visits Ireland, the Ruhr	*Babbling April*, 1925
1926	Working on the *Nottingham Journal;* received into Roman Catholic Church	
1926–1929	Sub-editor on *The Times*	
1927	Marries Vivien Dayrell-Browning	
		The Man Within, 1929
		The Name of Action, 1930
		Rumour at Nightfall, 1931
1932	Begins regular book reviewing for the *Spectator* (continues until early 1940s)	*Stamboul Train*, 1932
1933	Visits Denmark, Norway, Sweden; daughter Lucy Caroline born	
1934	Visits Paris, Latvia, Estonia, Germany	*It's a Battlefield*, 1934
1935	Journey to Liberia	*England Made Me*, 1935
1935–1940	Regular film critic for the *Spectator*	
1936	First of many film scenarios; son Francis born	*Journey Without Maps*, 1936 *A Gun for Sale*, 1936
1937	Co-editor and film critic for *Night and Day*	
1938	Journey to Mexico; visits Paris	*Brighton Rock*, 1938
		The Lawless Road, 1939
		The Confidential Agent, 1939
1940–1941	Literary editor and drama critic for the *Spectator;* works for Ministry of Information, London	*The Power and the Glory*, 1940

Year	Life events	Publications
1941	Wins Hawthornden Prize for *The Power and the Glory*	
1941-1943	Works for MI6, Sierra Leone	*British Dramatists*, 1942 *The Ministry of Fear, 1943*
1943-1944	Works for MI6, London	
1944-1948	Director, Eyre & Spottiswoode	
1945	Book reviewer for the *Evening Standard*	
		The Little Train, 1946 (first of four children's books with Dorothy Glover) *Nineteen Stories*, 1947
1948	Speaker, with François Mauriac, at Les Grandes Conférences Catholiques, Brussels; visits Vienna, Czechoslovakia, USA	*The Heart of the Matter*, 1948
1949	Wins James Tate Black Memorial Prize for *The Heart of the Matter; visits* Sierra Leone	
1950-1951	Reports about Malaya for *Life*	*The Third Man* and *The Fallen Idol*, 1950
1951	Visits Indo-China twice, reporting for *Life* (article rejected and published in *Paris Match*)	*The Lost Childhood*, 1951 *The End of the Affair*, 1951
1952	Received Catholic Literary Award for *The End of the Affair;* visits Indo-China for *New Republic*	
1953	Reports from Kenya for the *Sunday Times*	*The Living Room*, 1953 *Essais catholiques*, 1953
1954	Reports from Indochina for the *Sunday Times* and *Le Figaro;* visits Cuba, Haiti	*Twenty-One Stories*, 1954
1955	Reports on Vietnam and Poland for the *Sunday Times* and *Le Figaro;* first of many visits to Canada	*Loser Takes All*, 1955 *The Quiet American*, 1955
1956	Visits Haiti	
1957-1968	Director, The Bodley Head	
1957	Visits Cuba, China, Russia (twice)	*The Potting Shed*, 1957
1958	Visits Cuba	*Our Man in Havana*, 1958
1959	Visits Cuba, Congo; meets Yvonne Cloetta in Cameroon	*The Complaisant Lover*, 1959

1960	Given Pietzak Award in Poland; visits Russia, Brazil for PEN, USA	
1961	Made Honorary Associate, American Institute of Arts and Letters (resigns May 1970); visits Tunis, Russia	*In Search of a Character,* 1961 *A Burnt-Out Case,* 1961
1962	Awarded Hon. Litt. D., Cambridge; visits Romania	
1963	Made Honorary Fellow, Balliol College; visits Cuba and Haiti for the *Sunday Telegraph,* Goa for the *Sunday Times,* Berlin and East Germany	*A Sense of Reality,* 1963 *Carving a Statue,* 1964
1965	Visits Dominican Republic and Haiti	
1966	Named Companion of Honour; settles in France; returns to Cuba for the *Sunday Telegraph*	*The Comedians,* 1966
1967	Awarded Hon. D. Litt., Edinburgh; visits Israel for the *Sunday Times,* Sierra Leone for the *Observer,* Dahomey	*May We Borrow Your Husband?,* 1967
1968	Awarded Shakespeare Prize, Hamburg; visits Istanbul for the BBC, Paraguay, Argentina, Cuba	
1969	Named Chevalier de la Légion d'Honneur; visits Paraguay for the *Sunday Telegraph,* Argentina, Czechoslovakia	*Collected Essays,* 1969 *Travels with My Aunt,* 1969
1970	Visits Argentina	
1971	Reports from Chile for the *Observer,* visits Argentina	*A Sort of Life,* 1971 *Collected Stories,* 1972
1973	Awarded Thomas More Medal; visits South Africa and Switzerland	*The Honorary Consul,* 1973 *Lord Rochester's Monkey,* 1974 *The Pleasure Dome,* 1974 *The Return of A. J. Raffles,* 1975 *An Impossible Woman,* 1975
1976	Takes first of several trips to Spain and Portugal with Fr. Leopold Duran; visits Panama	

1977 Visits Panama; becomes member of the Panamanian delegation in Washington for the signing of the Panama Canal treaty	
1978 Made honorary citizen, Anacapri; visits Panama, Belize, Ulster	*The Human Factor*, 1978
1979 Awarded Hon. D. Litt., Oxford; visits Panama	
1980 Awarded John Dos Passos Prize; awarded Medal, City of Madrid; visits Panama and Nicaragua	*Dr Fischer of Geneva*, 1980 *Ways of Escape*, 1980
1981 Awarded Jerusalem Prize in Israel	*The Great Jowett*, 1981 *Monsignor Quixote*, 1982 *J'accuse: The Dark Side of Nice*, 1982
1983 Visits Nicaragua; awarded Grand Cross of the Order of Vasco Nunez de Balboa in Panama	*Yes and No* and *For Whom The Bell Chimes*, 1983 *The Other Man*, 1983
1984 Made Companion of Literature, Royal Society of Literature, London, and Commandeur des Arts et des Lettres, France	*Getting to Know the General*, 1984
1985 Visits Nicaragua, Panama, USA	*The Tenth Man*, 1985
1986 Awarded Order of Merit, London; visits Russia twice	
1987 Awarded Order of Ruben Dario in Nicaragua; visits Russia	
1988 Awarded Dr Honoris Causa, Moscow State University	*The Captain and the Enemy*, 1988 *Yours Etc.*, 1989 *The Last Word and Other Stories*, 1990 *Reflections*, 1990
1991 Died at Vevy, Switzerland (3 April)	*A World of My Own: A Dream Diary*, 1992

Introduction

It is nearly a quarter of a century since Graham Greene and I began to discuss *Reflections*. At the time I was writing *The Dangerous Edge*, a book about the juncture of his fiction and political reporting, and discovering in the archives newspaper and journal articles he could only vaguely remember having written. One day he sent me an essay which I had not seen before. 'All novelists, I suppose, have a box of rejected ideas,' it began. What followed were the openings of two unwritten novels and a short story he claimed to have saved from his dustbin. They were witty and provocative and seemed a fit ending for a collection of essays that would span his literary life, since their presence suggested they might have been retrieved for use in a new novel. The thought intrigued me as I worked my way through decades of papers. Perhaps the beginnings of other novels would turn up. In those now almost forgotten days before the ease of a computer search my hunt for material intrigued Greene. Could he disguise himself and come to help, he asked. Could we make a book of what I was finding in the archives, I asked. In less than a week another letter arrived from Antibes saying that Max Reinhardt, his publisher and friend, would be in touch.

Reflections turned out to be the last of Greene's books

published in his lifetime. To the original collection, I have added seven new pieces, two of which have not been published before. Had the essays in the first edition been remembered earlier, they might have been included in his *Collected Essays* or *Ways of Escape*. Here they combine to show the breadth and brilliance of his journalism and to add to our understanding of the development of his political thought. From his 1923 'Impressions of Dublin', which he published unsigned when he was only nineteen, his essays flow with perceptive and lively observations. This and other early articles established the pattern he would follow as a reporter for the rest of his life.

He travelled light and apparently without fear, absorbing the myriad details from which he would re-create the essence of contemporary life. June 1923 was a precarious time for an Englishman to walk from Dublin to Waterford questioning strangers about Republican feeling. Michael Collins had been assassinated less than a year before and in Dublin Greene sensed an 'expectant, but apathetic air'. Everyone was 'idle, but waiting'. His eye caught 'a small boy of about fifteen, in the green uniform of the Free State, fast asleep on a bench in St Stephen's Green, his head resting on the shoulder of a still younger girl'. A youth himself, Greene felt a 'fear at the heart that something terrible, unknown and unpreventable' was about to happen.

The following year he travelled to the French-occupied Rhineland with his cousin, Edward Greene, and Claud Cockburn, whom he later called one of the greatest journalists of the century. It was his second trip with Cockburn. On an earlier vacation they had disguised themselves as tramps and pushed a barrel-organ around Hertfordshire, fooling friends at Berkhamsted School and facing rough times by living on what they made. Soon after, Greene read a book of short stories about the conduct of the French troops at Trier and asked the German Embassy in London to pay his expenses in the Ruhr so he could report first-hand to an Oxford newspaper he edited. To undergraduates, the voyage looked more intriguing than tramping around Ireland or the English countryside because real espionage was involved. On the trip he and Cockburn talked about writing a thriller in the manner of John Buchan, but back in England Greene wrote 'In the Occupied Area' and 'The French Peace', two serious political articles which described the French treatment of the Germans as atrocious. He hoped that Count Albrecht von Bernstorff at the German Embassy would finance a return trip. At the same time, he was trying to record what he had seen dispassionately and to use observed detail to draw public sympathy for the underdog. Six years later he would fictionalize the situation in *The Name of Action*.

The seeds of Greene's double life as novelist–reporter are in these early journeys. The youthful search for adventure grew into the restless curiosity that made him one of the twentieth century's notable travellers. The distance achieved by disguise germinated into the critical detachment that allowed clear, unencumbered observations. The quick sympathy for the less fortunate matured into the political consciousness that gave moral urgency to his fiction. The schoolboy humour turned into irony and a healthy doubt about received views. Travelling, watching, recording – these were the means of moving outside one's class and cultural experience, outside one's consciousness 'to roam through any human mind'.

Greene's travels began with what seems to have been an

insatiable desire for adventure. The lightness with which he and his cousin Barbara decided to embark on a trip through unmapped Liberia after a few glasses of champagne shows the measure of his restlessness in the thirties. The very title, *Ways of Escape*, into which he incorporated much of his travel reportage, suggests that he continued to regard his expeditions as a fleeing from himself and the boredom he said plagued him all his life: incidents of truancy and self-mutilation marked his youth and led his father to send him to London for six months to be psychoanalysed by Kenneth Richmond. Yet to insist that escape was the only reason for his peregrinations is to ignore deeper motivations.

Greene belonged to that generation of writers who found themselves when young caught between a decaying liberal world and the threat of totalitarianism. By the mid-thirties he felt that centuries of cerebration had brought man only to unhappiness and the peril of extinction. Hastily taken as his decision to go to Liberia was, it sprang from a genuine desire to explore what he called in *Journey Without Maps* his 'place in time'. That meant looking back not in the manner of an historian, though it was history he had read at Oxford, but more in the way of an anthropologist or psychologist. 'What determines a journey,' he wrote in 'Analysis of a Journey', is the 'accumulation of the traveller's past' and for that reason 'the choice of a journey often deserves a writer's attention quite as much as the journey itself'.

While many of his contemporaries took up left-wing politics as the answer to Europe's problems, he tried to discover where things had gone wrong by measuring his own dying world against a more primitive one. 'A quality of darkness was needed,' he said, 'of the inexplicable, something which has to be taken as a symbol because it has no obvious meaning for the conscious brain.' That he had been influenced by his time with Kenneth Richmond seems obvious. But later in 'Letter to a West German Friend' he acknowledged that 'most of us have all our lives in this unhappy century carried an invisible frontier around with us, political, religious, moral' and that it was a relief 'sometimes to find oneself on a material frontier'.

To travel, if only vicariously as a reviewer at the cinema, was to explore the 'region of the imagination' – the region 'of a shape, a strangeness, a wanting to know'. Greene needed to see things for himself and was wildly impatient with those who wrote without first-hand knowledge of their subjects. Yet travel was difficult for a young man so obsessed with becoming a successful novelist that he gave up his sub-editor's job on *The Times* at the end of 1929 to risk keeping himself and his wife with his pen. Money was short. Reviewing and reporting barely enabled him to make ends meet and to pay for the experience that would feed his novels.

It was perhaps this cruel mixture of necessity and desire that released the full power of Greene's imagination as a novelist and drove him to embark on his own political odyssey. He had always been drawn to frontiers. The experience of crossing borders was deeply rooted in his childhood and as soon as he was old enough to journey on his own he began to contribute to the long tradition of travel writing in English literature. But even without the compulsive tramping about, the hard discipline of journalism forced him to cross borders that were aesthetic and political as well as geographic. In the thirties he reviewed close to eight hundred books and films. 'An author of talent,' he stated in one of them, 'is his own best critic – the ability to criticize his own work is inseparably bound up with his talent: it is his talent.' He was talking about Somerset Maugham, but he might have been talking about himself, for as he set standards of excellence for other writers and film-makers, he perfected his own skills.

In that formative decade he learned to make fictional dialogue dramatic, to cross-cut precisely from scene to scene and to use detail to create character and atmosphere – a technique we now recognize as perhaps his most distinctive artistic signature. In a letter to his mother in August 1936 when he was about to work on his first shooting script, a treatment of Galsworthy's 'The First and the Last', he told her that he had 'to visualize exactly the whole time, not merely what the person is doing, but from what angle you watch him doing it'.

In the thirties he also came to understand that 'if you excite your audience first, you can put over what you will of horror, suffering, truth'. In 'Subjects and Stories' he suggested that film-makers begin with the simplest popular drama – 'blood on a garage floor . . . the scream of cars in flight' – and then 'secretly, with low cunning' move 'towards a subtler, more thoughtful level' where human values could be suggested. In 'Is It Criticism?' he asked film critics to be satirically rude, 'to make a flank attack upon the reader, to persuade him to laugh at personalities, stories, ideas, methods, he has previously taken for granted'. Greene had no interest in middle-class escapism; he had been trying to escape middle-class life since his adolescence. His readers would recognize their own impoverished world in the vivid, exact descriptions of his novels, which caught the modern human condition as powerfully as those of any writer.

While much of Greene's fiction and reporting was set

in distant lands, as an essayist he often found his material close at hand. Taking off from the Café Royal and the area around Piccadilly, he chased images of what he might have been in 'Ghosts of Possible Adventure'. In 'Second-hand Bookshops' he led us through his favourite London haunts, speculating on how Freud would have interpreted his dreams. When he lived in Chipping Campden in the early thirties he wrote 'Death in the Cotswolds' about a man who padded about the village in rags, 'clutching a tall stick' and looking 'suspiciously like a stage madman'. He had been born into a wealthy family in Bombay two years before the Mutiny, at which time his father had fled panic and gunfire and taken the family to England. After growing up in ease, studying medicine, going to tennis parties, falling in love, he inexplicably became destitute and went mad. When he froze to death on his straw mattress, 'They did not care to undress him, his rags were too verminous, but put round his shoulders the web with which coffins are lowered into the ground, and dragged him head first down the stairs. Then they crammed him quickly into his coffin and nailed him down.' The story smelled of the Depression, personalizing in its squalid pathos the despair of an entire decade.

Greene learned quickly, whether at home or abroad, to draw the concrete detail of journalism into political metaphor. In 'Strike in Paris' he described a drunken man selling copies of *Action française* on the Boulevard Montmartre during the general strike of 1934. The man danced and sang and when no one bought his papers, he tore them in half. He was happy and amiable, but in ten minutes had emptied the café simply because he was making a noise. 'Any noise in Paris last Monday night might have started a riot,' Greene wrote, linking the tension in the city to the image he had seized.

Years later, with his novelist's skills honed, he wrote 'A Memory of Indo-China'. He had been on a vertical bombing raid, and recorded the physical sensations as the B26 bomber dived down, throwing him into a deep fear of humiliation, of vomiting, of not being able to stand the physical pressure pushing on his lungs, loosening his bowels. Then, as the bomber turned for home and in the relief of finding himself still alive even the fear of being shot down left him, the plane dived again, flattening out over the ricefields to aim 'like a bullet at one small sampan on the yellow stream. The gun gave a single burst of tracer, and the sampan blew apart in a shower of sparks; we didn't even wait to see our victims struggling to survive, but climbed and made for home. I thought again, as I had thought when I saw a dead child in a ditch at Phat Diem, "I hate war". There had been something so shocking in our fortuitous choice of prey – we had just happened to be passing, one burst only was required, there was no one to return our fire, we were gone again, adding our little quota to the world's dead.' In *The Quiet American* the sampan and the dead child would be in Fowler's mind when he decides that one has to take sides to remain human and chooses the Viet Minh.

The bombing raid and a good deal else of Greene's commentary about Vietnam found its way into that novel, as did his account of Mexico (*The Lawless Roads*) into *The Power and the Glory*, his reports from Haiti and Paraguay (included here) into *The Comedians* and *Travels with My Aunt*. Of course, the material is not simply transposed. The same words have an astonishingly different effect as part of the fictional structures. He told Marie-Françoise Allain he would never consent to appropriate other people's political sufferings for literary purposes. Yet a writer cannot deny what he sees. In *A Sort of Life* Greene recalled that in 1926 as a young man in hospital for an appendectomy he saw a mother with her dead child. Everyone else in the ward put on earphones to block out the scene, but Greene watched and listened and thought himself entirely selfish for doing so. 'There is a splinter of ice in the heart of a writer . . . This was something which one day I might need.' His eye and ear went on coldly recording, but the selfishness of which he accused himself was in reality a measure of the power of his empathy for human pain and grief. In 'Lightning Tour' we find him praising Ralph Ingersoll, an American newspaper-man who came to London to write about the blitz, for being similarly self-conscious. In *Travels with My Aunt* Henry excuses the same 'awful selfishness' in Aunt Augusta and recognizes her as 'one of the life-givers'. Still, Greene's own discomfort remained.

Suffering affected him profoundly. As a child he could faint at the mention of blood, but during the blitz his sensitivity came under control as he helped the injured. In 'Goa the Unique' he told of 'the enormous pressure of poverty' he encountered on his travels 'flowing, branching, extending like flood-water'. The very activity of writing, of trying to bring a scene to life, enabled him to bear its weight. Perhaps, as he said, it is the subject which chooses the author and not the other way round, for like the reluctant Fowler he too became involved in what he saw.

Greene's politics are reflected in the reports in this book. They were never attached to a particular ideology, and for all his public letters on specific issues, he refused to be pinned down generally on the grounds that a writer must be free of fixed affiliations. He was vehemently opposed to American intervention in the affairs of smaller nations and took up the causes of Vietnam, Cuba, Haiti, Chile, Panama and Nicaragua. At the same time his was one of the major voices raised in defence of human rights in countries like the Soviet Union. Late in life he allowed that he was something of an old-fashioned social democrat, which was consonant with his quick attachment to Omar Torrijos (described in *Getting to Know the General*) and his vision of what was then a moderately socialist Panama. But just as often he talked about the 'virtue of disloyalty' and the 'price of faith', about disinterested observation and the importance of doubt. In his novels he cultivated the dangerous edge of things so that faith wavers, love betrays and the uninvolved die for causes. In his articles he tried to maintain a distance by using his extraordinary powers of observation to evoke places and events – which he did again and again with memorable power – rather than analyse. It was for this reason that he preferred to be called a reporter than a journalist.

Of course it is impossible not to take sides. One by one Greene's characters learn this and find themselves driven, often against their will, to commitment – but that is fiction. Whatever Greene described – the plight of the refugees in Vietnam, the excitement of the early days of the Cuban Revolution, the macabre nature of Papa Doc's reign of terror in Haiti, the political chicanery at the signing of the Panama Canal treaty – his commitment to detached reporting, written from a position similar to that adopted by many of his protagonists, gave us an honest account of what he saw. But Greene the reporter and Greene the novelist were the same man, and what he saw forced him to become involved and to move a second time in his fiction through the dangerous political geography of his travels. Perhaps the way he got caught up in the struggles he observed, committing himself to people and causes sometimes against his own pre-conceived ideas, best shows the value of keeping an open eye, and the importance of dissent. His political articles bear witness to his moral as well as to his physical courage.

Most reporting is read only once, after which it is consigned to the archives to accumulate dust, or these days preserved digitally and stored in a cloud. Greene's has survived its half-life in newsprint and continues to amuse and invigorate here and in other collections. It has had a deservedly long life, and has been even more privileged in providing the backgrounds to his novels. Whether the journey he took was through the green baize door from the security of home into the torments of school, or from Oxford to Berkhamsted for fun, whether it was to the cinema where as critic a living could be had by travelling in the dark along other people's shadows, or to far-off places where one's own culture was thrown into sharp relief against the shifting politics of the Third World, it ended where reality and imagination merge in fiction. 'To a novelist, his novel is the only reality,' Greene said, and he was right. A novel has a meaning that reality, even as tellingly described as in Greene's reporting, does not. But that is one of the most fascinating things about a great writer's essays – to see what reality looked like before it was transformed into his unique vision of the world.

Judith Adamson
2014

Impressions of Dublin

As the train moved out of Kingstown for Dublin, my first feeling was that here was the Ireland of the Irish Players, the traditional comic Ireland.

The carriage was full. A farm girl and her 'boy', a mother with two small children, an elderly couple, an unattached female, and an old gentleman with a top hat and gold-rimmed eyeglasses were with us in the carriage. While we were waiting for the train to go, the mother suddenly realized that she was without her luggage, and rushed from the coach, leaving one of her children behind. The minutes passed and the child began to weep. After some time the unattached female took the boy upon her knee, where it continued to weep. Presently the guard appeared and inserted a key into the lock. After waiting to see if someone else would speak, the unattached female raised an indignant voice, 'Don't lock that door,' she cried, 'a woman's gone off and left her baby here.' 'Sure,' said the guard slowly, 'she wouldn't be deserting her baby. It's foolish you are.' With stern dignity, and with a perfect belief in his own logical behaviour, he locked the door and departed. The child cried harder than ever and would not be comforted. The elderly man in the corner sank quietly asleep; his wife made a tentative effort to silence the boy, but all was of no avail.

Of a sudden I was conscious of a movement beside me. The old gentleman in the top hat was slowly stirring, like a piece of disused machinery, put into unwonted movement. I could almost hear the creaking of the parts. After a long and laborious fumbling in some deeply hidden pocket, he abstracted a dilapidated chocolate cream, and still without a word presented it to the boy. Silence reigned in the carriage.

At last everything was settled comfortably, as in a popular novel, and the train started. The first indications of the new Ireland occurred just outside Dublin, in the shape of a barricade, behind which was stationed a sentry, with fixed bayonet. But as soon as we left the station, all signs of a comic Ireland vanished.

We were tired, our rucksacks were heavy, and we had looked forward in happy expectation to one night of comfort before our walk commenced. But when we inquired for our hotel from a passer-by, we learnt that the servants were on strike and had picketed the entrance. As we had no desire to be made conspicuous, we went elsewhere, and since the hotel dinner was too expensive for our moderate means, we asked a theatregoer the whereabouts of a moderately cheap restaurant. I dare not name the place to which we were directed lest an action for libel should be lodged against me. In a rash moment I ordered liver and bacon. The liver was the colour of good gorgonzola cheese; I will not speak of the bacon. My language might go too far. The prices, however, were higher than the average English restaurant, and this cannot have been due, as elsewhere, to our nationality, since the prices were clearly printed upon the menu.

It is the poverty and the expensiveness of Dublin that first impress visitors. The houses are dilapidated, the roads unswept. The two principal thoroughfares, Grafton Street and Sackville Street, would disgrace an English country town, and beggars are as numerous as in a Continental port. Every space of blank wall is painted in scarlet or red, 'The Republic Lives', 'Up the IRA'. General Mulcahy, whose Flogging Bill is very unpopular, and Mr Healy come in for most comment. 'Fight clean, Mulcahy, don't murder' decorates one building, while along the length of another wall runs, 'Tim Healy, traitor to both sides, swears allegiance to England. Don't be a fool, Tim, fight.'

These notices, it is true, mean very little. The greater number of them are written up at nightfall by young girls, still at the 'flapper' age, who seem at the moment to be the only active Republicans in the city, but they are the hardest with whom to deal. If they are put in jail, they hunger strike and become martyrs. Thirteen women were qualifying for this heavenly crown at the time when we were in Dublin, and the Government, though it had definitely stated that there would be no more releases, were forced to surrender Marie Camelford unconditionally. A more efficacious punishment was invented by a Free State soldier, who, finding a girl engaged on this work of propaganda, quietly emptied the pot of red paint over her head, and passed on his way.

Two bodies of men are to be seen in the streets, one is the Free State army, the other the Civic Guard. The Civic Guard, many of whom are old RIC men, look smart and well disciplined, but they carry no arms, and are useless save for ordinary police routine. The specimens of the army which we saw in the capital were not encouraging. There seemed to be little discipline, only one in fifty condescended to salute an officer, if he met him in the street, and they consisted chiefly of old men and boys. One picture remains firmly fixed on my mind, that of a small boy of about fifteen, in the green uniform of the Free State, fast asleep on a bench in St Stephen's Green, his head resting on the shoulder of a still younger girl.

But the most impressive thing about Dublin is its expectant, but apathetic air. Everyone is idle, but waiting. The stark ruins of the Four Courts and the Custom House, and a silent crowd of perhaps fifty people listening to a barrel-organ, or watching an officer giving orders to a sentry, are symbols of the Dublin of today. It is like that most nightmarish of dreams, when one finds oneself in some ordinary and accustomed place, yet with a constant fear at the heart that something terrible, unknown and unpreventable is about to happen.

Weekly Westminster Gazette
25 August 1923

In the Occupied Area

Yes; quaint and curious war is!
You shoot a fellow down
You'd treat if met where any bar is,
Or help to half-a-crown.

This is the English attitude to war that Mr Thomas Hardy voices, or at least it is the post-war attitude. England may be a nation of shopkeepers, but she bears no foolish grudge against those who have been worsted in the competitive fight. And it is this that makes Cologne a different town from Essen or from Trier. In Cologne the soldier is the exception; in Trier it may be most certainly said that the German citizen is the exception.

But England is walking on a very narrow edge of quibble and prevarication; her geographical separation from Europe has prevented her (for the moment) from slipping into the hateful and unquestioning spirit of Revanche, but there is a section of the nation who would rather see us fall into a slough of superficial success with France than stand dangerously alone. Yet to those who have seen, for however brief a time, the conditions reigning in the Ruhr and the Rhine Provinces, there can be no doubt that this last is not only the one right policy, it is the one safe policy.

Otherwise another war is inevitable, and within twenty years.

Dirt is the first impression that is gained in Essen, but dirt in itself is no unbearable thing. There are cheerful faces enough to be seen in Manchester or Liverpool, for misery is not the natural province of a manufacturing town. Yet in the Ruhr there is an atmosphere of misery and strain that silts into the pores of the mind, the kind of strain that is felt in the childish nightmare, when a vague and unknown something may happen at any moment, perhaps out of a cupboard, perhaps from behind a door.

In a world of shadows there are two realities, the French soldier, steel-helmeted as in war, and Poverty. As for the French soldier – well, there are worse things. He is quite often amiable, though always contemptuous, for is he not the conqueror? At least here in the Ruhr, he is white. It is well perhaps to walk on the edge of the pavement and not to obstruct him, however unintentionally, for his officer may have reprimanded him or his dinner may not have agreed with him. Yes, the man is well enough, but sometimes his wife is less agreeable, and if as well there should be a daughter and perhaps a mother-in-law, all quartered upon you, cooking in your stove, sharing your kitchen, affairs are apt to get irksome. The triviality of the friction may raise a smile, but when it goes on day after day, week after week, and the months slip by into the years, with no eventual relief for which to look, still the same small cares and petty indignities, a triviality becomes a tragedy.

And then there is the poverty. 'Look at the cafés,' some cry, 'they are packed every night.' That is true, but if such an ingenuous observer sat in a café from seven o'clock in the evening till eleven he would find that seventy per cent of those there span out an evening of talk and warmth and light on one glass of beer. For that small outlay they could get all they need – save food, but a man in these days must learn to work on one meal a day, save for an occasional burst of luxury, and some bean soup with the beer.

He is lucky indeed if he has work. Krupps in 1914 employed 88,000 men and women. After the temporary increase during the war, the firm converted its machinery towards the manufacture of peace articles with extraordinary speed, and were already employing 99,000 at the time of the French invasion. The passive resistance, however, that followed the breaking of the Treaty forced the directors to dismiss a third of their employees, and the work of pruning, as a director himself told me, was still going on. And what are these men to do? Hitherto their work, owing to the policy by which reparations are paid by a few industrialists, scarcely brought in a living wage. An ordinary skilled worker received about twenty-five renten marks a week, which roughly approximates to the wage paid to an English agricultural labourer, whilst food in Germany is twice as expensive as in England, and clothes at least three times as expensive. The dole, however, for unemployment – little danger here of its being voluntary – at its largest estimate for a family is six marks a week. The wolf has left the door, and apes the domestic cat at every hearth-side.

The children of the employed add to the difficulties of existence. Before the entry of the French there were schools to which they might be sent, perhaps for warmth even more than for education. But in the Ruhr or Rhineland districts two hundred of these schools have been closed. In many places the members of one school use the sole remaining building in the morning, those of the other in the afternoon.

The rest of the day the children are forced to wander round the town and play in the street, and as a consequence many unfortunate incidents cannot be prevented. Over 147,000 families have been expelled from the Ruhr alone. 'Oh yes, one must be careful,' said an old waiter in one of the cafés. He spoke a little English, having lived for many years in this country before the war. 'It is better to remain silent, even at home. I have two French women in my house, and they would report. The French soldiers, they do not behave badly, but they are strict. It is a hard thing for men of my age to leave their homes suddenly. And they can take nothing away. Perhaps they have to clear it up for the French before they go. It is hard, yes.' He flicked the table with his napkin and passed on.

It is not only a German tragedy, it is a French tragedy, for she is forgetting those great ideals of the Revolution that made her the benefactress of Europe:

> Liberty, chivalry, all we cherished
> Lost in a rattle of pelf and perished.

We are not the enemies of France. French policy is as fatal to herself as it is to us. But more and more often an inevitable thought arises in the mind of the English nation: 'Tu l'as voulu, Georges Dandin. Tu l'as voulu. Tant pis pour toi.'

Oxford Chronicle
9 May 1924

The French Peace

It is said that Pilate called for a basin of water and some soap and after a somewhat lengthy ablution declared that his hands were clean. This example England unfortunately is not as yet able to follow, but while the soap and water is impossible, she may at least keep free from unnecessary grime. There is no need for England to kneel and grab with her fingers in the silt because France insists on making mud pies, and calling them fortresses for future security.

The English occupation has, on the whole, been free from unnecessary precautions, and a certain type of bullying, which is only too common in the French provinces. On Sunday evening, 6 April, an officer in command of the troops at Coblenz decided apparently that sufficient distinction was not being made between his town and Cologne, and that the inhabitants were most regrettably lapsing into a state of comparative comfort. The cavalry therefore rode through the streets, breaking up all groups of more than four people, with blows from their whips. On this occasion their action did not go entirely unchallenged, as an American officer in mufti received a cut across the face. He immediately complained to his Consul, and the trooper in question was severely reprimanded, a lesson in future no doubt to distinguish more carefully between Germans and other nationalities.

I visited the town three days later and can most certainly declare, from the atmosphere of deadness that cloaked it, that the French had succeeded in their object.

Yet there have been cases where our own hands have not been entirely clean. I wonder how many read a small paragraph that appeared in the *Manchester Guardian* earlier in the year: 'August Schulze, charged at the Solingen Summary Court with the unlawful possession of two bayonets, pleaded "guilty". Accused stated that the bayonets had been in his possession since 1918. They were kept for purposes of decoration, and though he knew the possession of arms was forbidden, he did not know that the bayonets were considered as arms. Schulze, against whom there were no previous convictions, was sentenced to *six months' imprisonment*.' The italics are my own. It is not of the justice of punishment that I complain, it is of the brutality of the particular sentence. For six months Schulze's dependants were to be deprived of all support, for a piece of harmless sentimentality, which could have been satisfactorily met by confiscation and a small fine.

But in spite of a few such cases there is no more startling contrast than that between Cologne and a typical 'French' town, Trier. The soldier in Cologne is the exception, in Trier the German is the exception. Sixty per cent of the population is now French. For the French soldier's baggage in the occupied area includes his wife and mother and sister, and any relation, who is free to live at the expense of the German Government. And in Trier more than in any other town I visited, the 'black' is in evidence. One of the most startling indictments of the whole futility of French policy, of her cries of 'security' and 'revenge', was the sight of a small

Spahi, with his ragged beard and dirty khaki cloak, lounging beneath the Porta Nigra, the great Roman gateway that has stood there for sixteen hundred years.

It must be remembered, however, that the French claim that there are no blacks on the Rhine. Blacks, they say, are negroes, and their troops Senegalese or Moroccans. It is an interesting distinction, and in Bonn especially I 'imagined' many negroes. The fact, however, that a Frenchman is free from colour prejudice is no excuse for quartering them on a population that is known to possess it. It is a deliberate insult against a defenceless people.

There is another reason against their employment, their lack of discipline and self-restraint. It would be possible to quote a hundred charges of rape both of women and boys from the official, documented evidence of the German Courts, which I have myself seen. Occasionally the offender is punished, but now an easy road to acquittal has been found. One case is sufficient, as an encouraging precedent. A girl of sixteen was left alone one afternoon by her parents. A Spahi forced his way into the house and violated her. He then offered her five francs, and, on her refusal, forced her to take the money by threatening her with his bayonet. When the case was brought up before the military tribunal, the man was acquitted, because the girl had accepted the payment, and the father was fined four hundred gold marks for making a false accusation against a member of the occupying army. And now the French point with pride to the improvement in discipline of the troops, for no more of these cases are reported.

Repression has gone far in the occupied area. A man receives a month's imprisonment for the smallest offence. I talked with one such man. He agreed that there was no actual brutality on the part of his gaolers, but his companions in prison consisted of German thieves and mutinous Spahis; he was forced to stand at attention and salute his gaoler, whenever he entered his cell; he had to scrub out his cell every day, and he was allowed no books or papers. This man was fifty years old, sentenced for a so-called political offence, the offence being his refusal, on behalf of his town, to continue the pay of the Regie workers whilst they were on strike.

Whole families are liable to expulsion, on suspicion and without even a military trial, at a few hours' notice, and in many cases they have been forced to clean up their houses, for the French troops, before leaving. Over 147,000 Germans had been expelled from the Ruhr alone by November, 1923. During the election meetings of the last few months, it was declared that entire liberty of speech would be allowed to the parties. Indeed there was no actual interference before or during a meeting, but all those who spoke at meetings, other than that of the Centre Party, were expelled shortly afterwards, with no reason given.

And what is the final object of all these measures? That strange character, General de Metz, perhaps the most grotesque figure in all modern history, gives the answer. Separatism is his dream, and Separatism he will have. He is hardly a diplomat. Perhaps he would call himself a plain soldier, and his superiors in Paris could hardly have approved of that clear speech of his on 7 January: 'The people of the Palatinate have every reason to get used to the autonomous form of the state as soon as possible in their very own interests . . . For the next war, and that will be a war between England and France, will be fought out on the Rhine . . . It is urgent that the bridgehead of Mainz be enlarged and fortified to secure the Palatinate from an attack by troops coming from the east.'

The General's first efforts at Separatism failed in spite of big words. 'I will let all the devils loose on the Palatinate until the parties of the bourgeois come to their senses,' he declared, but his chief devils included a shoemaker and a brothel-keeper. Was it a sense of humour that made the last-named Commissioner at Bonn for Religion and Education? (See *The Times*, 2 and 12 November 1923.)

But General de Metz has not yet deserted his dream. The new name for his Separatists is that of the Rhineland Workers' Party, subsisting almost entirely on French funds. The natural leaders of labour in the Rhineland and on the Palatinate are the Burgomasters. Large numbers of them have been expelled. To take one instance, Trier has lost one-third of its Government. In the meanwhile the remnants of the Separatists are being re-formed, peacefully as yet, and though Heinz is dead, many of their leaders remain. One may be seen in the streets of Trier, a French police inspector. A couple of years ago he kept a brothel in the same town, but the wages of Separatism are higher than the wages for virtue.

For a few months now there has been a somewhat suspicious lull, while de Metz collects again his band of hired hooligans; in another two months shooting and pillaging will recommence, and the French peace will again be in full operation. Successful this time perhaps.

God rest you, peaceful gentlemen, but give us leave to pass,
We go to dig a nation's grave as great as England was . . .

But graves are shallow nowadays:

> *The time has been*
> *That, when the brains were out, the man would die,*
> *And there an end, but now they rise again*
> *With twenty mortal murders on their crowns*
> *And push us from our stools.*

Oxford Outlook
June 1924

Poetry by Wireless

. . . This was not what I had imagined at all. I had pictured in my mind a large bare steel room, dedicated to silence and science, inhuman, terrifying. At my most nervous moments I had even contemplated the possibility of some subtle mental torment, which evoked those heart-rending cries and shrieks, mingled with bubbles of derision, that I had heard floating from the depths of loud-speakers. So feared those who listened at the Union to the Oxford Symposium. But let me reassure them. Mr Harold Acton, the only man in Oxford who could mount the guillotine like an aristocrat, was not called on to show his courage; Mr Macleod did not go forth to meet his lord; Mr Rowse remained untouched by the arrows of the Shi.

Instead we sat in comfort in a large and overpowering drawing-room, in deep armchairs and sofas, upholstered in a somewhat symbolic shade of green. Thick curtains, and not steel walls, shut out all sound, and there was nothing which would have been out of place in Golders Green, save for a telephone box in one corner. At least it was probably not a telephone box, but a sound transmitter, or a radially active light wave, or an auricular intensifier, one of those things to which one refers casually in talks on psychic phenomena to ignorant old ladies: 'Oh, it's quite easy to get that effect. Radium, you know. Of course, Lodge is a quack, but Planke says . . . And after all light waves travel in inverse proportion to the ratio of the atomic sound transference. No, I never did agree with Einstein. Read Ray Lankester.'

Above the telephone box – I call it that because it is shorter than the other names – was an electric bulb, which shone, while we talked, like ourselves. In the centre of the room was a small occasional table, in rather good taste, on which was a casket, draped in a Liberty shade of mauve. It was at the casket that we talked.

When the red light appeared Mr Acton began. To it he confided with admirable suavity the title of his poem. Then he grew indignant, scornful, derisory. He lashed the casket with his satire. His body made a perfect geometrical curve in front of it. One hand gesticulated to it, furiously but gracefully. Yet the box remained inert, unresponsive, upon the table.

Mr T. O. Beachcroft wooed it next with more honeyed words. He leaned forward towards it softly, caressingly, for he had known another similar box at Manchester now for many months. He treated this as quite a family friend. He reminded it of a quotation from Crashaw. He talked philosophy to it for quite a considerable time, but the box seemed unimpressed.

Next came my turn. Satire had been tried, philosophy had been tried, I would try sentiment. As Earl Harold at William's Court spoke over the casket of saints' bones, I spoke over this box that I hoped contained the great heart of the British public. The box did not deign a smile, not a glimmer of a glance.

Mr Bryan Howard wooed it with aloofness and a distant

superiority to convention. He talked of naked ladies, but he gained no blush. The box seemed entirely lacking in all maiden modesty, though well covered itself in its Liberty dress.

Mr Macleod thundered at it in a voice which was heard doubtless in New York. As Macaulay would have said, 'His vowels brought terror to the inhabitants of Vancouver; his consonants re-echoed through the courts of Canton', yet to that box they might have been no more than the soothing chant of a siren.

I think that Mr Monkhouse voiced the feelings of the whole room towards that confounded box when he swore at it very loudly and distinctly. 'Had I the heart to call you a damned fool,' he cried, and then proved very conclusively that he had the heart. The box seemed quite insensible to his oaths; not so the British Broadcasting Co., who were filled with consternation and visions of enraged persons breaking their earpieces. They pictured themselves 'damned for a fretful d—', bankrupt, starving. The storm in their hearts was still raging when Mr Rowse proceeded to calm them with the cool twilight of Ireland, in that deep mellow voice which has so often stilled the Conservative frenzy of the Oxford University Labour Club.

Then all was over. The red light flashed back into vacancy, and weary and defeated we left the box, scornful and victorious. 'What a lot of fuss about nothing,' it seemed to whisper. 'Poetry – toys. Who wants it? Give me Einstein.' And the worst of it all is, that in one's moments of sanity one knows that the Box is Always Right.

Oxford Chronicle
30 January 1925

A Walk on the Sussex Downs

The Downs by Ditchling Beacon were washed by a pale yellow surge of sun. In the slowness of the ebb, which left for a long while the moon an indistinct wraith in the transparent blue, lay spring, and in the breeze, salt from a distant Channel out of sight, gorse-laiden, prophesying green. There was no green yet in the woods, which lay on the lower slopes like bands of soft brown fur, but green crept cautiously, afraid still of an ambush from winter, into the flat ploughed fields below, advancing from pastures where small white sheep were grazing. Dotted across the distance were toy farms. Along a white road a scarlet motor-car was scrambling recklessly, like a ladybird along the vein of a leaf. The Surrey hills peered through a silver veil, as though they were an old nun's face, austere, curious, and indestructibly chaste. A cock a mile away crowed with frosty clarity and a lamb bewildered and invisible cried aloud.

The turf underfoot was fresh with past rain, yet crisp with salt from the sea. A man riding with uncovered head passed across the brow of the Beacon, the horse stepping high and delicately, in the manner of a great lady conscious of a crowd. With ears pricked it watched its rider out of the corner of one desirous eye, heart yearning for the gallop, and was gone. The olive-green slopes lay alone once more to the spring, which came as Jove to Danaë in a shower of gold doubloons. They were scattered and untouched, for no heart delirious with spring could stoop to gather gold, when a mile of gorse and thirty miles of sea were carried in the breeze down over Plumpton and Ditchling and on past Lindfield and Ardingly to fade only before that quiet, impassive silver veil. Save for the passing wind and the small dots of moving men and cattle below, the world was motionless. Above a round blue dewpond a singing bird floated in the air like a scrap of charred paper, too light to stir.

By Harry's Mount the moon breasted a tide grown darker blue and came out proudly clear. Somewhere away by Hassocks the sun had sunk to the level of the downs, which lay, sleepy, listless slugs, barred in parallel lines by the gold rays pointing to Lewes. In gold and brown and blue the spring departed and left Lewes crouching dark in the valley, a fierce remnant of old winter.

Lewes in the dark was a disquieting mystery. A town in a valley, it yet seemed to stand upon a hill. There was the one dimly lighted High-street of shops and houses belonging to the period most at peace in English history — square Georgian fronts, with bow-windows — orderly and controlled glimpses of the imagination. Then on each side the streets dived steeply down into a darkness made chaotic by one lit lamp, which disclosed only a few huddled fronts leaning forward, signboards of ancient inns, six steep feet of cobbles and then vacancy.

Spring lay dead outside upon the downs, and one person at least in Lewes High-street did not mourn her death as he sat before a coal fire bathed in a warm content. Let winter be left with the mystery on either side and spring to her burial place. Here was neither spring nor winter, frozen nor restless heart, but two feet quietening their weariness, two hands spread to an orange glow, and two drowsing eyes that watched the warring sparks and came to no conclusions.

The Times
9 March 1928

Barrel-organing

Those who have barrel-organed in a hard December may
be said to have graduated in that peculiarly classical
profession whose gamut of tunes, in the form of a numbered
dial, ranges from the Dead March in *Saul* to the Toreador's
Song. The latter was the gayest tune which my organ
contained, and was intended, perhaps, to combat with its
cheerful bludgeoning the searching rapier of the wind. It
was the former's velvet-hung pomp, however, which
brought in the pennies, until the organ, slipping from cold,
clutching fingers, tumbled over and over down a steep
Hertfordshire hill and came to rest at the bottom with all
its bass notes broken. What seemed at first disaster and
bankruptcy, for my friend Claud Cockburn and I were far
from home with no money in our pockets but our scanty
earnings, and with nothing to pawn but our elaborate and
careful rags, proved a blessing. In the first street in which
we played four separate elderly ladies gave us four separate
sixpences on condition that we moved on to a neighbour's
house.

And in this connection it may be noted that in the
country – I have no experience of London – the barrel-
organist's principal income is derived not from the rich
but from the poor – from youths 'walking out' who wish

to impress their companions with the measure of their charity and from women who bring their children to the door to listen to the music, bad music, perhaps, but music with a hint of a hot south – 'des fruits, des fleurs, des feuilles et des branches'. These do not pay sixpence to the organist to go away, but pay him a penny for another tune. This is less profitable but more warming to the heart, and was very welcome on the three bitter December days during which I followed the profession and graduated, if not with the legendary motor-car, at least with a few pence profit.

Perhaps to begin with the organ was a little too polished in its performance to carry conviction of poverty, for it was only after disaster had marred its notes that we were admitted to the *camaraderie* of the profession. Among itinerant musicians there is a very real fellowship. Trundling the barrel-organ along a frozen lane, we met at the approach to a village one time a lean, drooping figure, curled round a forlorn pipe, who, passing, indicated, without staying his steps, the street in which the wealthiest harvest could be reaped; another time a fat, red fellow with a gramophone perched on a perambulator, who warned us between wet, pendulous lips of the presence of skinflints. Little do those who throw an organist sixpence in order to drive him away know that they are thus ensuring the arrival of a succession of similar players.

I do not know whether London is the Mecca of the barrel-organist, as it is of the more legitimate musician. Certainly during the winter it has great advantages over the country in the matter of lodgings. In London there is the crypt of St Martin between the common lodging-house and the Embankment; in the country there is little, as we proved to our cost, between the public house and the frost-gnarled field.

Of all but one of the five towns in which I have barrel-organed I have nothing but pleasant memories. The exception should surely have been foremost in charity, since it was the birthplace of the one English Pope, Nicholas Breakspear, friend of poor men and enemy of emperors. But in this town, because of our dirty faces and our rags, we were rejected at every inn. One inn, more friendly than the others, offered a stable for our organ, if we paid, but from his organ, as from his horse, a man should not be separated.

There seemed only to remain an iron-bound field, but here, after a few hours' attempt at sleep, cramp knotted every muscle. Thence we made our way to a half-built house with a roof and floor, but only unlidded gaps for windows, through which the wind swept in a regular succession of chilling gusts. We woke again before dawn in the grip of cramp, and finally left the suspicious and uncharitable town for the comparative warmth of walking between high hedges, followed on our right hand by a spectrally coughing cow — and so trundled out of the profession for ever.

Listen! Outside the window a gradually growing tinkle of sound — small scented sugar-plums of brittle music dropping rapidly one by one into the blue dusk. Here is sixpence, organist. Do not go, but turn the handle of your dial and play another tune.

The Times
27 December 1928

Death in the Cotswolds

Amazing the amount of useless experience which can be gathered in a lifetime. To have been born in the blaze and glare of Bombay two years before the Mutiny, a doctor's son, and to have died, frozen, last month in a Cotswold cottage on a bed of straw – this is to touch the extremes of life as nearly as any man. Amahs and black servants, cattle droving and begging, panic and gunfire on the edge of the young consciousness, the terrible tedium of the three months' voyage, work for a medical degree, encounters with the police, childhood in England, tennis parties and searching the dustbins on a Friday morning; it is an irony that this experience should so completely have been lost, forgotten or jumbled together like a puzzle, in the mad brain of Mr Charles Seitz.

He was the kind of figure round whom legends clustered. Even his real name was lost in common speech, so that he was known among the Campden villagers as Charlie Sykes, as he padded down the High Street bent double under the weight of incredible rags, clutching a tall stick, his bearded Apostle face bent to the pavement, but his eyes, flickering sideways, aware of everyone who passed. He was suspiciously like a stage madman, and it is certain that he played up to strangers, bellowing at them unintelligible words and shaking his great stick, so that they shrank away a little daunted, while those who knew him smiled from doorways. Sometimes in summer he went berserk in the market place, shouting and shaking, all alone in a desert of indifference; no one took him seriously, least of all himself – his humorous eyes showed that. He would earn money from Americans with kodaks, 'snapped' picturesquely in front of the seventeenth-century butter market, and occasionally the sly indecency of his words had almost too much meaning for a man so lunatic.

There were two rival stories of how his madness started. The one, most romantic and most unevidenced, spoke of an unfortunate love affair; the other, and I think the true one, that his brain gave way from overwork for a medical degree. Once an inhabitant of Campden spoke in his hearing of an operation; Charlie Sykes, beating his chest between every word, described the operation in detail. That was how he would speak, gruffly and disconnectedly, beating his chest. He had a grudge against God. 'There He is,' he would say, 'up there. We think a lot about Him, but He doesn't think about us. He thinks about Himself. But we'll be up there one day and we won't let Him stay.' His accent changed with his audience: to some pretentious ladies whom he wished to insult, he would speak in broad Gloucestershire.

He had an extraordinary vitality. There was a time when five men could not hold him, and once when two policemen tried to arrest him at Evesham for begging, he flung them both over a hedge. He would walk several times a week into Evesham, eight miles each way by road, but he did not go by road. He knew every gap in every hedge for miles around, and once campers in a field above Broadway woke to see his face in the tent opening. That was the occasion of his most subtle indecency. His knowledge of the hedgerows made it easy for him to be present at any fête or open-air entertainment without paying, though once inside he took no further interest, but went to sleep under a tree with his hat over his eyes.

He had several hundreds of pounds in the bank which he never touched. The only work he ever did, after his reason went, was cattle droving. He begged, if that word can be given to his friendly demands. 'Now, what about potatoes? Or a cabbage? Well, then, turnips? What have you done with all that dough?' I never saw him in a shop, but on Friday mornings he toured the dustbins in the long High Street, turning over their contents in an interested, unembarrassed way like a lady handling silk remnants on a bargain counter.

He had a two-roomed cottage in Broad Campden, with one broken chair and a pile of straw in the corner, and sixteen pairs of old shoes. He stopped a sweep in the village once and asked him to clean his chimney, repeating the one word, 'Shilling – shilling.' The sweep began to clean, but he could not finish in the airless room and the appalling stench. But the stench could not keep out the cold of this last long frost, and when a policeman broke in because no smoke had been seen from the chimney, he found Mr Charles Seitz frozen to death on his straw in the upper room. They did not care to undress him, his rags were too verminous, but put round his shoulders the web with which coffins are lowered into the grave, and dragged him head first down the stairs. Then they crammed him quickly into his coffin and nailed him down. If one remembers the birth in Bombay, it seems the perfect ironic ending, but there is some horror to me in the thought that the skull of a man can case so many contrasts, such knowledge of comfort and poverty, that the same membrane can vibrate to such an extreme of heat and cold.

Spectator
24 February 1933

Gold Bricks

Consider the Financier: at school apt for sharp practice; in love secretive and promiscuous; diffident and charming to his guests, blushing often (only at the end of his life are the blushes regarded as something less than a mark of modesty); he has a sweet tooth and a craving for mystery (at the office there is a 'silent room', and at the theatre he takes three seats for himself in the stalls, sitting alone, mysterious and not inconspicuous). He is so used to juggling with astronomical figures (even at school he spoke in non-existent millions), that he buys even his underclothes wholesale; has enough shirts and vests to stock a shop; buys walking sticks, cameras, snapshot albums by the dozen, and this because he is not an ordinary man; he is a Great Man, a Napoleon of finance. His Gold Bricks are not ordinary gold bricks, but he takes your money just the same, and presently he is a little less than ordinary, lying on his bed with a bullet through the heart. There is generally forgery before the end; in this particular case 25 million pounds of Italian 6 per cent Treasury Bills. The figures are astronomical to the last, for this man is Ivar Kreuger, though he might almost as well be Whitaker Wright or even Uncle Ponderevo.

Mr Soloveytchik tells the story well; it can never fail to

be exciting, this curve up to success and down to death. The figures in the case of Kreuger were more than usually astronomical. The mind can grasp them no more easily than the position of a new star a few more light years further away. This man lent money to half the governments of Europe. Less than five years before his suicide, and when his swindles were well advanced, he lent 75 million dollars to the French Government and his credit stood five points higher than the credit of the Republic. Less than three years before his death he arranged to lend 125 million dollars to the German Government, and no one questioned his ability to raise the money. Mr Soloveytchik guides one through this jungle of figures and ambitions and chicaneries with great skill. As it is generally a business man who buys the gold brick in a public house, so it was one of the greatest American trusts, the ITT, closely connected with J. P. Morgan's, which was finally swindled by Kreuger, and there is some ironic pleasure in the sight of these hard-bitten men paying 11 million dollars in cash for shares in a company whose books they did not properly examine until after the deal.

A great deal has been read into Kreuger's face. Since his death it has been described as that of 'a reptile with sunken and stinging eyes'. To me the smooth, bald face of the frontispiece seems peculiar only in its anonymity. There is as little to distinguish him in feature from other men as there is little, except the extent of the ruin he left behind, to distinguish his swindles. His fall had the usual superficial pathos; he was hounded by people asking questions; his nerves gave way and he was found weeping at his desk. It has all happened so many times before. One remembers the little old world-worn swindler Uncle

Ponderevo: 'They asked me questions. They *kep'* asking me questions, George . . .'

Review of *Ivar Kreuger* by George Soloveytchik
Spectator
3 March 1933

Two Capitals

At Oslo the editor played yo-yo, in evening dress, over Bjornson's grave: it was nearly midday; and the learned professor was too drunk to compose a speech, the one he had prepared having been stolen; and the King was there and members of the Government, honouring Bjornson's memory. (At Stratford the margarine in the dairies is modelled into Shakespeare's bust, the girls in Elizabethan dress sell rosemary at a high price for remembrance, and all the ambassadors take off top hats and unfurl their countries' flags.)

A little patch of careless culture at the edge of the sea and of the forest: on the table Eliot's Poems, and, a few miles behind, a clearing in the forest where all the bears in Norway pass once a year, migrating. At dinner the champion quarter mile runner talked of the influence of *Anna Livia Plurabelle* on his prose style, and nobody dreamed of going home till four, and the level of the great wine cask in the cellar sank. The soldiers before the palace sat on the grass all day and smoked; all down Karl Johannes Gatan, the only fine street in Oslo, strolled the politicians and the typists and the authors, but the demi-monde was away on holiday up country. A balloon bobbed in the air at the end of the street and a band played above the harbour and all down the fjord brown children see-sawed up and down in boats and swam and dived. The little river steamer crept down the fjord, waited five minutes at every quay, and at every quay the captain took up a rod and fished for five minutes.

The business man nodded and drank and talked of Faulkner and Hemingway. Once, not far from Oslo, after an accident, he had dragged the girl he loved for hours at night over the snow on a stretcher formed of skis and found when he reached a house that she was dead. So in the background of literary gossip, wildness and death; just as past the bathing in the fjord, the four days' continuous drinking at the university gaudy, defiles the long depression of the autumn, beginning in October with the first cold spatter of rain, the season when all the books are published, when the stoves are lit and the windows shut and darkness overtakes luncheon and no one stirs outside, and it is hard to look forward to the real winter, the midnight toboggan parties and the lamps lit all down the mountain side between the pines. It is the October of Edvard Munch's 'Autumn', hanging in the National Gallery: two pigtailed schoolgirls on a verandah in shapeless coats, staring out at the richness and the decay of the fields, in the slope of their shoulders a sickening boredom, not the will to endure, but the knowledge that, will it or not, they have to endure. All through the autumn the whiskered frock-coated statues of Ibsen and Bjornson outside the National Theatre remain undecorated by revellers; Ibsen with whiskers sunk on the waistcoat, Bjornson hands behind back, one foot forward, spectacled face thrust out, grey as old ice.

But in Stockholm the moon glinted on the sentry's bayonet parading on the palace terrace; and at midday a beating of drums and flashing of swords and prancing of chargers as the royal guard changed. Our little country, our little country, the Swedish lawyer and the Swedish publisher kept repeating with sentimental humility and a deep hidden arrogance. (In Oslo they said, our small country, our small country, meaning the latest census result, the extent of the herring fisheries.)

In his formal house, where every piece of furniture was like a child in a charity school, well-scrubbed, in place, at attention, the Swedish pacifist supported war between races. He grew excited at the thought of Russia, spoke of the glory of a war of extermination: poison gas, germs, aerial bombardment, savouring the words; after the schnapps and the beer and the wine (Skoal, with the glass held at the fourth button of the waistcoat, while the charity children stood stiffly around) and the glasses of punch and three whiskies and sodas, he became vehement about women, ears back, eyes popping: no woman has character . . . made to be the mates of men . . .

The publisher with the military carriage and the bristling red moustache said, If the Socialists really came to power, I should be the first to take up arms . . . I do not, of course, believe in God, but if our Church was threatened, I should be the first . . . He said, We haven't any need of Socialism here. I will show you how the workmen live. Poor, but so clean, so contented. He thrust his way into strangers' cottages, leant in at their windows, opened their doors, displayed their bare rooms. The young man out of work with the fine starved features played an accordion for us, as we stood in the one room he shared with his mother. You see, Red Moustache said, speaking through the music, he has been unemployed for three years, the State gives them just enough to live on, but it is all so clean, they are so contented. He threw a krona on the table, and the young man played on, paying no attention. He rapped the krona on the table, and the young man nodded and went on playing and paid him no attention.

That could not happen here, they said in Oslo, Red Moustache would have been half killed. But the Swedes are like that. Have another drink.

Spectator
20 October 1933

Strike in Paris

One of the chief merits of flying is that it affords sudden and astonishing contrasts: it was a rare aesthetic pleasure to leave London last Sunday morning, driving out to Croydon through a thin yellow fog, through the late-rising suburbs (three men in bowler hats led out Pekinese dogs for a stroll round the pillar boxes and back before Matins), to leave England for France (the white distinct gravestones round the Sussex churches like sheep grazing in groups, Ashdown forest spilling out against hills curiously flattened into plains, the row of villas on the sea front casting regular shadows the shape of piano keys, the great wheel suspended over sea, over cloud, over Beauvais Cathedral, over the Oise, tilted above Le Bourget), to arrive in a Paris guarded and patrolled and plastered with dramatic appeals.

The contrast might have been less startling if within an hour of my arrival I had not been dubiously honoured by an invitation to march with a party of the National Front in a demonstration against the Communists: but in any case it would have been impossible to mistake the signs of war, the broken windows along the Rue de Rivoli, the burnt patches on the streets where fires had been lit, the smashed pavings, the bent rails of a Metro entrance, above all the notices, faultlessly phrased, the marble appeals of politicians to keep calm, to gather at Vincennes on the morrow, to strike, to remain at work, to bring 'the criminals' of 6 February to justice, to forgive and forget. 'Citoyens!' 'Peuple de Paris!' 'Travailleurs!' 'A Bas la Grève!': an impression of sculptured rhetoric, of innumerable politicians facing every way with carved open mouths and hands raised in the silence of stone. And all round the Place de la Concorde the Paris bourgeoisie took a sullen Sunday stroll; they would have resembled groups of tourists led round a cathedral if they had been less serious; but there was nobody to ask silly questions or to laugh at the guide; they stopped under the pedestal of each hideous statue and poked their fingers into the holes the bullets of the Gardes Mobiles had drilled on 6 February. They could not have been more careful in distinguishing bullet holes from the pockmarks of age or more solemn if they had been examining the relics of a criminal act with the intention of bearing evidence.

Sunday night was a night of talk and uneasy waiting. No one knew what the extent of the General Strike would be, whether it would be the occasion of an attempted *coup d'état* by the Left. Everywhere the talk was in terms of weapons, of who would take to the streets. The middle-aged, fanatical rather bandy-legged woman, Mlle B, who had given me so dubious an invitation, turned out to be one of the leaders of the National Front which now claims 50,000 members and possesses what the Croix de Feu lacks, money. All that large section of the middle-class which has cared nothing for politics, for Left or Right, has been baptized by fire in the Place de la Concorde and become suddenly politically conscious. Everywhere there was rumour, conspiracy, anger. The Gardes Mobiles had committed this and that atrocity, they had been drunk when they fired; a regiment had mutinied at Fontainebleau rather than be sent against unarmed Parisians; fourteen regiments of artillery were in Paris in readiness for the General Strike. All were agreed that the Government figures of the casualties on the Place de la Concorde were far from the truth, that there had been over sixty deaths. When Mlle B claimed that a fortnight hence her organization would take to the streets with the rifles and machine-guns they already possess, one was almost prepared to believe her. The bullet marks, some as low as a man's knee, most breast high, show what the bourgeoisie, men and women, have been able to face.

But this was at dusk. Next morning one was sceptical. There were so few signs of a General Strike. Buses were running in the centre of the city fairly frequently; some of the stations on the Metro were closed and a few shops were shut, a platoon of Republican Guards sat decorative in plume and brass on their horses beside the Louvre. That was all. The Socialist demonstration in the Place de la Nation melted noisily away. But curiously the air did not clear; the buses went off the streets, the Metro closed, the streets emptied, the dusk came. With the streets taxiless and busless, the difficulty of locating a revolution, if one was going on, became extreme. Revolutions, I was told, always follow the same road in Paris; and the authorities obviously thought the same. Driving with a friend between the Louvre and Vincennes we could see how Paris had become suddenly since the morning an armed camp. Soup kitchens rolled noisily through the dark, the Place de la Bastille was surrounded, rows of lorries on one side, cavalry on another, the Gardes Mobiles with slung rifles everywhere. In their dark uniforms, in their steel helmets which shone like scales in the lamplight, in their ubiquity, they resembled woodlice in a rock garden. Move any stone and you would find them: they sheltered close behind every corner house in every street. The centre of Paris was cut off from Vincennes. The Socialists had been beaten by an amazing show of force.

There remained the Communist districts round Belleville and Combat from which the rioters emerged last Friday night. Just before midnight I walked up to Belleville. Between the Place de la République and Belleville there were no police or guards. It would have been useless to try to police all the narrow gullies and cross-streets. But by the closed Belleville Metro, in the great boulevard which runs from Combat to Ménilmontant, one came again on the preparations for civil war. About fifty Gardes Mobiles waited in lorries to drive wherever they were needed; outside the café La Vieilleuse, there was a dressing station with half a dozen Red Cross men, and up and down the road moved a cordon of police in steel helmets, stopping passers-by and questioning them. The café proprietor stood in his shirt sleeves staring through the windows of the empty bar, a man moved round and round a billiard table practising shots, and outside on the pavement men held their hands above their heads while they were searched for arms. Every ten minutes an ambulance drove up to Combat or down to Ménilmontant.

But the incident which represented to me more vividly than anything else the state of tension which held Paris through the night occurred on the Boulevard Montmartre. A drunken man was selling copies of *Action française,* the only paper which appeared that day, outside Les Princes. He danced and sang and orated; when people would not buy his papers he tore them in half; he was very happy and very amiable, but in ten minutes he had nearly emptied the

38

café. He was making a noise. That was all, but any noise in Paris last Monday night might have started a riot.

Spectator
16 February 1934

Analysis of a Journey

The choice of a journey often deserves a writer's attention quite as much as the journey itself. Travel, like dreaming, is a form of emotional satisfaction, and though you may explain the act of dreaming by the cheese eaten at dinner, you cannot explain so easily the particular images which formed the dream. When X chose West Africa, and in West Africa Liberia, for the object of his journey, it interested me to try to trace in his sub-conscious mind the reason of his choice.

The psycho-analyst takes the images of a dream one by one. 'You dreamt you were asleep in a forest. What is your first association to forest?' and he starts his stop-watch and times the patient's reaction. Some images have immediate associations: before others the patient finds it difficult to bring out anything at all; his brain is like a cinema in which the warning 'Fire' has been cried; the exits are jammed with frightened people trying to escape. It is to these last images that the analyst returns. They are the important images, and when I say that to X Africa was an important image, that is what I mean. 'You dreamt you were in Africa. Of what do you think first when I say the word Africa, Africa?' and a crowd of words, death and forest and maps and school and dust and darkness, unhappiness and the Gare St Lazare, the face of an unpleasant boy and evensong and a pair of dividers crowd together and block the way to full consciousness.

But I noticed, as I acted the analyst with the stop-watch, that if I said 'South Africa' the reaction was immediate: Rhodes and British Empire and an ugly building in South Parks Road and Trafalgar Square. If I said 'Kenya', there was no hesitation: gentleman farmers, the seedy aristocracy, gossip columns and Lord Castlerosse. 'Rhodesia' produced: failure, Empire Tobacco, and, after a long pause, failure again.

It was not, then, these particular parts of Africa which strongly affected the unconscious mind; certainly it was not that part of Africa where the white settler has been most successful in reproducing the conditions of his country, its morals and its popular art. A quality of darkness was needed, of the inexplicable, something which has to be taken as a symbol because it has no obvious meaning for the conscious brain. This Africa may take the form of an unexplained brutality, as when Conrad noted in his Congo diary: 'Thursday, third July . . . Met an off^{er} of the State inspecting. A few minutes afterwards saw at a camp^g place the dead body of a Backongo. Shot? Horrid smell'; or a sense of despair, as when M. Celine writes, 'Hidden away in all this flowering forest of twisted vegetation, a few decimated tribes of natives squatted among fleas and flies, crushed by taboos and eating nothing all the time but rotten tapioca.' The old man whom X was to see beaten with a club outside the poky little prison at Tappee Ta, the naked widows at Tailahun covered with yellow clay, the great wooden toothed devil swaying his raffia skirts between the huts; these, like the images in a dream, stood for something of importance to himself. If he were to follow his associations with these images he felt he would be carried very far.

In his African novel, *The Inner Journey*, Herr Kurt Heuser wrote: 'The interior: that might signify the heart of the continent, but also the heart of things, the mystery: and finally, the comprehension of himself in nature and in Time.' What determines a journey in fact is the whole accumulation of the traveller's past. You must take into account a witch which haunted the corner by a linen cupboard, jumping on X's back as he fled by to the nursery, tickling with pointed nails; a dead dog at the bottom of a pram; a tin motor-car; a man by a canal bridge who wanted to kill himself with a razor but other people wouldn't let him; French bayonets in an Essen slum.

'We feel the past like a pain,' Herr Heuser's surveyor thought, and any journey, like a form of dreaming, is an attempt to express the pain in harmless images, slipping it past the censor in the shape of a casino, a cathedral, a *pension* at Rapallo. A psycho-analytical study of travel, if it is ever written, will throw, I think, an amusing and unexpected sidelight on the psychology of the ordinary man at certain periods; it was, one remembers, the Victorians who first exploited the full emotional satisfaction of a holiday in Switzerland.

Spectator
27 September 1935

The People's Pilgrimage

King George this afternoon goes back to Westminster Hall.

Less than a year ago the King stood there to receive the address of congratulation from Parliament; today he lies there, as his father lay, and tomorrow he will receive the last respects of the common people who mourn him.

In Westminster Hall he lies in the centre of the history of which he is a part, under the huge dark span of Sussex oak cut for Richard II, under the faces of the flying angels on the grey walls, with his Bodyguard of Gentlemen-at-Arms, with halberds reversed, to watch his catafalque under the wreaths and the draped Standard and the Crown.

On a dark day this huge hall, where Richard II could feast 10,000 people, is like a vault. The only brightness is in the great perpendicular window at the south end above St Stephen's Porch, which casts its colour on the stones which commemorate some of the most tragic scenes in history: the trial of Sir William Wallace and of Charles I, the impeachment of Strafford and Warren Hastings, the attainder of the English saints, Moore and Fisher, the lying-in-state of Edward VII. It was to these memories that King George himself referred when he opened Westminster Hall again thirteen years ago, after the magnificent hammer-beam roof had been saved from the death-watch beetle.

'For centuries,' King George said, 'the hall has witnessed the growth of the Constitution and has been, as it were, a link between the Crown and the people.'

Perhaps he was remembering the one occasion on which the link was broken, when Charles I stood here on trial for his life by the only dictator who has ever ruled in England.

'I die,' Charles said, 'for the common people of England and their liberties', and in a sense every King since that time has stood his trial too in this hall.

For since that age the earlier, more boisterous, memories have been effaced: of William Rufus, who first built the hall and kept his noisy Court there; of the 6,000 poor men and women who were feasted here on New Year's Day exactly 700 years ago by Henry III; of King Richard Lionheart's Christmas feast, cooked for him by his 2,000 cooks, when 10,000 guests were entertained with a meal of 28 oxen, 300 sheep, and more fowls than could be counted.

Here, too, until the accession of William IV, the head of the House of Dymoke would ride up the hall in full armour during the coronation ceremony and fling down his gauntlet in defence of the new King's title.

Perhaps where that challenge used to be given it is most fitting that a King should meet his people for the last time. The white-plumed soldiers, the tall candles burning at every corner, the Crown, the Cross, the empty Throne do not disguise the fact that he is closer now to his people than he has ever been, closer even than on Christmas Day, when his deep, rather husky voice made him familiar to millions. This is his dock and this is his trial, and it is the ordinary man now who judges him – the city clerk, the unemployed workman, the woman from the suburbs – who will pass round the catafalque. Their silence and grief are his acquittal.

This is no empty show: the people *can* condemn. When William IV lay in state Greville noted in his Journal how *'I saw two men in an animated conversation, and one laughing heartily at the very foot of the coffin as it was lying in state'.*

Compare that glimpse of empty show — Greville compared the chamber of death with *'a scene in a play'* — with what is felt today, the sense of personal loss.

Kipling wrote when King George's father lay in state in Westminster Hall:

> *Who in the Realm today lays down dear*
> *life for the sake of a land more dear?*
> *And unconcerned for his own estate toils*
> *till the last grudged sands have run?*
> *Let him approach. It is proven here*
> *Our King asks nothing of any man more than*
> *our King himself has done.*

That is the significance of the draped flag, the arms reversed. Just as much as Charles I, the King has laid down his life 'for the common people of England and their liberties'.

And here the common people will come to him, a long line of trudging feet and bared heads passing for hour after hour through the huge dim hall; hastily improvised mourning, black bands, black ties, dresses last worn at a family funeral.

During his life the King met many of his commons: the men who had travelled in wild places, mountaineers, flyers, motorists, sailors; they would be commanded to the palace to relate their adventures or their discoveries.

It is the fate of royalty to meet only the outstanding and to see the millions of his subjects only in the mass, a cheering crowd outside a building to be opened, the mob beside a slipway when a new giant liner takes the water.

It is only now that he meets them one by one as they go slowly by: the woman with six children, the ex-Service man, lovers, and strangers from country towns. It is *their* sorrow that we mean when we talk of a nation saying good-bye to its King.

Daily Mail
23 January 1936

Two Tall Travellers

'Unknown Liberia' – fortunate indeed for Mr Greenwall, of the *Daily Express,* and Mr Wild, 'one of the first unofficial Englishmen to enter Afghanistan and "debunk" the country', that Liberia *is* comparatively speaking unknown, so that there will be few people to call their bluff or question their almost incredible effrontery. 'We have investigated,' they say, on the strength of a good many pages of potted history, sometimes inaccurate, and gossip, often absurd, 'the charges of Slavery and Cannibalism', and again, 'Let us say here and now that we went to considerably more trouble to explore all roads leading to the truth than did the League of Nations Commission.' They speak of 'weeks of painstaking enquiry', and in a passage closely following a chapter on native bush schools, which might well have been written by a careless and muddled reader of popular encyclopedias, we get the proud Munchausen claim: 'We had gained an insight into Liberian native lore that is given to few white men.'

'All roads leading to the truth': this audacious claim, so typical of our less honest newspapers even when they deal with European affairs, the storming of Badajoz or atrocities in Madrid, is worth examining. *Unknown Liberia* has 260-odd pages; of these less than 40 deal with the authors' personal observations (if one may call their culinary grumbles by that name) in the hinterland. The rest of the book is compiled from published histories, from interviews in a far from unknown capital served by regular steamship services (their tallest story is of Leopard Men who roam the streets of Monrovia after dark), from League of Nations reports and from unreliable gossip. As for the trek into the hinterland, it leaves unknown Liberia more unknown than ever. The authors (it is amusing to read that they took with them twenty hammock carriers but could not afford the extra weight of a book) seem to have spent some uncomfortable days. I can hardly treat seriously their claim to have trekked 'week after week' – going up the main route from Monrovia to Kolahun and the English border, the regular official route from the capital used by missionaries and Government servants and about as little known as the Ridgeway. They had difficulty with their overpaid carriers, not surprising considering their attitude, suspicious, bullying, nervous and hostile (' "My God," we would mutter to one another, "here comes another of those blacks . . ." '), and as for anything they saw with their own eyes they might just as well have stayed in England, where indeed almost all their material might easily have been compiled.

It is only from scraps of internal evidence, for they print no map of their route and all details are for reasons of their own carefully shrouded, that I conclude they went up by Belliyella and Jenne to Kolahun (a route the Liberian Government always suggests to travellers, which is presumably why these two gentlemen found a shortage of chickens and eggs), where they saw Mr Reeves, a District Commissioner whom they picture (Munchausen again) as 'a black Mussolini' capable of one day marching a negro army to Monrovia, a comic idea to anyone who has met Mr Reeves. On the dust cover we are told that the authors stayed 'with the virtual ruler of Liberia', another mystery, for there is no word about this in the text, though I suppose it refers with equal ineptitude to the same little parochial tyrant. Perhaps these mystifications have the same motive as the curious form this book takes. For example, a chapter on their trek is followed by a chapter on Chief Nimley, the rebel Kru, written partly from unreliable hearsay, partly from League reports, which to the uninstructed reader may well give the impression that the authors had themselves passed through his district, making 'painstaking enquiries'. Throughout the volume unacknowledged second-hand sources are carefully mingled with the trivial personal anecdotes to give the former the appearance of direct reporting. Even the photographs are misleading, for many of them are borrowed without acknowledgement, one from Lady Dorothy Mills's book on quite a different part of Liberia, two from Sir Harry Johnston's, and one from the late H. R. Reeve's *Black Republic*. This is pretty good for a book entitled *Unknown Liberia*; indeed, as at least one other photograph I gather from internal evidence cannot have been taken by either of the authors, I begin to wonder whether any of these snaps of the undiscovered are by the intrepid explorers. Through the haze of mystery nothing is quite certain, except that Mr Greenwall and Mr Wild did visit Monrovia and presumably did make a short journey in hammocks from Monrovia to Kolahun. Ten days is a more usual allowance than 'week after week' for 'our long and arduous trek of several hundreds [*sic*] of miles', and surely President Barclay had his tongue in his cheek when he offered them an armed escort.

Review of *Unknown Liberia* by Harry J. Greenwall and Roland Wild
Spectator
11 September 1936

Is It Criticism?

Film criticism, more than any other form of criticism except perhaps that of the novel, is a compromise. The critic, as much as the film, is supposed to entertain, and the great public is not interested in technicalities. The reader expects a series of dogmatic statements: he is satisfied, like any member of the Book Society, with being told what is good and what is bad. If he finds himself often enough in agreement with the critic, he is content. It never occurs to him to ask why the critic thought this film good and that film bad, any more than it occurs to him to question his own taste. The fictional film is more or less stabilized at the level of middle-class taste.

One need not deny to either books or films of popular middle-class entertainment a useful social service, as long as it is recognized that social service has nothing to do with the art of cinema or the art of fiction. What I object to is the idea that it is the *critic*'s business to assist films to fulfil a social function. The critic's business should be confined to the art.

It is this which presents serious difficulties, for a critic concerned with an art needs at least two things: material for his analysis, for comparison and instruction, and a mind which, however sympathetic, is not prone to quick enthusiasms. But, to take the first difficulty, what in the cinema is the critic to write about? He is lucky if two or three films in the year can be treated with respect, and if week after week he produces an analysis of the latest popular film, showing how the scriptwriter, the director and the cameraman have failed, he will soon lose his readers and afterwards his job. He has got to entertain, and most film critics find the easiest way to entertain is 'to write big'. One leading reviewer adopts a very masculine, plain man manner, which is as uncritical and has the same effect as the fulsomeness of more hack reviewers; it catches the eye easily. *Their* praise is usually unequalled by the official publicity writers. Indeed I once knew a daily journalist who never troubled to write his own copy, but handed in the publicity man's 'blurb' with a few adjectives knocked out. The public eye accustomed to the weekly 'masterpiece' and the daily 'tragedy', demands from these journalists Poignant Dramas and Tragedies of Frustrated Love rather than unenthusiastic and accurate estimates. A Hungarian producer at Denham, turning out a number of commercial films of rather low technical value, becomes – in a recent magazine – a Man of Destiny.

Reviewing of this kind contributes nothing to the cinema. The reviewer is simply adding to the atmosphere of graft, vague rhetoric, paid publicity, the general air of Big unscrupulous Business. He is not regarded by his employers as a critic so much as a reporter. One day he is required to write a fulsome interview with a visiting film star at the Savoy, the next to criticize a film in which she appears. The double role is too much for the reviewer, and his criticism reads like an extended interview, gossiping little paragraphs about the stars, an inaccurate sketch of the story, no mention of the director unless he is, like Capra or Clair, world-famous, and no mention at all of the film as a film, that is to say, sequences of photographs arranged in a certain way to get a certain effect.

For some months I, too, received from a patient American company about two telegrams a week addressed to my home inviting me at great length (they usually ran to forty words) to be present next day at the Savoy or the Carlton when a film personality, sometimes of remarkable obscurity, would 'hold court'. This was the invariable phrase. There would be, the telegrams usually added, refreshments.

Refreshments: it is a key word to the murky business, to the world in which a new critic finds himself. Even publishers, with their cocktail parties, have not developed the racket to this pitch. It is still possible to review books, among books, in quiet, and I believe dramatic critics are not yet given free drinks at the bar between acts or offered, before the curtain rises, a glass of sherry and a cigarette (one film company even goes as far as champagne). It is assumed that the film critic is invariably thirsty and alcoholic even at the oddest hours. Nowhere else, except on the West Coast of Africa, have I been expected to start drinking by 10.30 in the morning, when the taste of the morning marmalade is still on the tongue. Sometimes the dubious hospitality extends to a lunch at the Carlton.

The film companies, of course, are not bribing the critics. No one is going to be bribed with a glass of sherry and a cigarette. The motive is less obvious and more kindly. The daily press is to a great extent controlled by advertisers. The film critics are not free to damn a bad film. Almost the only papers where you can find uncontrolled criticism are the periodicals: the *New Statesman,* the *Spectator,* the *London*

Mercury, and the *Listener.* The glasses of sherry, so I believe, are charitably intended to make it easier for the so-called critic to tap out his fore-ordained notice: it would be a grim business otherwise.

The same motive perhaps lies behind the Gala performances: a Gala performance is usually allotted to an expensive but bad film: *Moscow Nights, The Dark Angel,* the two worst films of 1935, both had this curious setting of blue lights, squealing peeresses, policemen to keep back a crowd which wouldn't have assembled without the policemen, a strained attempt to make a bad film, if it can't be entertainment, at any rate something, a Show, a social occasion. It is in this atmosphere that, if ever there is a Shakespeare of the films, he will have to get a hearing. His films will not be damned, they will be praised, praised as highly and in the same terms as *The Dark Angel.* And it is in this atmosphere, too, that a Coleridge of the films would have to work. Indeed, when once his little vice became widely known, his kindly host would see that he was served with his individual opium pill instead of the glass of sherry.

It is not that one wishes the cinema to be precious, eclectic, unpopular. The novel has long ceased to make any effort at being a really popular art: the novels of Mr Priestley or Mr Brett Young represent the people about as much as do the prosperous suburbs of Balham and Streatham. I doubt if we have had any popular art in England since the Shakespearean theatre, and I welcome the chance the cinema offers. Millions go to the cinema, but do they really get what *they* want or do they get what the middle-class public wants? – the cinema of escape. The thousands who come down to Wembley in charabancs from the north with favours in their caps don't want to escape. They want something as simple and exciting as a cup-tie, just as the Elizabethan public wanted something as brutal and exciting as what went on in the bear-pit. *The Texas Rangers* is nearer to popular art than *Anna Karenina*. I admire a film like *Song of Ceylon* more perhaps than anything else I have yet seen on the screen, but I would rather see the public shouting and hissing in the sixpenny seats. Instead – I look at my paper this week: *The Great Ziegfeld, Sins of Man, Follow Your Heart, East Meets West, The Singing Kid*.

What, to return to my earlier question, is the critic to write about? Almost the only approach possible at the present stage for a critic who is writing for readers uninterested in technical detail is the satirical. This is to make a flank attack upon the reader, to persuade him to laugh at personalities, stories, ideas, methods, he has previously taken for granted. We need to be rude, rude even to our fellow reviewers, but not in the plain downright way, which may help to kill a particular picture, but leaves its kind untouched. The cinema needs to be purged with laughter, and the critics, too (critics who can write: 'By sheer diligence and enthusiasm the cinema, which twenty-five years ago was producing such morsels as *What Drink Did* has now arrived at the point when the Queen, the Prince of Wales, and the President of the United States, are all prepared to patronize its shows within a fortnight'). Indeed, I am not sure whether our fellow critics are not more important subjects for our satire than the cinema itself, for they are doing as much as any Korda or Sam Goldwyn to maintain the popular middle-class Book Society *status quo*.

Sight and Sound
Autumn 1936

Ideas in the Cinema

Not even the newspapers can claim so large a public as the films: they make the circulation figures of the *Daily Express* look insignificant. The voice of Mr Paul Muni has been heard by more people than the radio voices of the dictators, and the words he speaks are usually a little more memorable. The words of dictators do not dwell in the brain – one speech is very like another: we retain a confused impression of olive branches, bayonets and the New Deal. How easy it would be to draw an optimistic picture of the film industry, the perfect method of communicating simply and vividly to the greatest number the ideas of the artist, the reformer, the moralist. *Zola* after all preaches Truth; whatever we may think of its aesthetic falseness, the moral is impeccable. The moral indeed is always impeccable; whether we are present at a gangster picture or a news film there is always the villain and the hero. In *The March of Time* the bombs fall on the babies of Madrid and not on the babies of Granada: the Japanese imperialists wage ruthless war on – whom? The Chinese warlord whose methods were described with such convincing horror in *La Condition humaine*, in which officers – according to M. Malraux – burned their Communist prisoners alive in the boilers of locomotives. No, Time Marches On and the warlord is oddly transformed. It isn't altogether an ideological purpose which dictates these simplifications: the huge public has been trained to expect a villain and a hero, and if you're going to reach the biggest possible public, it's no good thinking of drama as the conflict of ideas; it's the conflict – in terms of sub-machine-guns – between the plainest Good and the plainest Evil.

But does reaching the public necessarily mean reaching the biggest, most amorphous public possible? Isn't it equally possible to reach a selected public with films of aesthetic interest? The artist needs an audience to whom it isn't necessary to preach, in whom he can assume a few common ideas, born of a common environment. I don't mean a small intellectual *avant-garde* public, but a national public, the kind of trench kinship which isn't a matter of class or education, but of living and dying together in the same hole. The cinema, of course, should be a popular art, but need that popularity be worldwide? What common ideas can be assumed between the middle-western farmer and the Cockney clerk, between the New York stockbroker and the unemployed man in a Welsh village? Few, I'm afraid, less vague and sentimental than the ideas of *Lost Horizon*. And yet the other day at a private discussion I heard one of the best English commercial directors (English by birth, a rare thing) state that he wasn't interested in making English films: he wanted to make international films.

Was it a commercial boast or was it a confused relic of the political ideal we most of us shared till it was routed in the African mountains? Probably it was a little of both – the idealist dreaming of an art dimly connected with Geneva and the great dead Palace of the Nations, and the merchant trying to muscle in on the American market, and perhaps too the wise man making the best of his limitations. For art has never really left the cave where it began, and you cannot live, as an English ace producer does, between Denham and Hollywood, with a break in New York for business conferences, and betweenwhiles make a picture which is the product of saturation, saturation in a particular environment. What can you do in those circumstances – your territory the office, the liner, the aeroplane, the studio – but make an international picture? That is to say a picture without atmosphere or theme, of which the literary equivalent, I suppose, is something like *La Madonne des sleepings*.

I daresay the producer (an intelligent man) would have admitted, if he had been pressed, that there's no such thing as international art, but art was not a word which came up at that discussion. England, it was assumed, was too small for a self-supporting industry. English films couldn't be made. A curious and disingenuous notion when you consider how much money English producers have lost with their international pictures. If the financial consideration was the only one, it would surely occur to them that nationality might *pay*. For if the expression is fine enough the world in time will listen, but the fineness of the expression depends on the integrity of the source – Shakespeare is English first, and only after that the world's. And to compare small things with great, *Mr Deeds* was an American and not an international picture. Mightn't it be the sensible, the economic thing to aim at the English markets alone and leave the world's to fate?

Possibly, but that is to leave out of account human megalomania. Film magnates have this affinity to newspaper barons – they are really less concerned with money than with themselves, their own publicity. Better to make a picture for £200,000 and lose half your money than make a picture for £20,000 and clear a paltry profit. There's a kind of wild impracticability about these men – they don't really want money, they want noise. (I have myself played a modest part in the construction of a 'cheap' film which was shot hurriedly without a finished script and scrapped uncompleted at a cost of £45,000 – the total cost of the French spectacular film, *Mayerling*.) You can't, these men will tell you, make a film pay in this country alone. The French can, and the Swedes can, but apparently, with our much greater population, it remains for us an impossibility. Of course all they mean is that their productions would be too small for glory, and to justify themselves they compute merit in terms of pounds. I have heard one of the leading men in the industry state confidently that a picture which costs £100,000 *must* be a better picture than one which cost £50,000 . . . and yet we all know that the 50,000 extra pounds may all have gone on a single star, on bad organization so that the script was not finished when the star arrived from Hollywood. The sense of glory is the main thing that stands between the artist and his public.

There's another. The artist belongs to the cave: he is national: and the men through whom he must transmit his idea, in whose company he must retain the integrity of his conception, are – very frequently – foreign. In what can with technical accuracy be termed an English company you may have a Hungarian producer assisted by a Hungarian art director and a Hungarian scenario editor. Among its directors there may be Frenchmen, Hungarians, Germans and Americans. The language is strange to them, the ideas are strange: little wonder that the characters are slowly smoothed out of existence, the English corners rubbed away. The public – you may say – has been reached by something, and they'll be reached again next week and the week after by so many thousand feet of celluloid; they haven't been reached by an idea: that has died on the way, somewhere in the central-heated office, at a conference, among the foreign accents.

Spectator
19 November 1937

Homage to the Bombardier

The best autobiographies are written by old ladies: malice trained over the tea-tables, the sharp eye for foibles, and a nostalgic memory of the days when top hats were worn to church. We learn curious details about hot-water bottles and the way Sunday dinner was served. An old way of life, close enough not to be history, comes alive. The worst autobiographies, I suppose, are written by politicians – interminable details of what went on behind the scenes of old Home Rule Bills now of academic interest: these memoirs should be mimeographed and circulated to historians 'on request'. Somewhere in between the two come the autobiographies of people who have known people – anecdotes of the great according to a private computation. Stories about Henry James I always enjoy: he has the suavity and abstraction of legend; Mr Wyndham Lewis's stories – in the literary part of his autobiography – are about Mr Eliot, Mr Joyce, Mr Pound. Somehow these great and good men lack, for me, the legendary excitement – perhaps a younger generation may find these the most thrilling pages: the publication of *Blast*, the moment when Mr Eliot unwittingly presented Mr Joyce with a present of old boots . . .

To me the aesthetically exciting section of this always entertaining autobiography is that which deals with the war, and that is because Mr Wyndham Lewis writes about those savage and irrational events with beautiful objectivity, sometimes tinged with malice. This is magnificent writing, without personal passion, a series of images rendered exactly and memorably:

'Mobilization was everywhere; the train was quite full. Ten people, chiefly women, slept upright against each other in one carriage. They revealed unexpected fashions in sleep. Their eyes seemed to be shut fast to enable them to examine some ludicrous fact within. It looked, from the corridor, like a séance of imbeciles.'

It is better than Mr Douglas Jerrold's account of the Gallipoli campaign in *his* recent autobiography – and that is saying a great deal. Both authors take – like the old ladies – a refreshingly protestant view: they don't belong to the great pacifist-class-war-racket: Mr Jerrold is the more revolutionary with his view that the war was right and that we were on the right side: Mr Wyndham Lewis is only a pace behind, for though he thinks the particular war was a stupid one, he doesn't object to war in theory. So we have an account of a scene, untainted by moral indignation or patriotic fervour, and the effect is odd and stimulating. It is as if for the first time we are being shown the common factor in men's experience (can a writer aim higher?). This is what men *saw* – however they felt about it. Herr Remarque, Mr Blunden, Mr Graves, Mr Sassoon, the long roll of war writers, distinguished and less distinguished – they have no common subjective experience, but at least this, we feel, is what they observed – the landscape of their differing thoughts.

'The sunset had turned on its romantic dream-light and what had been romantic enough before was now absolutely operatic. A darkening ridge, above a drift of saharan steppe, gouged and tossed into a monotonous disorder, in a word the war-wilderness; not a flicker of life, not even a ration party – not even a skeleton: and upon the ridge the congeries of "bursts", to mark the spot where we had been. It was like the twitching of a chicken after its head had been cut off.'

There are, one notices as one writes the passage down, a few subjective adjectives – romantic, operatic, but they are not there to support a private judgement but to convey an appearance. Surface writing I suppose it could be called, but how close the nerves are to the skin, and what homage we ought to pay to a writer – in this dark age of prose – with a rhetoric like this at his command (he is describing a visit – as an artillery officer – to the front line):

'More German batteries were firing now, and a number of shells intercepted us. We met an infantry party coming up, about ten men, with earthen faces and heads bowed, their eyes turned inward as it seemed, to shut out this too-familiar scene. As a shell came rushing down beside them, they did not notice it. There was no side-stepping death if this was where you *lived*. It was worth *our* while to prostrate ourselves, when death came over-near. We might escape, *in spite of* death. But *they* were its servants. Death would not tolerate that optimistic obeisance from them.'

Review of *Blasting and Bombardiering* by Wyndham Lewis
London Mercury
December 1937

India Unvisited

India, unvisited, has always been to me a literary region; the region of Mr E. M. Forster, of Kipling, vague memories of Flora Annie Steel and Henty. An hysterical woman in a cave, adultery at Simla, a Calcutta newspaper in the heat, greased cartridges, heroic Gurkhas advancing to the drums of the Fore and Aft, mutinies on barrack squares.

Indian writers have done little to help. Occasionally a student at Oxford may win a local reputation as an officer of the Union, and on the strength of it publish a thin volume of essays, which have previously appeared in the *Isis*, and shrink in the indifferent London air. Nor are these ever concerned with India: they represent always an Indian view of England. As for Rabindranath Tagore, I cannot believe that anyone but Mr Yeats can still take his poems very seriously. One associates him with what Chesterton calls 'the bright pebbly eyes' of the Theosophists.

It was Mr Narayan with his *Swami and Friends* who first brought India, in the sense of the Indian population and the Indian way of life, alive to me, and in *The Bachelor of Arts* he continues to fill in his picture of Malgudi, a small town in Mysore. *Swami* is the story of a child written with complete objectivity, with a humour strange to our fiction, closer to Chekhov than to any English writer, with the same underlying sense of beauty and sadness. *The Bachelor of Arts* is the story of a young Indian in his last year at college, and his first year of freedom. Some readers will admire it for its humour, some for its sense of implicit – I was going to say tragedy, but that word is too blatant for a pathos as delicate as the faint discoloration of ivory with age.

A few readers may be puzzled. English novelists, I am afraid, have never been chary of expressing openly their point of view, of telling the reader how he should judge a character or situation. The Victorian novelists were always ready to step into the foreground to point their moral, and it was this habit more than anything else which brought the objective novel into disrepute. Alas that the way out discovered was subjectivity, for though the new method has produced its masterpieces it is too easy a solution for permanent satisfaction. The author can state his point of view, it is true, without destroying the fictional illusion, but only by becoming himself one of his characters, by losing the clear line, the vivid visual grasp of something observed from without.

Mr Narayan has chosen a more difficult way, and his novels, as a consequence, are of more than topical or utilitarian value. They increase our knowledge of the Indian character, certainly, but I prefer to think of them as contributions to English literature, contributions of remarkable maturity, and of the finest promise too, when we consider that Mr Narayan is writing in what is to him a foreign tongue. This complete objectivity, this complete freedom from comment, is the boldest gamble a novelist can take. If he allows himself to take sides, moralize, propagand, he can easily achieve an extra-literary interest, but if he follows Mr Narayan's method, he stakes all on his creative power. His characters must live, or else the book has no claim whatever on our interest.

And how vividly Mr Narayan's characters do live: Natesan, the Union Secretary who has bribed his way to office with coffee and tiffin: Gajapathi, Professor of English, who finds errors in Fowler and corrects Bradley on Shakespeare: the holy and dignified thief who steals flowers to lay before the gods: the talkative revolutionary, Veeraswami, with his huge optimism: the poet Mohan ('the poems were on a wide variety of subjects – from a Roadside Grass Seller to the Planet in Its Orbit; from Lines suggested by an Ant to the Dying Musician. All conceivable things seem to have incited Mohan to anger, gloom, despair, and defiance'): Kailas, the sentimental drunken debauchee ('Mother is a sacred object . . . It is a rare commodity, sir. Mother is a rare commodity'): Chandran himself, always drawing up detailed plans for living and always finding them disarranged by this and that, a visit to the cinema, the sight of a girl by the river side ('How old was she? Probably fourteen. Might be even fifteen or sixteen. If she was more than fourteen she must be married. There was a touch of despair in this thought'), the absence of a letter.

And behind these characters we are aware not of an individual author, with views on politics or social reform, or with a personal mysticism to express, but of a whole national condition: the huge Indian spaces into which friends disappear to take up railway clerkships and never to write letters: the fine plans which under the pressure of life narrow down into getting so many new subscribers for a paper at so much a commission. Perhaps it is no coincidence that Mr Narayan's light, vivid style, with its sense of time passing,

66

of the unrealized beauty of human relationships, so often recalls Chekhov; perhaps there was a similarity between the position of the educated Indian under British rule and that of the student class of Tsarist Russia: the same wasted intellectual effort (all those four years at the Malgudi College, the political science, the history of the medieval papacy, Shakespeare and Milton, leading to nothing more important than the local agency of a newspaper): the same Siberian distances (friends leaving Malgudi, letters not arriving, the group photo fading). How often in Chekhov a story ends with a waving handkerchief, a departure, a looking back to something beautiful, a looking forward to something which we know will never happen. But it would be wrong to emphasize more deeply than Mr Narayan himself this sad and poetic background: the humour of the book is enough to enchant.

Introduction to *The Bachelor of Arts* by R. K. Narayan
1937

Subjects and Stories

There is no need to regard the cinema as a completely new art; in its fictional form it has the same purpose as the novel, just as the novel has the same purpose as the drama. Chekhov, writing of his fellow novelists, remarked: 'The best of them are realistic and paint life as it is, but because every line is permeated, as with a juice, by awareness of a purpose, you feel, besides life as it is, also life as it ought to be, and this captivates you.' This description of an artist's theme has never, I think, been bettered: we need not even confine it to the fictional form: it applies equally to the documentary film, to pictures in the class of Mr Rotha's *Shipyard* (one remembers the last sequence of the launching: the workers who have made the ship watching from the banks and roofs the little social gathering, the ribbons and the champagne) or Mr Wright's *Song of Ceylon*: only in films to which Chekhov's description applies shall we find the poetic cinema. And the poetic cinema – it is the only form worth considering.

Life as it is and life as it ought to be: let us take that as the only true subject for a film, and consider to what extent the cinema is fulfilling its proper function. The stage, of course, has long ceased to fulfil it at all. Mr St John Ervine, Miss Dodie Smith, these are the popular playwrights of the moment: they have no sense of life as it is lived, far less even than Mr Noël Coward, and if they have some dim idea of a better life, this is expressed only in terms of sexual or financial happiness. As for the popular novel, Mr Walpole, Mr Brett Young, Mr Priestley, we are aware of rather crude minds representing no more of contemporary life than is to be got in a holiday snapshot: Mr Walpole the house and garden, Mr Brett Young the village street, the old alms-houses and the vicar, Mr Priestley the inn, the forge, the oldest inhabitant.

I think one may say that *Dodsworth* represents about the highest level to which this type of writer can attain on the screen. *Dodsworth* as a book was far less readable than as a picture it was seeable. The dimmest social drama can be given a certain gloss and glitter by a good director and a good cameraman. No one, I think, could have been actively bored by *Dodsworth*. It had the great virtues of natural acting and natural speech; it did in its way, its too personal and private way, fulfil one of the functions we have named; it at least presented life as it presumably appears to an American millionaire, unhappily married to a wife who is determined to climb socially: perhaps one is rash in making even that claim, for the number of people who can judge its truth must needs be strictly limited. But as for life as it ought to be, the nearest *Dodsworth* comes to that is a quaint Italian villa on the bay of Naples and the company of a gentle, refined and flower-like widow. It is alas! still true of the theatre what Mr Ford Madox Ford wrote in 1911, in an essay on the functions of the arts in the republic, 'that, in this proud, wealthy and materially polished civilization, there was visible no trace, no scintilla, no shadow of a trace of the desire to have any kind of thought awakened'. In those days before the great four years' deluge Mr Ford found that 'it is to the music-halls we must go nowadays for any form of pulse stirring', the popular entertainment of that day. The cinema has to a large extent killed the music-hall, but has it absorbed its virtues or 'the sinister forms of morality' Mr Ford found in the theatre?

Writing this in the third week of February, 1937, I turn to the list of films now to be seen in London (perhaps it may amuse a few readers when this book appears to try to recall these films, and if a few do still stick obstinately in the memory, to try to recall their subjects, a few sequences): *Ernte, Maid of Salem, Magnificent Obsession, Mazurka, This'll Make You Whistle, The Great Barrier, Devil Takes the Count, The Texas Rangers, Beloved Enemy, Dreaming Lips, O.H.M.S., Aren't Men Beasts, Ramona, The Plainsman, Girls' Dormitory, His Lordship, Accused, La Kermesse héroïque, Good Morning Boys.* It is not on the whole such an unfavourable week. I think three of those films may be remembered in a year's time. But how many of them show any inkling of the only subject-matter for art, life as it is and life as it ought to be, how many even fulfil what Mr Ford defines as the functions of merely inventive literature, of diverting, delighting, tickling, of promoting appetites? Only, I think, three which I have mentioned: *La Kermesse héroïque, The Texas Rangers, The Plainsman.* The first had at least an adult theme, that the sexual appetite is a great deal stronger than patriotism: it did present life – in fancy dress for safety – as it is; it had the characteristic personal exaggeration that Mr Ford demands of the imaginative writer: it was a Feyder film. The other two had good, if less interesting and more obvious themes: that when you have settled a new country, you must make it safe for the unarmed and the weak, themes which do contain of their very nature the two halves of Chekhov's definition.

But I am afraid in the plots of the others you will get the more representative film. *Mazurka:* fallen woman shoots her seducer to save her child from a similar fate; *Magnificent Obsession:* a woman loses her eyesight when a drunken young plutocrat smashes his car, the drunken young plutocrat turns over a new leaf, studies medicine, becomes the greatest eye surgeon of his day in time to cure and marry the girl while both are young; *Dreaming Lips*: a young wife falls passionately in love with a musical genius; unable to choose between the genius and the boy husband, she kills herself; *Girls' Dormitory*: an innocent and dewy schoolgirl falls in love with her headmaster, writes an imaginary love letter which is discovered by a prying mistress, is expelled for immorality, runs away in the rain pursued by the headmaster who then discovers the truth.

It is difficult to see what critical purpose is served by subjects like these. (I say *critical* purpose because the sense of life as it should be must always be a critical one. An element of satire enters into all dramatic art.) Is it possible that the glittering prizes the cinema offers defeat their purpose? The artist is not as a rule a man who takes kindly to life, but can his critical faculty help being a little blunted on two hundred pounds a week? A trivial point perhaps, but one reason why we do not look first to Hollywood or Denham for films of artistic value, for the poetic cinema.

I use the word poetic in its widest sense. Only of quite recent years has the term poet been narrowed down to those who write according to some kind of metrical or rhythmical scheme. In Dryden's day any creative writer was called a poet, and it would be difficult to justify any definition

71

which excluded James or Conrad, Chekhov or Turgenev from the rank of poets. Mr Ford Madox Ford has given us the most useful definition for the quality which these prose writers have in common with Shakespeare and Dryden: 'not the power melodiously to arrange words but the power to suggest human values'.

So we need not consider, I think, the various screen adaptations of Shakespeare. It isn't that kind of poetry we are seeking (the poetry made tautological by the realistic settings), nor will we find in the smart neat *Dodworths* and *Dreaming Lips* the power to suggest human values. We come nearer to what we seek perhaps in a picture like *Hortobagy,* the film of the Hungarian plains acted by peasants and shepherds. The photography was very beautiful, the cutting often superb, but photography by itself cannot make poetic cinema. By itself it can only make arty cinema. *Man of Aran* was a glaring example of this: how affected and wearisome were those figures against the skyline, how meaningless that magnificent photography of storm after storm. *Man of Aran* did not even attempt to describe truthfully a way of life. The inhabitants had to be taught shark-hunting in order to supply Mr Flaherty with a dramatic sequence. *Hortobagy* did at least attempt to show life truthfully: those wild herds tossing across the enormous plain, against the flat sky, the shepherds in their huge heavy traditional cloaks galloping like tartar cavalry between the whitewashed huts, the leaping of the stallions, the foaling of the mares shown with meticulous candour, did leave the impression that we were seeing, as far as was humanly possible, life as it is. It was documentary in the finest sense: on the documentary side it has been unsurpassed: but Mr Basil Wright's *Song of Ceylon,* faulty in continuity as it was, contained more of what we are looking for, criticism implicit in the images, life as it is containing the indications of life as it should be, the personal lyric utterance.

It was divided, it may be remembered, into four parts, and opened with a forest sequence, huge revolving fans of palm filling the screen. We then watched a file of pilgrims climb a mountain side to the stone effigies of the gods, and here, as a priest struck a bell, Mr Wright used one of the loveliest visual metaphors I have seen on the screen. The sounding of the bell startled a small bird from its branch, and the camera followed the bird's flight and the bell notes across the island, down from the mountain side, over forest and plain and sea, the vibration of the tiny wings, the fading sound. Then, in a rather scrappy and unsatisfactory movement, we saw the everyday life of the natives, until in the third movement we were made aware of the personal criticism implied in the whole film. As the natives followed the old ways of farming, climbing palm trees with a fibre loop, guiding their elephants against the trees to be felled, voices dictated bills of lading, closed deals, announced through loud-speakers the latest market prices. And lest the contrast between two ways of life should be left too indecisively balanced, the director's sympathy was plainly shown in the last movement: back on the mountain side with the stone faces, the gaudy gilded dancers, the solitary peasant laying his offering at Buddha's feet, and when he closed the film with the revolving leaves, it was as if he were sealing away from us devotion and dance and the gentle communal life of harvest, leaving us outside with the bills of lading and the loud-speakers.

Here, of course, with the director who acts as his own cameraman and supervises his own script, with the reduction of credits to a minimum, and the subsidized film, we are getting far from the commercial picture. The *Song of Ceylon* will always stand outside the ordinary cinema. We are getting closer to the poetic and yet commercially possible cinema with a picture like *The Song of Freedom,* an inexpensive picture made by a small British company, full of muddled thought and bad writing: the story of a black dock-hand who becomes a famous singer and goes back to his ancestral home to try to save his people from the witch-doctors. Full of muddled thought and absurdities of speech, it is true, yet this film had something which *Dodsworth* lacked. A sense stays in the memory of an unsophisticated mind fumbling on the edge of simple and popular poetry. The best scenes were the dockland scenes, the men returning from work free from any colour bar, the public-house interiors, dark faces pausing at tenement windows to listen to the black man's singing, a sense of nostalgia, of what Mann calls 'the gnawing surreptitious hankering for the bliss of the commonplace'.

The commonplace, that is the point. The poetic drama ceased to be of value when it ceased to be as popular as a bear-baiting. The decline from Webster to Tennyson is not a mere decline in poetic merit – 'Queen Mary' has passages of great beauty – but a decline in popularity. The cinema has got to appeal to millions; we have got to accept its popularity as a virtue, not turn away from it as a vice.

Only the conviction that a public art should be as popular and unsubtle as a dance tune enables one to sit with patient hope through pictures certainly unsubtle but not, in any real sense, popular. What a chance there is for the creative artist, one persists in believing, to produce for an audience incomparably greater than that of all the 'popular' novelists combined, from Mr Walpole to Mr Brett Young, a genuinely vulgar art. Any other is impossible. The novelist may write for a few thousand readers, but the film artist *must* work for millions. It should be his distinction and pride that he has a public whose needs have never been met since the closing of the theatres by Cromwell. But where is the vulgarity of this art? Alas! the refinement of the 'popular' novel has touched the films; it is the twopenny libraries they reflect rather than the Blackfriars Ring, the Wembley final, the pin saloons, the coursing.

> *I'm not the type that I seem to be,*
> *Happy-go-lucky and gay,*

Bing Crosby mournfully croons in one of his latest pictures. That is the common idea of popular entertainment, a mild self-pity, something soothing, something gently amusing. The film executive still thinks in terms of the 'popular' play and the 'popular' novel, of a limited middle-class audience, of the tired business man and the feminine reader. The public which rattles down from the north to Wembley with curious hats and favours, tipsy in charabancs, doesn't, apparently, ask to be soothed: it asks to be excited. It was for these that the Elizabethan stage provided action which could arouse as communal a response as bear-baiting. For a popular response is not the sum of private excitements, but mass feeling, mass excitement, the Wembley roar; and it is the weakness of the Goldwyn Girls that they are as private an enjoyment as the Art Photos a business man may turn over in the secrecy of his study, the weakness of Bing Crosby's sentiment, the romantic nostalgia of 'Empty saddles in the old corral', that it is by its nature a private emotion.

There are very few examples of what I mean by the proper popular use of the film, and most of those are farces: *Duck Soup*, the early Chaplins, a few 'shorts' by Laurel and Hardy. These do convey the sense that the picture has been made by its spectators and not merely shown to them, that it has sprung, as much as their sports, from *their* level. Serious films of the kind are even rarer: perhaps *Fury*, *The Birth of a Nation*, *Men and Jobs*, they could be numbered on the fingers of one hand. Because they are so rare one is ready to accept, with exaggerated gratitude, such refined, elegant, dead pieces as *Louis Pasteur*: the Galsworthy entertainments of the screen: or intelligently adapted plays like *These Three*.

'People want to be taken out of themselves,' the film executive retorts under the mistaken impression that the critic is demanding a kind of Zola-esque realism – as if Webster's plays were realistic. Of course he is right. People are taken out of themselves at Wembley. But I very much doubt if Bing Crosby does so much. 'They don't want to be depressed', but an excited audience is never depressed; if you excite your audience first, you can put over what you will of horror, suffering, truth. But there is one question which needs an answer. How dare we excite an audience, a producer may well ask, when Lord Tyrrell, the President of the Board of Censors, forbids us to show any controversial subject on the screen?

The cinema has always developed by means of a certain low cunning. The old-clothes merchants who came in on a good thing in the early days and ended as presidents of immense industries had plenty of cunning. It is for the artist to show his cunning now. You may say with some confidence that at the present stage of English culture, a great many serious subjects cannot be treated at all. We cannot treat human Justice truthfully as America treated it in *I am a Fugitive from the Chain Gang*. No film which held the aged provincial JPs up to criticism or which described the conditions in the punishment cells at Maidstone would be allowed. Nor is it possible to treat seriously a religious or a political subject.

But this is not all to the bad. We are saved from the merely topical by our absurd censorship. We shall not have to sit through the cinematic equivalents of Mrs Mitchison's emotional novels. We are driven back to the 'blood', the thriller. There never has been a school of popular English bloods. We have been damned from the start by middle-class virtues, by gentlemen cracksmen and stolen plans and Mr Wu's. We have to go farther back than this, dive below the polite level, to something nearer to the common life. And isn't it better to have as your subject 'life nasty, brutish, and short' than the more pompous themes the censor denies us? He won't allow us a proletarian political drama, and I cannot help being a little relieved that we lose the lifeless malice of Pudovkin's capitalist automatons, that dreadful shadow of Victorian progress and inevitable victory. Our excitements have got to have a more universal subject, we have the chance of being better realists than the Russians, we are saved from the tract in return for what we lose.

And when we have attained to a more popular drama, even if it is in the simplest terms of blood on a garage floor ('There lay Duncan laced in his golden blood'), the scream of cars in flight, all the old excitements at their simplest and most surefire, then we can begin – secretly, with low cunning – to develop our poetic drama ('the power to suggest human values'). Our characters can develop from the level of *The Spanish Tragedy* towards a subtler, more thoughtful level.

Some such development we can see at work in Fritz Lang: *The Spy* was his simplest, purest thriller. It had no human values at all, only a brilliant eye for the surface of life and the power of physical excitement: in *Fury* the eye was no less sure, but the poetry had crept in. Here in the lynching was the great thriller situation superbly handled; but not a shot but owed part of its effect to the earlier sequences, the lovers sheltering under the elevated from the drenching rain, good-bye at the railway station with faces and hands pressed to wet fogging windows, the ordinary recognizable agony, life as one knows it is lived, the human, the poetic value. And how was this introduced? Not in words — that is the stage way. I can think of no better example of the use of poetic imagery than in *We from Kronstadt*. At one level this was a magnificent picture of schoolboy heroics, of last charges and fights to the death, heroic sacrifices and narrow escapes, all superbly directed. But what made the picture remarkable was the poetry, critical as poetry must always be (life as it is: life as it ought to be). We were aware all the time that *We from Kronstadt* had been written and directed by the fellow countrymen of Chekhov and Turgenev, and curiously enough among the gunshots, the flag waving, the last stands, the poetry was of the same gentle and reflective and melancholy kind as theirs.

Indeed there was a scene in this picture of humorous and pathetic irony which might have been drawn directly from one of the great classic novelists. The hall and stairs of a one-time palace on the Baltic shore are packed nearly to suffocation with soldiers and marines; they lie massed together like swine: at dawn a door opens at the stair-head and a little knot of children, lodged for safety in the palace, emerges, climbs softly down, ready to start like mice at any movement. They finger the revolvers, the rifles, the machine-guns, climb quickly away when a man moves, percolate down again among the sleepers persistently, to finger a butt, a holster, the barrel of a Lewis gun.

There were many other examples in this picture of the poetic use of imagery and incident: the gulls sweeping and coursing above the cliffs where the Red prisoners are lined up for their death by drowning, the camera moving from the heavy rocks around their necks to the movement of the light, white wings; one sooty tree drooping on the huge rocky Kronstadt walls above a bench where a sailor and a woman embrace, against the dark tide; the riding-lights of the battleships, the shape of the great guns, the singing of a band of sailors going home in the dark to their iron home. Life as it is; life as it ought to be: every poetic image chosen for its contrasting value, to represent peace and normal human values under the heroics and the wartime patriotism.

The poetic cinema, it is worth remembering, can be built up on a few very simple ideas, as simple as the ideas behind the poetic fictions of Conrad: the love of peace, of country, a feeling for fidelity: it doesn't require a great mind to conceive them, but it does require an imaginative mind to feel them with sufficient passion. Griffith was a man of this quality, though to a sophisticated audience he sometimes seems to have chosen incidents of extraordinary naïvety to illustrate his theme. Simple, sensuous and passionate, that definition would not serve the cinema badly: it would enable us at any rate to distinguish between the values say of *Way Down East* and *Louis Pasteur,* and beside that distinction all other discussion of subject-matter seems a little idle.

From *Footnotes to the Film,* edited by Charles Davy 1937

Vive le Roi

'Godd saive aour grechieuss Kinng. Longg laïve aour nobeul Kinng. Godd saive ze Kinng.' That is *Paris-Soir* teaching Paris in phonetics to sing the National Anthem, and that, too, I like to think, is what happens when democracies entertain each other – something a little comic and a little moving as well – like the small boy dressed in a Guards uniform out with his mother, the slightly inaccurate Union Jacks, the postcard sellers who offer you pictures of the Royal Family – furtively: they can't change the habit of a lifetime. We are already familiar with the meetings of dictators – 'stone, bronze, stone, steel, stone, oakleaves, horses' heels over the paving'. The monuments look made to last for ever, and the friendship is over at the railway station. Here in Paris the decorations are as transient as flowers, but the friendship – it is inconceivable that it can ever seriously be threatened, and so we can take the celebrations lightly between friends.

The flags, of course, are everywhere, little splashes of bright colour against the grey Paris stone. They hang in trophies on the lamp-posts and wave in pairs on the hoods of the little green buses: they are to be seen above the advertisements of Byrrh – 'recommendé aux femmes' – and in the shop windows, among the Chaussures Walk-Over, the Walk-Over Unics and the Walk-Over Seductas. And as one might expect there is an elegant variation on our flag below Maggy Rouff's windows on the Champs Elysées – an impression of Union Jack rather than real Union Jacks.

A democracy doesn't have to be dignified all the time – there are the odd attractive monsters on the Seine, a whole school of them, grey and rocky and old, with gold teeth like all Latins and a brood of young like scorpions or whiting – though it can vie with the dictatorships when it chooses: the Place Vendôme, great royal red hangings, embroidered with golden crowns, falling down the front of the grey eighteenth-century stone, green laurel wound above the highest windows as if it had grown like moss with time. The façade of the Opéra is not spoiled by elaborate decoration, only red hangings with gold loops below the tall windows. In the Champs the standards are a little faded by the long delay – it might be a charming French compliment – and obelisks of mirror glass, as sharp as icicles, reflect the banners and trophies as they stir in the grey air and the spray of the fountains, a crystalline triumph. And the little ugly Bois de Boulogne station has been transformed – or rather avoided, pushed aside by a small graceful pavilion with thin white pillars and a white canopy and a great fall of scarlet curtain and golden seal-like lions of unleonine intelligence who gaze sidelong at the golden statue of France on a white pediment across the way.

One is aware all the time that it is a Republic which is welcoming the King. There are, therefore, amusing contrasts – in the Place de la Concorde are giant plaques which light up at night: in one the axe which killed a king under the Sansculotte cap that reminds most Englishmen, I think, of the demned elusive Pimpernel and old women extras knitting under the guillotine and Sidney Carton saying: 'It is a far, far better thing . . .'; and next to it the Royal lion and unicorn – sleek and svelte with tiny vicious waists and little wicked decorative faces. One reads with interest in the Press about the King's chauffeur, M. Duthoit – 'C'est un excellent père de famille, il a une fille de douze ans qui fait de très brillantes études.'

It is a Republic too undoubtedly at night, when there are free performances of *Othello* at the Odéon in honour of the King, and people shout and push and the police get rough and shrill, and there are little flurries and fights and excitements – in honour of Shakespeare. And everywhere are street dances – bystreets marked off by paper streamers. 'It is very good,' a French poet said, 'to dance in the street. It is a symbol', and the motor-cars and buses line up and wait for the dance to finish, while the fireworks play above the Seine and giant golden fountains rise and fall and the monsters sit like idols in green spray.

But at last comes Tuesday afternoon. The King's arrival is imminent – he must have left Boulogne. Workmen are still dodging about behind the great trophies, shifting ladders. It is often said that Paris is not France. That was not, on Tuesday, true. Old ladies in black veils from the Provinces stared at Paris over the tops of buses – like Judy, and let themselves heavily down on stools in the Champs – like blocks of Epstein stone. People got argumentative over the elaborate police precautions – no window boxes allowed along the route, special passports for apartment owners opposite the station and no guests allowed, police agents in place of concierges, armed chauffeurs. But, as a taxi–driver said to me, in that marbled prose which seems to come as naturally to Paris drivers as humour to London bus conductors: 'Today every Frenchman is a police agent.'

The Gardes Mobiles arrive: whippet tanks – camouflaged as in war – line one side of the Place de la Concorde: soldiers distribute themselves among the shops and houses which overlook the route. It reminded me of the day of the General Strike – steel helmets down every side street: shift a stone and you disturb a soldier – but this is not a national crisis but a social call. It is the technique enforced by one assassination and the methods of dictatorships.

The Gardes Mobiles line the route in front of the police and troops are placed in front of *them*. Field guns and Spahis make a circle round the Arc de Triomphe – small dark fanatical faces above the white robes: police officers are silhouetted on all the roofs, among the chimney pots. A plain-clothes man at the corner of the Rue de Tilsitt searches a working girl's attaché case – one is suddenly granted an intimacy one doesn't want with a private life among the balls of wool – as when a bombed house discloses its interior.

Then the standards go by and the buglers twirl their bright brass instruments in the sun and the people clap. It is not too solemn. Black soldiers march side by side with white – and that too is republican, no racial nonsense, a fading dream of human equality. And there is a little good-humoured laughter as the President is whisked quickly past towards the station in a flurry of plumes and breast-plates. The sun has come blindingly out, and the mannequins lean decoratively down over Paris like gargoyles.

And when the King at last went by, preceded by Spahis and surrounded by the Republican Guard riding at a canter, so that all you saw was a cocked hat and some gold lace between the horses and plumes, and he had gone, what you chiefly felt was pity. It was very moving, of course, when a foreign band played 'God Save the King' and the cheers came rattling down past the Arc de Triomphe and the Spahi sabres flashed and a fierce old gentleman in a beard barked 'A bas les chapeaux' and Frenchmen cried out 'Vive le Roi!' and then 'Vive la Reine!' (though they didn't sing 'Godd saive ze Kinng'), but it was a pity one felt most of all – pity for the human race who have made it impossible for a simple and kindly gentleman to visit another in the way of friendship without these elaborate precautions, just because he represents his country. The King is among friends, but that in these days is not enough – Paris must put herself in a state of siege to protect him. I shall remember for a long while the black Senegalese soldiers who lined the Avenue Marigny when the King drove to the Élysée to call on the President, and their gentle and destructive smile – this was not Africa, this was civilization.

Spectator
22 July 1938

Twenty-four Hours in Metroland

The little town always had an air of grit about it, as one came in under the echoing tin railway arch associated with shabby prams and Sunday walks, unwilling returns to Evensong – grit beside the watercress beds and on the panes of the station's private entrance which the local lord had not used for generations. Now it appeared from the elderly lady's conversation and the furtive appearances in the lamplight that the grit had really worked in. Neither country nor city, a dormitory district – there are things which go on in dormitories . . .

Sunday evening, and the bells jangling in the town; small groups of youths hovered round the traffic lights, while the Irish servant girls crept out of back doors in the early dark. 'Romans,' the elderly lady called them. You couldn't keep them in at night – they would arrive with the milk in a stranger's car from Watford, slipping out in stockinged feet from the villas above the valley. The youths – smarmed and scented hair and bitten cigarettes – greeted them in the dark with careless roughness. There were so many fish in the sea . . . sexual experience had come to them too early and too easily. The London, Midland and Scottish Line waited for everyone.

Up on the hillside the beech trees were in glorious and

incredible decay: little green boxes for litter put up by the National Trust had a dainty and doily effect; and in the inn the radio played continuously. You couldn't escape it: with your soup a dramatized account of the battle of Mons, and with the joint a Methodist church service. Four one-armed men dined together, arranging their seats so that their arms shouldn't clash.

In the morning, mist lay heavy on the Chilterns. Boards marking desirable building lots dripped on short grass where the sheep were washed out. The skeletons of harrows lay unburied on the wet stubble. With visibility shut down to fifty yards you got no sense of a world, of simultaneous existences: each thing was self-contained like an image of private significance, standing for something else – Metroland, loneliness. The door of the Plough Inn chimed when you pushed it, ivory balls clicked and a bystander said, 'They do this at the Crown, Margate' – England's heart beating out in bagatelle towards her eastern extremity; the landlady had a weak heart, and dared not serve food these days in case she went off just like that in the rush. In a small front garden before a red villa a young girl knelt in the damp with an expression abased and secretive while she sawed through the limbs of a bush, the saw wailing through wet wood, and a woman's angry voice called 'Judy, Judy', and a dog barked in the poultry farm across the way. A cigarette fumed into ash with no one in sight, only a little shut red door marked Ker Even; 'the leading Cairn Terrier Farm' was noisy on the crest of the down, the dogs like the radio, never ceasing – how does life go on? And at the newsagent's in the market town below the Chiltern ridge there was a shrewd game on sale, very popular locally, called 'Monopoly', played with dice and counters – 'The object of owning property is to collect rent from opponents stopping there. Rentals are greatly increased by the erection of houses and hotels . . . Players falling on an unoccupied square may raise a loan from the bank, otherwise property will be sold to the highest bidder . . . Players may land in jail.' The soil exacted no service and no love: among the beechwoods a new house was for sale. It had only been lived in a month: the woods and commons were held out by wire. The owners, married last December, were divorced this summer. Neither wanted the house. A handyman swept up the leaves – a losing fight – and lamented the waste. 'Four coats of paint in every room . . . I was going to make a pond in that dell – and I was just getting the kitchen garden straight – you can see for yourself.'

Kick these hills and they bleed white. The mist is like an exhalation of the chalk. Beechwoods and gorse and the savage Metro heart behind the Whipsnade wire: elephants turning and turning behind glass on little aesthetic circular platforms like exhibits in a 'modern' shop window, behind them dripping firs as alien as themselves; ostriches suddenly visible at thirty yards, like snakeheads rising out of heaps of dung. A wolf wailing invisibly in the mist, the sun setting at 4.30, the traffic lights out in the High Street and the Irish maids putting the door on the latch. In an hour or two the commuters return to sleep in their Siberian dormitory – an acre of land, a desirable residence for as long as the marriage lasts, no roots, no responsibility for the child on the line. 'The object of owning property. . .'

New Statesman and Nation
13 August 1938

Bombing Raid

I had been reading Halévy's Epilogue to his *History of the English People* on the way to the aerodrome, bumping through the flat salty eastern county when the first labourers were going to work; yesterday's posters still up outside the little newsagent's which sold odd antique highly-coloured sweets; the squat churches surrounded by the graves of those who had had placid deaths. Halévy is depressing reading – 1895–1905; the old power politics which have returned today: secret arrangements between politicians: words astutely spoken at social gatherings: agreements which were anything but gentlemen's: the sense of middle-aged men with big ideas in a shady racket. One always prefers the ruled to the rulers, and the servants of a policy to its dictators: this hardbitten unbeautiful countryside, this aerodrome – belonging to Eastland – where none of the officers flying the huge camouflaged Wellington bombers was over twenty-three.

Presumably the war between Eastland and Westland had the same political background one found in Halévy – human nature doesn't change; but the war was on and nothing mattered except careful navigation, so that you descended from the clouds on the right target, and a delicate hand and eye, so that you didn't crash while hedge-hopping half a dozen counties at 200 miles an hour. You could even enjoy yourself now that war was on. At tea time a bomber zoomed down and up, almost brushing (so it seemed to the inaccurate eye) the mess room window, making everybody jump – you could shoot the mess up without a court-martial because it gave practice to the machine gunners round the aerodrome in sighting an enemy target.

I hadn't realized the amount of clothes one had to wear; one felt like a deep-sea diver, in overalls, with the heavy shoulder-straps and steel clamps of the parachute equipment and the inflated waistcoat for saving one's life at sea, the helmet with the padded ear-pieces and the microphone attachment dangling by the mouth with a long flex to be attached to a point near one's chair. But then this is not the kind of war which entails much walking; it is a sitting war from which it is impossible to run. Nor, knowing only passenger planes, had I realized the fragile look of the huge bombers inside, all glass and aluminium, tubes coiling everywhere, a long empty tunnel like a half-built Underground leading to the rear gun; a little cramped space in front behind the cockpit for the navigator at his table and the wireless operator. In the cockpit you feel raised over the whole world, even over your plane: space between your legs and glass under your feet and glass all round, enclosed in something like the transparent bullet-nose of a chlorotone capsule.

Under the feet at first there was water as we drove for half an hour out over the North Sea, climbing to 12,000 feet, hands and toes chilling. We were the leading plane of four, and it was odd up there in the huge din (the Wellington is the noisiest bomber these pilots have handled), in the immense waste of air, to see the pilot use the same trivial gestures through a side window as a man might make signalling to a car behind. Then as an indication to the other pilots that he needed room, he wobbled his plane and the whole squadron turned, a lovely movement in the cold clear high altitude light: the great green-brown planes sweeping round in formation towards Westland and the distant inland target.

Then the Blackwater: Gravesend – with the oil tanks like white counters on the Tilbury side. Cloud obscured everything, and afterwards it seemed no time at all before the engines were shut off and each plane in turn dived steeply down, cutting through the great summer castles of cloud, and it was Hampshire below. So far no fighter squadron had intercepted us; whether we had been a mark for anti-aircraft guns we couldn't tell, but they had had their last chance. It was low flying from now on to the target in Berkshire – a maximum height of about 200 feet at 200 m.p.h., too low for gunfire; nor could any fighter squadron in the upper air observe us as we bumped just above the hills and woods the same colour as ourselves. Once, miles away, little black flies at perhaps 8,000 feet, three fighters patrolled a parallel track and slowly dropped behind: we were unspotted. One felt a momentary horror at the exposure of a whole quiet landscape to machine-gun fire – this was an area for evacuation, of small villages and farms where children's camps might possibly be built, and it was completely open to the four aircraft which swept undetected from behind the trees and between the hills. There was room for a hundred English Guernicas.

In an air liner one doesn't recognize speed – a Hercules seems slower than a cross-country train, objects below move so slowly across the window pane; but at 200 feet, and we were often at 100 and sometimes as low as 50, the world does really flash – county giving place to county, one style of scenery to another, almost as quickly as you would turn the pages of an atlas. We were out of Hampshire, climbing down so close to the turf that it was like combing a head, up the forehead and over, into Berkshire, above our target, wheeling round, one great wing revolving like the sail of a windmill against the bright summer sky, off again, and five minutes later cutting across a fighter aerodrome, with the planes lined up and the men idling and no chance of taking off before we were away, driving a long route home along the Thames, above the film studios of North London and back into the flat Dane-drenched eastern counties. It must be the most exciting sport in the world, low flying, but the bumps are hard on the stomach, and I wasn't the only one sick – the second pilot was sick, too, and the navigator passed me an encouraging note – 'Not feeling too good myself.'

Over the coast at 100 feet, the popular resort, people resting on the beach after boarding-house luncheon or taking reluctant exercise on the pier, and out to sea again, climbing into the comfortable smooth upper air: then the last turn, the pilot signalling to his squadron, and the four planes closing up – the sense of racing home. Everybody began to smile, the navigator packed up his maps and instruments and drawing pins in a big green canvas bag, and the Wellingtons drove back in close formation at 260 miles an hour. It had been a good day: even if the war had been a real one, it would still have been a good day – the six-hour flight over, sweeping along to the buttered toast and the egg with the tea and the radio playing in the mess.

Whatever causes a future Halévy might unearth of the war between Westland and Eastland, these men would not be responsible – action has a moral simplicity which thought lacks.

Spectator
18 August 1939

A Happy Warrior

Enter in the shade General von Fritsch & Marshal Tukhashevsky.

> *Both together:*
> *Are you the happy warrior, are you he*
> *Whom every man in arms should wish to be?*

> *Marshal T.*
> *I was a traitor: I was heard confess*
> *By chosen members of my national Press;*
> *A visionary – oh, the dream was wild*
> *Of Germany & Russia reconciled*
> *My leader knew how wild: he proved his case*
> *By an odd silence, a vacuum, a disgrace*
> *Hinted in foreign papers, an exile,*
> *Enforced by nervous friends afraid to smile,*
> *From counsel, conversation, till at last .*
> *The gunbutts grounded as the Ogpu passed.*
> *Five sleepless nights they stayed to question me,*
> *Then Pravda dug the grave which set me free.*

> *General von F.*
> *You lived a year too early, I too late.*

Unused to public love & private hate,
I read my Moltke, lived with men & maps,
Modelled the Western Wall, dug-outs, tank traps,
Studied statistics, knew the exact strength
Of enemy divisions & the length
Of hangman's rope allowed us. Better far
Have endlessly applauded at Lehar,
With Goebbels censored films, with Marshal Goering
Have tickled tiger cubs to set them purring.
My only aim to make my land securer
I warned too often — thus far & no Führer.
They shot me in the back, lest I should be
A crying witness to stupidity.

     Marshal T.
My plot unfinished   Stalin completes it.

     General von F.
My army withdraws — Hitler defeats it.

Spectator
13 October 1939

The Winter War: Finland

We were liberators: so the bands played,
Ice on the mouthpiece & the fingers frozen:
We were friends, so the old tanks went ahead
And the broken boots let in the snow.
The portrait of Stalin wilted on the windscreen,
And we carried films called Earth & Mother.
But the rifles jammed & the boots let in the snow,
And the tanks stopped.
They were our friends, so they gave us bullets:
They were liberators, so they freed us,
Here in the blizzard, from the shared room,
The awful repetition of the how-many-years plan,
The edited texts of Lenin & the million sale of Marx.
Here died fear, clutching a child's toy from Petsamo,
Or a water colour sketch,
On the arctic road from Petsamo:
Fear of the informer & the whisper of sabotage,
The grit in the dynamo & the foreign expert,
The long trial & the longer confession.
Lubianka died in the forest, bundled up with the film called
    Mother.
And the bodies stiff like logs
Are freed at last from the loudspeaker,

In a land where White is only snow,
And Red is only blood.

Spectator
8 March 1940

Escape

Many people lying at night on a cement floor in the company of total strangers must catch themselves dreaming of some other period of history in which they would prefer to have lived. For them Mr Sitwell's book will prove the perfect escape. It consists of two autobiographical compositions written by members of consecutive generations of the Sitwell family – one, Mrs Swinton, looks back as an old lady on the 1840s, and the other, Miss Florence Sitwell, writes of events as they occurred, a young girl's journal of the seventies. Both are works of art, catching without self-consciousness the whole atmosphere of two lives. They have in common a gentleness, a seriousness and a kindliness: they represent a way of life that was graceful, unhurried, and responsible (not only to the deserving poor). We may smile when young Florence Sitwell talks earnestly at a party about Dean Farrar's *Life of Christ* or becomes excited in the company of a ubiquitous Archdeacon, but we smile – on that cement floor – with the wrong side of our mouths. Life through these two generations was becoming progressively more civilized: there was no reason then to suppose that the progress was to lead nowhere.

In Mrs Swinton's time, of course, there were still elements

of romantic savagery: her reminiscences belong to a period only just emerging from the Gothic: her eyes 'pale blue with a dash of green' look out on a Brontëesque world in which servants freeze to death on the dickey seats of carriages carrying the family to Scotland, and strange passionate men, like Frank Sitwell, famous for 'the Squire's Leap' on his horse Clansman, appear restlessly in churchyards after death. These reminiscences are beautifully illustrated with family portraits: hobby horses and ringlets and long thin dogs and battledores flung down on the parquet.

Mr Sitwell, who has so admirably edited these compositions, does not altogether care for the change to the seventies: to the Archdeacon and the favourite hymn and meeting Dean Farrar. But nobody could resist the naïve poetry of Miss Sitwell's journal: the stovepipe hat loses all its ugliness: when the coming millennium is the talk of the drawing-rooms, clergymen have the romantic air of officers on active service. Of course it is sometimes very funny: we can't resist laughing at the Archdeacon who pops up everywhere, even on a Channel steamer: the ghost of Mrs Heber in high-heeled shoes has taken the place of the passionate apparition in the graveyard: infectious diseases, tea parties for 'bad girls' ('it was so interesting to watch the Archdeacon talking privately to each in turn'), the American organ and the Archdeacon explaining about vestments – you wouldn't think that these could become symbols of poetic suggestiveness; but when the book is done we are left with the impression of a quiet world of Sunday afternoons, where the dark falls early, and carriage lights come up the drive, and somebody somewhere is playing a harmonium, and the linen is being laid out in the guest-room. Everywhere is great kindliness and confidence and hope. The last words are:

'Next day, I was rather late for chapel and did not like to go in, but I stood close by the door, and could hear some of the service, and at the end the Archbishop's deep voice, praying that the world might be prepared for the Second Coming of Christ.'

But things didn't happen that way: something went wrong. The collapse of a whole way of life can be read into Mrs Compton Mackenzie's book of gossip – gossip about herself and Capri and her friends, the distinguished and the not so distinguished, and Monty, above all 'Monty' – Monty in a cherry-red smoking suit, Monty 'flashing like a meteor', Monty's nervous system, Monty's cats, Monty's first kilt, Monty's gramophone records, Monty's books. For those who do not share Mrs Mackenzie's belief in her husband's importance, this book may seem trivial, exaggerated, a little vulgar. It is rather horrifying to turn from the world (and the style) of:

'When I was dressed ready for dinner, I sat down on the stairs so as to be able to see when the brougham came up. It was nearly dark, and so quiet, with the lights shining through the swing door, and down below, and Leckly and Grace's voices, talking over Mamma's luggage, and Mrs Leach, walking about arranging the rooms, and the people walking about now and then with dishes, in the passage below; and I thought of John Huss's prayer, and of some of our favourite hymns, and of Christ

to the world (and the style) of Mrs Mackenzie: 'Life at Capri in the last year of the Great War and after might well be described as highly spiced.' It makes one more reconciled to the cement floor: this had to happen.

Review of *Two Generations*, edited by Osbert Sitwell, and
More Than I Should by Faith Compton Mackenzie
Spectator
4 October 1940

A Lost Leader

There were many of us who, before war made such disagreements seem trivial, regarded Mr Priestley with some venom. We felt that as a novelist he represented a false attitude to the crumbling, untidy, depressing world; that he had clothed himself in the rags of a Victorian tradition. He was continually speaking for England, and we very much doubted whether *The Good Companions* or *Let the People Sing* represented England at all. Then, after the disaster of Dunkirk, he became a voice: a slow roughened voice without the French polish of the usual BBC speaker; we had been driven off the Continent of Europe with a shattering loss of men and material: in a few weeks we had watched the enemy obtain what he had failed to win previously after four years of war, and the voice on Wednesday, 5 June, began to lead the way out of despair: 'Now that it's over, and we can look back on it, doesn't it seem to you to have an inevitable air about it – as if we had turned a page in the history of Britain and seen a chapter headed "Dunkirk"?' Mr Priestley, the dramatist, had often experimented with Time; but never so effectively as in that single sentence.

He became in the months that followed Dunkirk a leader second only in importance to Mr Churchill. And he gave us what our other leaders have always failed to give us – an ideology. We had seen the strength of an ideology, how it could turn the Maginot Line and send the French armies back in hopeless defeat beyond Paris, and there was a real danger that in this country we should fail simply for lack of a unifying idea. The ordinary man didn't want war aims, but he did want to be told more than that he was fighting to survive. Self-preservation is not the deepest instinct: we have learnt from childhood the Christian doctrine of the greater love. Mr Priestley gave us this ideology: he gave us the idea of the two orders, the Nazi and our own, in simple terms, as moving as poetry, and his Sunday broadcasts gave far more confidence in the future than the inclusion of a few Labour men in the Cabinet. Surely it was a sign of something that the BBC should allow a speaker to refer to the old false peace, 'the defeat of goodwill', to appeal openly for a new order in England after the war.

The result, of course, could have been foreseen. When he spoke of the Nazis and their sympathizers as 'middle-aged dead-end kids', he had dug deep into the truth. He said:

'Nazi-ism is not really a political philosophy, but an attitude of mind – the expression in political life of a certain very unpleasant temperament – of the man who hates Democracy, reasonable argument, tolerance, patience and humorous equality – the man who loves bluster and swagger, uniforms and bodyguards and fast cars, plotting in backrooms, shouting and bullying, taking it out of all the people who have made him feel inferior'

and in no time angry letters were being received, accusing

him of trying to divide the country. He was told to get off the air 'before the Government puts you where you belong'. It was obvious that 'the old hands, the experts, the smooth gentry', 'the pundits and mandarins of the Fifth Button', the people 'who, for years, have been rotten with unsatisfied vanity', had recognized a dangerous enemy. And so, on Sunday, 20 October, Mr Priestley went off the air. He explained that his relations with the BBC had always been excellent, he said that he was tired by five months of broadcasting, but he also said: 'There are other reasons.' He didn't feel the same exaltation as during the earlier period. 'The high generous mood, so far as it affects our destinies here, is vanishing with the leaves. It is as if the poets had gone and the politicians were coming back.' His loss will be more deeply felt before this hard winter is through, for the return of the politicians means also the return of suspicions and doubts which lead the mind towards despair.

These postcripts read admirably. In his description of the little boats at Dunkirk, of deserted war-time Margate, of the country 'Parashots', there is an accuracy and economy of expression which produce phrases with the validity of poetry. We shall never know how much this country owed to Mr Priestley last summer, but at a time when many writers showed unmistakable signs of panic, Mr Priestley took the lead. When the war is over we may argue again about his merits as a novelist: for those dangerous months, when the Gestapo arrived in Paris, he was unmistakably a great man.

Review of *Postscripts* by J. B. Priestley
Spectator
13 December 1940

Three Score Miles and Ten

One cannot, unless one belongs to the Army of the Nile, travel very far these days, but a little book on *Colloquial Persian* which I picked up recently set me turning over all the old phrase-books which an Englishman gathers and puts away like the stray copper pieces left over from Mediterranean cruises – the piastre, the zloty and the rest . . . An indefinable smell like sewage, a squashed raisin, complicated attempts to work out the price – of what? – in shillings on an inside cover, they bring back the hopes, the terrors, the illusions of travel that the accomplished linguist never knows. How the hopes of my first visit to Germany – in the happy days of Weimar and Wandervögel – were conditioned by a sentence in my English–German phrase-book which had been compiled by a German: 'At least let the lady have a bed: as for myself, I can sleep upon straw.'

Before going abroad we used to read guide books, look at picture postcards, but Gothic cathedrals and dubious anecdotes about Barbarossa go in at one ear – or eye – and out at the other. It is in the phrase-book that the whole spirit of a country seems, however fallaciously, to reach out an Ancient Mariner's hand and grip our imagination once for all. 'At least let the lady have a bed . . .' There is a hint of romantic and illicit passion, of obscure Black Forest inns, of large pink knees and green corduroy knickerbockers, chivalry and sentimentality and the smell of sausage . . . It is no use telling me that Germany is not like that.

No other phrase-book was ever quite so appealing: French ones were full of arguments with taxi-drivers – 'I have given you your full fare', and all the intricate business of buying a ticket in a theatre – it was all fun and finance – and one friendly country has left altogether too abrupt and unfair an impression: 'Waiter, this fork is dirty.' But Persian – no modern book of travel has promised so much as this phrase-book. Dust and boredom in Teheran: statesmen in bowler hats: how right one was to believe that there was more to it than that. Never mind that you are feeling very ill already in Exercise 2 and the doctor is not in the house and Hassan is away in the bazaar and there is only bread on the table: the magic question is asked, 'Where is your home?' and the answer comes, 'My home is Isfahan.'

In Isfahan there may not be a very good hotel – though one is rather too promptly recommended, probably by somebody with a financial interest, in Pahlavi Street ('Go by droshky, you will arrive there sooner'), and 'actually there is no water', but life is decorative, lazy, timeless. 'When were you born?' 'Actually, I do not know, but my identity certificate says 1294.' No wonder the bargaining over the hand-drawn Isfahan work has an unurgent quality about it.

'The price is 100 rials each.'

'What! I will not give more than 50 rials.'

'Sir, I gave 90 rials myself; but never mind, I will accept 70.'

'All right, I will take two, and give you 120 rials.'

'Very well, Sir; goodbye.'

And the workmen born in 1294 do not feel it necessary to conform to crude industrial standards.

'Ali Jan, you are the laziest of all the men; why don't you do your work?'

'What are you saying, sir? There is no compulsion; if I don't wish to work, I won't.'

'Very well; as you like. You are discharged; go to the office and get your money.'

'I shall complain to the police.'

Compared with that of the German phrase-book, it is an oddly masculine world, and compared with the French it is frivolous in an unorganized hazy way. Domestic life is chancy and interrupted – 'What is the matter with the house-boy? Why is he shouting?' 'He is fighting with the cook.' And the butcher in Shah Street has a sinister way with him: 'Come inside, Sir. I have some unusual things to show you.'

Little wonder that in another exercise we read: 'Where had you gone yesterday? I came here to call on you, and your servant said you had gone out.' 'I am sorry; I was rather ill through eating bad meat.' Perhaps it was the kabobs, for the cook, when he is not fighting with the house-boy, has dubious suggestions to make.

'Can you make pilau? I am very fond of Iranian pilau.'

'Yes, Sir, I can; I can also cook kabobs. Would you like some?'

Food in Isfahan seems always a bit like that – strange in its appearance and unpredictable in its results. One remembers Flecker's Hassan, the confectioner, and his sweets: 'Sweets like globes of crystal, like cubes of jade, like polygons of rubies', and the pastries celebrated by the Second Kalandar in *The Thousand and One Nights*:

Sweet fine pastries
Rolled between white fingers,
Fried things whose fat scent lingers
On him who in his haste tries
To eat enough!
Pastries, my love!

'Take this pill,' the Isfahan doctor tells us in Lesson 6, 'you will soon be better.'

It is a much fuller world this than that of the French and German phrase-books, which seem to be inhabited almost solely by functionaries – policemen and postmen and porters, and those people just as forbidding as functionaries: the lynx-eyed woman who showed you to your seat in a French theatre, the aggrieved taxi-driver, and the unrelenting hotel-clerk. Europe is so old: it is as if history has borne too heavily on all these. Bismarck stands at the elbow of the railway guard: 'This ticket is only available for a slow train', and the tumbrils have rumbled constantly in the dreams of the concierge as she knits and knits. But the world for whom these young men were born in 1294 is altogether sunnier, and where can we find a more complete escape from the ruins of history than in the poetic pages of *Colloquial Persian,* in the company of Eshaq, and Ahmid's father who is a painter, and Reza's son whose house is 'tall', and Mr Hazar, the company's clerk; where the water is bad and the child's father is absent and Hassan, the driver, is always in the bazaar and the Qum mosque is beautiful and 100 cases of tea have arrived in the Customs and the carpet-seller has brought some beautiful carpets, geleems and curtains, and 'the ambassadors of the nations of the world are present'?

'I want to go to Isfahan; how can it be done?'

'Do you want to go by taxi, or by charabanc?'

If only it were as easy as all that; if only we could say like this phrase-book, 'Have we not come quickly? We left yesterday, and arrived today.' How many miles to Babylon? Three score miles and ten. Can I get there by candle-light . . .?

'Sit down there; now tell me, what did you see on the road?'

'Sir, I was asleep in the back of the car; I saw nothing.'

'You always tell lies; the road has many holes — how could you sleep?'

Spectator
14 February 1941

Through American Eyes

Mrs Miller is a popular American novelist; her novels have such titles as *Forsaking All Others*, *Five Little Heiresses*, *Less Than Kin* – a play of hers called *The Charm School*, I seem to remember, had a success over here soon after the last War. Now her short story in verse, *The White Cliffs*, has swept across the States. Eleven editions were sold in a month (it came out a fortnight after the blitz on London began), and it has been read in serial form over the wireless by Miss Lynn Fontanne. In England it deserves to have the same welcome: this simple, rather trite, but oddly moving tale of an American girl who marries an Englishman before the last War, and lives on here after her husband is killed, bringing up her son, only to find herself faced in 1939 with the problem whether to stay or go. The concluding lines are:

> *I am American bred,*
> *I have seen much to hate here – much to forgive,*
> *But in a world where England is finished and dead,*
> *I do not wish to live.*

How many of us have thought in those terms of France, and to hear it said of ourselves is like overhearing praise from strangers. We feel surprise, and pride, and gratitude.

The popular writer in war-time – or at any period of

social convulsion – comes into his own. He knows how to speak to people who are not interested in aesthetic problems; nobody will waste his time analysing the literary qualities of *Uncle Tom's Cabin* – the book belongs to history and not to literature. In the same way Mrs Miller's book may prove of some historic importance; it expresses, with the minimum of art and the maximum of sincerity, a genuine love of England – an England simplified perhaps for an American audience, an England of great manor houses and impoverished peers, of receptions in Belgrave Square and Tudor ghosts and Scottish nurses, a rather Edwardian privileged England, but in one passage an England we need not be ashamed to own:

> *Frenchmen, when*
> *The ultimate menace comes, will die for France*
> *Logically as they lived. But Englishmen*
> *Will serve day after day, obey the law,*
> *And do dull tasks that keep a nation strong.*
> *Once I remember in London how I saw*
> *Pale shabby people standing in a long*
> *Line in the twilight and the misty rain*
> *To pay their tax*

A war is not fought with literature, but it is fought with popular jokes and popular songs and popular verse, and Mrs Miller's poem is capable of creating the kind of legend that does move common men to action.

Review of *The White Cliffs* by Alice Duer Miller
Spectator
28 February 1941

Lightning Tour

Mr Ingersoll, editor of a New York paper, *P.M.*, came to London last autumn to see things for himself. He arrived after the worst of the blitz was over, and rather too much publicity was given to the statement on his return that 'in the month of September, between Saturday, 7 September, and Sunday, 15 September, Hitler almost took London – and didn't know it'. Mr Ingersoll is a newspaper-man, and occasionally (but how occasionally compared with most of his colleagues!) he finds it necessary to catch the attention with a startling point of view. Now that all his articles have been collected in book-form we can see that remark in proportion – as the barker's cry which calls attention to his account of our domestic war, an account more accurate, more level-headed and entertaining than any that has previously appeared.

The blitz has produced only one work of literature – Mr Strachey's *Post D*. Otherwise we have suffered from an enormous number of personal records – of which Miss Vera Brittain's is the worst – in which accuracy and objectivity have gone down under the surf of emotion. Mr Ingersoll, just because he was not personally involved and was enormously interested, allows us to see the war momentarily from the outside. We think 'How exciting, how fascinating this would be if it was happening to someone else'; with fresh eyes we suddenly realize the changed face of London, as we drive into it with Mr Ingersoll from a south-coast port after a strange flight from a strange Lisbon, where the planes for England taxi off side by side with swastikaed Fokkers bound for Berlin. We notice the tank-traps by the roadside, the fields bristling with stakes, the blacked-out place names – and then the first bombed houses, the shelter signs, the diversions, the paper labels, each bearing the new address of a bank or a shop, dangling from a rope which bars off a devastated street, the first black-out – the dramatic change from the day-world to the night-world, peace or war separated by a short twilight. It is fascinating so long as we believe that it is not happening to us. Watch the old lady sleeping by the *hors d'œuvre* stand in the Dorchester; note the cubicle in the elegant shelter, once the Turkish baths, 'reserved for Lord Halifax'. (The editor of *P.M.*, unfortunately, does not care for Lord Halifax: when other Ministers talked to him on the work of their departments 'Lord Halifax talked to me about the spirit of sacrifice'.)

Mr Ingersoll visited the shelters, and had the good fortune denied to Mr Willkie of journalistic rather than official guides, so that he saw the worst as well as the best (his contrast between the Isle of Dogs and the Dorchester is sardonic but hardly unfair): he saw the East End and the West End; he talked to psychologists and Cabinet Ministers and Cockneys, wardens, firemen (whose organization he admired profoundly) and airmen – they told him frankly of the deficiencies of American planes ('the American fighter-planes which we have sent to England are not fighting' – this, of course, was in October). He was struck as any stranger must inevitably be by the Government's failure to face the air-raid situation before it occurred. 'Despite a year of war there was really no shelter-provision at all until the bombs actually came down, and then they were makeshift.' (How makeshift they still are, after nine months of blitz, any ARP worker will witness.) The book is not written in terms of adulation; there are as many stories of muddle as of heroism; of selfishness as of self-sacrifice, but it does give an honest picture (inaccurate only in small details), and it is written with imaginative sympathy – which is better than emotional sympathy.

One point is puzzling: in his description of our air-defences there are blanks. Apparently the Ministry of Information cabled to the author: 'Two passages relating our secret devices . . . earnestly plead omission for security reasons . . . emphasize this very important.' Were the Ministry really so lavish in their information to a foreign journalist as to give him the means to endanger our defences, at the very time when they were promoting the Silent Column at home?

Review of *Report on England* by Ralph Ingersoll
Spectator
13 June 1941

The Turn of the Screw

We are all of us emigrants from a country we can remember little of: it haunts us and we try to reconstruct it, but all that is most important about it escapes us. We feel that we have never been so happy since we left it or so miserable, but we can't remember how happiness felt or the quality of the misery: we watch our children's eyes for hints. Knowledge has altered the taste of every emotion: during an air-raid we may occasionally hear a child crying, but we know no more of what he feels than we know of the dog wailing in a locked and empty house; but just because we know so little we feel the heavy responsibility of not understanding – horror happening to a child seems twice the horror because we don't know what he feels and can't help him: it is James's *Turn of the Screw*.

It is our sense of responsibility that makes this diary of a twelve-year-old Dutch boy who was living on the outskirts of Rotterdam when the invasion started so terrible. We feel the weight of the millstone round our own necks. His mother was killed by a bomb on the second day of the invasion, his father is a veterinary surgeon and is still in Holland. An uncle brought Dirk and his sister Keetje, aged nine, to England and sent them off to another uncle in the States. 'Keetje never mentions Mother and neither do I.'

We watch all the repressions of experience which will help to form the adult character painfully initiated. Here are the vivid scraps of childhood-horror which the psycho-analyst, stop-watch in hand, may later have to lead his patient back to by way of dreams or faulty memories.

On Wednesday, 8 May 1940, Keetje had a cold and did not go to school. 'I went as usual and Mijnheer van Speyck gave me a composition to do – 150 *words* on the life of Erasmus by *Friday*.' But on Friday the scene had changed: Rotterdam had been bombed intermittently all day: the children had taken refuge in one of the few air-raid shelters in the neighbourhood – the private one of the Baron, who pops up intermittently like the friendly comic Barons of pantomime.

'The noise was worse than fireworks or thunder and went on all the time. It made my head ache and it made me a little sick to my stomach again. I wasn't frightened, but I felt a way I can't describe. Maybe I was frightened. The raid only lasted a few minutes this time. One bomb came down very near us and people all hurried back into the shelter. We heard the glass falling upstairs. Keetje sat up in the bed during the raid. She was neither all awake nor asleep but she was tired and her hair was stringy and her face pale and she wanted the noise stopped.'

On Saturday Dirk begins his diary: 'This was another bad day. The war didn't stop, but got worse everywhere.' The children's father had gone away to the Army. Their mother had gone to work at the hospital: they were left alone with the neighbours, and the war came closer all the time. Keetje was the first to see a parachutist come down behind the Baron's barn. 'We saw Mijnheer van Helst take out his pistol and aim and then he fired three times. He came back a moment later looking very sad and said the German was shot.' Then the bombs reached their street. A child, Heintje Klaes ('pretty silly looking . . . and his eyes stick out like tulip bulbs'), was killed and three men. 'One of the men was our postmaster and I loved him very much.' In such flashes the child communicates to us *his* sense of values: the love that may light anywhere – on a postman or a baron: his measurement of terror: 'it is worse than anything I ever heard about and worse than the worst fight in the cinema': his play-instinct that seems to older people callousness.

'We got up a game with several other children playing soldiers and bombers. We took turns jumping off the high back steps holding umbrellas and pretending we were parachutists, but we had to quit this because the grown-ups said it made them nervous.'

And then at the end of Saturday:

'The ambulances coming and going and so many dead people made it hard for me not to cry. I did cry some while the bombing was going on but so many other little children were that no one noticed me I think. I just got into bed with Keetje and hid my face. I was really frightened this time.

Later
'Uncle Pieter came back. He didn't find Mother because she is dead. I can't believe it but Uncle Pieter wouldn't

lie. We aren't going to tell Keetje yet. The ambulances are still screaming. I can't sleep or write any more now or anything.'

The Baron's cat shrieking in a chimney, Keetje vomiting, the machine-gunned woman dying on the road to Dordrecht, the two lost children who wouldn't talk (Keetje gave one of them her doll – 'Keetje was nice to do this: she is often very selfish, but she was good to do this'), the wasted essay on Erasmus, the fear that suddenly returns in America when it rains ('I thought I was back in Holland and that what was striking the windows were pieces of bombs') – all this is war, and it is just as well for us sometimes disturbingly to see the conflict of ideologies, the great Democracies and the great Dictatorships, the clarion-calls, the heroisms and the speeches, through the undimmed window of the innocent eye.

Review of *My Sister and I: The Diary of a Dutch Boy Refugee* by Dirk van der Heide
Spectator
20 June 1941

A Mission and a Warning

On the night of 12 September 1919, the first train to leave Paris for Berlin after the first German War drew out of the Gare du Nord. Officers talking in five languages stood in the corridors.

They were the advance guard of the Allied Control Commission on the way to Germany to enforce the disarmament and demobilization clauses of the peace treaty. The British military representative, Brig.-General J. H. Morgan, in *Assize of Arms*, tells the story of the mission.

Let no one be deterred by the idea that the subject is a dry and technical one, however important. The story is as exciting as any adventure novel could be, and it is told by General Morgan with great literary skill.

The disarmament clause in the treaty was on the face of it so simple. 'Within two months from the coming into force of the present Treaty German arms, munitions and war material, including anti-aircraft material, existing in Germany in excess of the quantities allowed must be surrendered to the Governments of the Principal Allied and Associated Powers to be destroyed or rendered useless.'

'Two months!' General Morgan exclaims. 'It took us seven years, and even then the "surrender" was anything but complete.' The German Ministry of Defence had been handed a perfect instrument of evasion. For what was war material? Was a spade a spade or an entrenching tool? How were they to distinguish between war explosives and commercial explosives?

The questions were innumerable, and the Germans showed immense tactical resource in their evasions and delays. Control officers were systematically hampered, and sometimes as systematically assaulted; a whole department was formed to control the Control; for days the mission was isolated by revolution, and all the time they were conscious of their defencelessness in the enemy capital: a few hundred men without arms in the middle of a population which was incited by the Press day in and day out to violence.

And all the time, too, they were aware – or at any rate, the British representatives were – of the Press campaign from the Left in their own country in favour of letting the Germans be. Sympathy had been well organized.

I saw myself something of that magnificent organization when I spent a few weeks in the occupied zone in 1923. I was only an undergraduate, but I was not beneath the organizers' notice. Letters of introduction were stacked at my hotels: rooms were booked for me. I remember an editor in the Palatinate telling me how every letter from the area was opened by the French authorities (untrue, as I easily proved), an industrialist outside Cologne piling my plate with food and talking of the workers' starvation: in Heidelberg, outside the occupied area, the secretary of the Society for the Relief of Exiles from the Palatinate told me how his society kidnapped collaborating mayors and tried these exiles for high treason.

Even this contributed to the general effect. He was a

sporting man, a stag hunter, and he lent to these stories of kidnapping a high romantic flavour which went down well with youth. Now one thinks of Dachau, and the romance is soured.

Many of us who have felt doubtful about the policy of unconditional surrender will be converted by General Morgan's book. This is how conditional surrender worked. The only complaint I have against a fascinating book is an occasional outbreak of moral indignation. It is, after all, the duty of a defeated country to evade the consequences.

Review of *Assize of Arms* by Brig.-Gen. J. H. Morgan
Evening Standard
3 August 1945

Books in General

The novelist is the victim of a passion. Whether it is one of those absurd, unequal passions from which it always seems to be our friends and not ourselves who suffer, depends on the measure of his talent. It might – mightn't it? – so nearly have been Mrs Amanda McKittrick Ros who sang to her Muse of Fiction: 'I turn, I screw round, and bend my lips to passionately, in my gratitude, kiss its hands', instead of Henry James. Mr Robert Liddell in his interesting, though sometimes rather aggravating essay, has set out, more completely than Mr Percy Lubbock or Mr E. M. Forster, to analyse the methods of these victims and to describe their behaviour:

> 'The present study aims at making some use of the information which many writers, great and small, have left us about their art, about the raw material presented to them by life, about the form they wished to impose on it, about their struggles with it, and about those gifts of inspiration which have seemed to come to them from nowhere'

and we can sincerely echo his own words:

> 'Any attempt to treat the novelist seriously, as an artist, not

as a medium or a reporter, is at the present time a service, however humble, to literature.'

For how serious, how desperately serious, this passion must be to its victims to make them continue enslaved and not at the end of their first book renounce this form of love for ever. By comparison with the lyric poet's or the painter's, the novelist's life is a despairing one. A work which takes him so long a time, a time that has to be measured in years rather than months, that has, therefore, to be written against so many varying and warring moods, how can it ever attain the satisfactory unity of a poem or a picture? His passion may give him moments of contentment or even of happiness, but he is aware all the time of how this love affair will close. This is not a marriage: this is a passion doomed sooner or later to end. It already contains the hatred and the dryness of heart that will succeed it. Mr Liddell quotes, among others, Proust:

'Nous sommes obligés de revivre notre souffrance particu- lière avec le courage du médecin qui recommence sur lui-même la dangereuse piqûre.'

And there are a crowd of other witnesses I would suggest for a later edition. Tolstoy turning back unwillingly to work:

'Now I am settling down again to dull commonplace *Anna Karenina*, with the sole desire to clear a space quickly and obtain leisure for other occupations.'

Flaubert rounding on the hated Bovary:

'My accursed Bovary torments and confounds me . . . I am utterly weary, utterly discouraged. You call me master – what a sorry master I am. There are moments when it all makes me want to die like a dog.'

Chekhov:

'My soul has wilted from the consciousness that I am working for money and that money is the centre of my activity. This gnawing feeling . . . makes my authorship a contemptible pursuit in my eyes; I do not respect what I write'

and that terrible scene of exhausted irony in Conrad's letters when, shut in a small Swiss hotel with two sick children demanding his compassion, he tries to conclude *The Secret Agent*:

'I seem to move, talk, write in a sort of quiet nightmare that goes on and on. From the sound next door . . . I know that the pain has roused Borys from his feverish doze. I won't go to him. It's no use. Presently I shall give him his salicylate, take his temperature and shall then go on to elaborate a little more the conversation of Mr Verloc with his wife. It is very important that the conversation of Mr Verloc with his wife should be elaborated . . .'

Isn't this a passion, an obsession and a self-disgust comparable to that of Rossetti when he left his wife, for the sake of a sexual adventure, to die alone?

'The contemporary novel falls roughly into two main categories, each of which may be sub-divided into two sub-categories' – so Mr Liddell, trying to deal coolly and dispassionately with this degrading passion. The quotation does not really do him justice, for we are conscious, even when he seems to us over-dogmatic or even a little naïve, that he is himself a victim; Mr Percy Lubbock, on whose admirable *Craft of Fiction* my literary generation was brought up, was an outsider; and for that reason, perhaps, saw rather more clearly than Mr Liddell the main technical problems of the novelist and at the same time, like a wise schoolmaster, trained us for freedom. Never surely since his time has a novelist shifted a 'point of view' without being conscious of the danger he was running, or spoken in his proper person without arguing with himself the merits and demerits of the pure objective novel. He established Henry James and Flaubert like monitory statues in the forecourt of our minds, but we felt that expulsion would not necessarily follow a sufficiently studied act of rebellion.

Mr Liddell, partly perhaps because he is a much younger man, partly because he is himself a victim of the passion he is trying so objectively to treat, is much more of a partisan. As a novelist himself he has learned at certain venerable knees, and he would have us all kneel there too. Sometimes he writes as unfairly as George Moore (whose books of literary criticism, *Conversations in Ebury Street* and *Avowals* are now too much neglected). Moore, it will be remembered, wrote of Hardy: 'The best prose is usually written by poets . . . and I do not think I am going too far when I say that Mr Hardy has written the worst', while Mr Liddell compares him as a craftsman unfavourably with Miss Charlotte M. Yonge, and in a rather naïve passage of his essay (naïvety is sometimes apparent in a dogma insufficiently reasoned): 'Highbury is really a more satisfactory background for a work of fiction than Egdon *apart from the fact* that the people of Highbury are of incomparably greater interest.' (The italics, of course, are mine.) Mr Liddell follows George Moore too in treating Tolstoy a little disdainfully: George Moore felt that a yacht race might well have been included among the 'properties' of *War and Peace* and Mr Liddell seems to suggest that the Napoleonic War might be excluded. From this it will be concluded correctly that Mr Liddell is an admirer of Jane Austen.

This is not a criticism of Mr Liddell's attempt to show us how a novel is made, but it is a classification of his essay. Both his predecessors in this field, Mr Lubbock and Mr Forster, have followed the same particular stream in the history of the novel: it winds from Jane Austen to Henry James and then on to Mrs Woolf and Mr Forster himself (Mr Liddell adds an excellent essay on Miss Compton Burnett). A curve is made to bring Flaubert in: it would have been, we feel, rather to his own surprise, and certainly to the surprise, and modified disapproval, of James. The novel, explained, described, analysed, with these examples mainly in mind, takes on a curiously uniform, but oddly feminine – or even 'sissy' air. It would be interesting for once to read an essay on the technique of the novel in which a different stream was followed: the stream perhaps Defoe, Fielding, Dickens, Dostoevsky, Tolstoy, Balzac, and on in contemporary times to M. Mauriac. I think it is assumed wrongly by followers of the Austen tradition that these other figures – writers of genius though they may have been – were not interested in the technique of their profession, that there is nothing we can learn from them. No one, it is true, before or since has examined his craftsmanship and explained it with the care and profundity of Henry James, but James had the good fortune to build on foundations laid by his great contemporaries, Turgenev and Flaubert; while Fielding, living at a period when the novel was in its infancy, made revolutionary experiments which were not to be adopted for more than a century after his time. Think of the experiment with Time in *Amelia* (dull novel though it be, it anticipates Conrad) and his attempt to exclude the author from the novel and yet retain the author's viewpoint in *Tom Jones*. Tolstoy worked so hard on *War and Peace* that he even pursued his much corrected proofs with telegrams to the compositors, and I refuse to believe that Dickens was unaware of the methods he was pursuing. If we disagree with the method we are too apt to believe that there is no method. Flaubert, and James after him, have made us so conscious of the value of the 'pure novel' that we forget there are other values other writers have pursued, that the novel's purity, like the chastity of Clarissa, may involve too great a price. Mr Liddell here is a little disingenuous. At some moments as wildly dogmatic as an undergraduate in his first tutorial essay, at others he leaves statements bristling with loopholes for escape at the *viva*:

'While admitting a degree of legitimate difference in taste, it is reasonable to claim that such structurally perfect novels as *Emma*, *Madame Bovary* and *The Ambassadors,* whose underlying principle is dramatic rather than epic, belong to a higher artistic order than the more rambling of the Waverley novels or *Martin Chuzzlewit*.'

He has deliberately, you will notice, chosen one of Dickens's worst books and assumed one of Scott's least capable. If he had substituted *War and Peace* his sentence would have contained a clearer intention, but one he would have found it hard to defend.

No, *A Treatise on the Novel* cannot, as technical criticism, rank with Mr Lubbock's *Craft of Fiction,* but nevertheless it deserves praise for the reason Mr Liddell has himself given. The dignity of the novel has been neglected in the past twenty years and a book of this kind does a service to the reader as well as to the practitioner. Trollope wrote of 'the unconscious critical acumen of the reader' but the novelist is not likely to complain if his reader's acumen becomes more conscious. No service to literature will be done, however, if he becomes conscious only of winds from one quarter. I should like to warn this innocent reader (who exists probably only in the reviewer's mind): Don't forget the use of the word 'why?' – don't hesitate to question Mr Liddell's dogmas. We have already quoted one, on the background in Hardy's novels. When he writes 'too grand a scene in the background may overpower the people in the foreground, so that the author may lose more than he gains by his scenic effects', give Hardy the credit for being quite conscious of what he was doing (it was his desire to dwarf his people at moments just as, in the stage directions of *The Dynasts*, he watched the peoples of Europe warring across the landscape, with an Immortal's eye). When Mr Liddell criticizes Joyce because in *Ulysses* 'it is impossible to develop any other character in the book on the same scale (as Bloom)', give Joyce too the credit of knowing exactly what he was about. This sentence of Mr Liddell's is not criticism: it is merely description. *Ulysses* would not be what it is – or *The Odyssey* – if it contained more than one character of epic proportions. When Mr Liddell writes:

'Novels are nearly always concerned with life as it is or has been lived, and only very exceptionally (and seldom satisfactorily) with life as it might be', realize that he is, deliberately, twisting Chekhov's apothegm into a meaning Chekhov never intended. Chekhov was contrasting the action and setting of his stories with the mood of the author: the mood of the author, Mr Liddell happily and truly remarks, should be one of Justice and Mercy, and while Justice sees and draws the world as it is, the mood of Mercy is aware of what it might be – if the author himself, as well as all the world, were different. In a passage admirably free from dogmatic assumption or narrowness of appreciation, Mr Liddell writes:

> 'A novelist may be Protestant, Catholic, agnostic or atheist; he may be imperialist, pacifist, conservative, liberal or socialist, independent or apolitical. He maybe any of these things with complete conviction – a conviction firm enough for him to think all other points of view mistaken. But he may not have an angry conviction. He must be able to understand and to sympathize with views he does not share. He must not think that everyone who differs from him is ill-informed, unintelligent or acting in bad faith.'

Review of *A Treatise on the Novel* by Robert Liddell
New Statesman and Nation
11 October 1947

The Last Pope

No doubt because he continues an uninterrupted tradition
of Christian state of mind, thought, and style, the French
novelist seems to move easily among abstractions: they
surround his childhood, and the liturgy is as familiar to him
as his nursery rhymes. When a door opens in a novel by
Mauriac, even before one leaves the shadows to enter the
well-lit room where the characters are assembled, one is
aware of forces of Good and Evil that slide along the walls
and press their fingers against the window-pane ready to
crowd in. This awareness is, in general, banished from the
English novel. Perhaps it is because we live in a northern
island where the sun shines so spasmodically and where we
can be cut off from the Continent for days at a time by
fog or storm, an island to which Christianity came like a
stranger from across the sea – perhaps because of this we
tend to be more materialistic in our reactions and more
concrete in imagination than those who live in sunnier
lands who can permit themselves the luxury of shadow.
The English novelist has become accustomed to bypass
eternity. Evil appears in Dickens's novels only as an
economic factor, nothing more. Christianity is a woman
serving soup to the poor. How vivid are his images of the
still Sunday streets, the dark, mean little courts near the

river, the prison buildings, but how barren and dim is the life of the spirit! In Dickens, Evil has lost its supernatural quality, it has become something that the power of money, an amendment to the law, or perhaps simply death can abolish, for when a character dies, the evil dies with him. The English novel always makes us live within time.

Is Christian civilization in peril? For each of you these words possess the solidity of statues. You move freely among them like a man making his way past the overpopulated side-chapels of a great cathedral: the Immaculate Conception stretches out its arms of stone to you; the Sacred Heart is there made out of carved and painted wood; the candles burn with a tangible flame. But I feel as though I am surrounded by shadows. Civilization is a thing I learned in books, and Christianity is something that happens somewhere else, beyond my range of vision, perhaps in another country, certainly in another heart. I cannot touch the words unless they are given a human shape. The Apostle Thomas should be the patron saint of people in my country, for we must see the marks of the nails and put our hands in the wounds before we can understand.

So this question, even before I begin to consider it, becomes three questions. First, what is a Christian civilization in terms of human characters, human acts, and the daily commerce of human lives? Second, has this civilization ever existed, and does it exist today in any part of the world? It is only if the reply to this second question is affirmative that it will be necessary to ask whether Christian civilization is in danger.

Naturally, it would be convenient to adopt a rigid and clearly defined attitude, to represent Christian civilization as a corporate arrangement of human life that would permit everyone to follow, without the least hindrance from his fellows, the teaching of the Sermon on the Mount. In that case, without further ado, we could examine our own age, retrace the course of history, and declare that such a civilization has never existed. But in adopting such an attitude – and the enemies of Christianity have often used this kind of argument – we are confusing the city of man and the City of God. The perfect imitation of Christ is impossible here, but our very imperfection is sanctified, for didn't God imitate man, and weren't man's despair and failure expressed by God himself on the cross? So in our definition of a Christian civilization we should not be led astray by the presence of wars, injustice and cruelty, or by the absence of charity. All those things can exist in a Christian state. They are not marks of Christianity, but of man.

But if we give up all thought of achieving or even of pursuing perfection, what clues can we hope to find that will help us distinguish a Christian from a pagan civilization? Perhaps, truthfully, we can count on nothing more than the divided mind, the uneasy conscience, and the sense of personal failure.

Of course this sense of guilt was already present in Greek civilization; it hangs over Greek drama like a heavy cloud. But it is a kind of impersonal guilt that a Christian literature might have produced on the theme of the fall of man if there had been the Revelation without the Incarnation, or if we had experienced personal failure without having had the model. In Greek literature any excess is synonymous with fear – excess of riches, happiness, luck, or power – but this fear is only an abstract fear. The fortunate man believes in justice operating like a pendulum; he follows like all men the swing of the pendulum; he has no sense of an individual failure which differentiates him from other men equally fortunate.

My conviction that the Christian conscience is the only satisfactory sign of a Christian civilization is reinforced by the fact that this trait was completely lacking in the pagan powers that so recently reigned over the world. How the Nazis strutted in their hour of triumph and how they justified themselves in their defeat! How deliberately and explicitly they followed the doctrine which consists in doing evil to achieve good — their own personal good! The totalitarian state contrives, by educating its citizens, to suppress all sense of guilt, all indecision of mind. Let the State assume the responsibility for the crime, I am innocent. My only crime is my loyalty. The parrot voices proclaim with a terrifying pathetic resignation, 'My chief gave the order.' No soldier makes a cross of sticks to hand his victim.

The years we have just lived through are perhaps not the worst Europe has known. Many times in Christian civilization cities have been sacked and prisoners tortured, but doesn't one always find these tyrants of the past haunted by a sense of guilt? Let me read you a passage from the Anglo-Saxon Chronicles which describes the situation in England in the twelfth century, in the reign of Stephen. It is a contemporary report. It is at least equal in horror to anything we have seen in Europe in the past few years.

'They sorely burdened the unhappy people of the country with forced labour on the castles; and when the castles were built, they filled them with devils and wicked men. By night and by day they seized those whom they believed to have any wealth, whether they were men or women; and in order to get their gold and silver, they put them into prison and tortured them with unspeakable tortures, for never were martyrs tortured as they were. They hung them up by the feet and smoked them with foul smoke. They strung them up by the thumbs, or by the head, and hung coats of mail on their feet. They tied knotted cords round their heads and twisted it till it entered the brain. They put them in dungeons wherein were adders and snakes and toads, and so destroyed them. Some they put into a "crucethus"; that is to say, into a short, narrow, shallow chest into which they put sharp stones; and they crushed the man in it until they had broken every bone in his body.

'. . . Then was corn dear and flesh and cheese and butter, for there was none in the land. The wretched people perished with hunger; some, who had been great men, were driven to beggary, while others fled from the country. Never did a country endure greater misery, and never did the heathen act more vilely than they did.

'. . . If two or three men came riding towards a village, all the villagers fled for fear of them, believing that they were robbers. The bishops and the clergy were for ever cursing them, but that was nothing to them, for they were all excommunicated and forsworn and lost.

'Wherever the ground was tilled the earth bore no corn, for the land was ruined by such doings; and men said openly that Christ and His saints slept. Such things and others more than we know how to relate we suffered nineteen years for our sins.'

I would not refuse the name of Christian civilization to those sombre years. Don't we, in fact, in reading this chronicle get the distinct impression of a bad conscience, of an acute sense of guilt? There were still some who raised voices in protest, the chronicle tells us so. The saints slept, but they were not disowned. Darkness covered the face of the island, but Christianity continued to move in the shadows. The possibility of an enormous repentance counterbalanced the possibility of enormous crimes. Take an example from English history. Our great king Henry II, in his grief, made a deliberate pact with the enemy of God. When he saw his native city burned in Normandy he made this great oath (so Christian even in its denial of Christ). 'O God, since you have seen well to take from me the thing I loved most, the city where I was born and bred, I swear that I, too, will take from you that which you love the most in me.' How could one class among the enemies of God this saint in reverse who gave us a true saint, Thomas of Canterbury, and who, after the murder of Saint Thomas, demanded to be whipped publicly by the monks. Contrition was born at the same time as the crime: twin births of sin and punishment.

Our enemies can call to witness many crimes committed in Christ's name. But in the long run what importance do such crimes have? In all our poetry you can hear a common note, the note of what I have called the divided mind – in the words of Sir Thomas Browne: 'There's another man within me that's angry with me.'

. . . This is the signature of a Christian civilization. Challenged by our enemies we can admit our crimes because throughout history it is possible to point to our repentance.

If you accept my definition of the distinguishing mark of a Christian civilization, we can now easily answer the second question, 'Has such a civilization ever existed?' The answer is 'Yes.' In a large part of the world man's conscience remains sensitive to moral failure. To cite only one recent example, it was not just political opportunism that determined the liberation of India. Half a century ago it would have seemed absurd to suggest that Christian civilization was in any danger. There have been so many wars and revolutions that a few more or less matter very little in the eyes of history. No new weapon can kill the impetus of Christianity. If that were possible, gunpowder would have finished it off. The atom bomb is powerless against conscience. But in the last twenty years we have witnessed an attempt to kill it by means of a new philosophy designed to persuade men that Lazarus is without importance. Dives, in a fancy dress uniform, receives the acclamations of the crowd in the streets of Berlin or from a balcony in Red Square. Perhaps my countrymen are not entirely wrong to mistrust those abstract words which allowed Dives to become a hero, by replacing Lazarus with 'the people' or 'the proletariat' or 'the working class'. In countries that were formerly democratic, and nowadays in countries that are still democratic, we have seen abstractions extend their domain in man's thought and leave their rightful place in philosophy and theology to invade history, economics and politics, subjects which, by their very nature, should be treated in concrete terms. Read any article in the popular press, even if the subject is as matter of fact as the extraction of iron ore, or estimates of this year's crop yield – one seeks in vain for a concrete image. Abstractions have been administered to our democracies like a drug. A phrase like 'render unto Caesar' is translated by political journalists into 'our responsibilities towards the State'. Abstract expressions help dictators to power by troubling the clear waters of thought. William Blake said that whoever wishes to do good to his neighbour should do so on small occasions, for the general good is always invoked by scoundrels, hypocrites and flatterers.

We can no longer take lightly the danger that threatens Christian civilization. Between 1933 and 1945 civilization was almost completely destroyed in Germany. That abscess has been lanced, but the totalitarian poison can still spread to countries which escaped the first infection. It is terrifying to think of the distance Russia has travelled in less than a hundred years. Remember in *The Brothers Karamazov* Aliosha stripping himself of everything for the service of God: 'I cannot give up two roubles instead of "all thou hast" or just go to morning mass instead of "come and follow me".' And remember Father Zossima and his all-embracing charity: 'Hate not atheists, the teachers of evil, materialists, even the most wicked of them, let alone the good ones among them . . , Remember them in your prayers thus: "Save, O Lord, all who have no one to pray for them, and save those, too, who do not want to pray to thee."' And then think of the Moscow Trials and of Prosecutor Vishinsky and of that inaccessible grey figure in the Kremlin with his skin-deep bonhomie reserved for state banquets and the dark in the depths of his eyes.

And yet it would surely be a sin against faith to exaggerate the danger. We are bound to believe that Christianity cannot die. A hundred years is, after all, a very short time. Perhaps it will turn out that it is Mitya Karamazov who rules in Russia today. You remember his words: 'If I am to precipitate myself into the abyss, I shall do so without a moment's reflection, head over heels, and indeed I shall be glad to fall in such a degrading attitude and consider it beautiful for a man like me. And it is at this very moment of shame and disgrace that I suddenly begin to intone this hymn.' Perhaps if we were well enough informed we could discern here and there in Russia, too, the signs of an uneasy conscience. For we must not forget that in Germany's darkest days the voice of conscience was heard intermittently, never among the leaders of the State, but among the leaders of the Church – Faulhaber, Galen, Niemöller, and others too obscure or too unimportant to escape death. I remember one of my friends, von Bernstorff. Before Hitler's rise to power he was First Secretary of the German Embassy in London. He resigned in 1933 and was executed in 1944 in Dachau because he belonged to a secret organization that continued to help Jews escape from Germany even during the war. What a strange fate that this heavy, superficial man, who loved the good life and a good laugh, with his aristocratic indolence and his taste for old cognac, should be transformed into a martyr for the cause of charity!

As I have said, we are bound to believe that Faith cannot die. It can suffer reverses, large parts of the world can be conquered by its enemies, but there will always exist pockets of Christian resistance. In England during the sinister year 1940 we used to say, 'But just look at the map of the world', meaning that if our island seemed tiny and desperately imperilled in relation to Europe, all the same, hope was rekindled at the sight of allied territories in Africa, Australia and Canada. Christians, too, should look at the map of the world from time to time. Suppose the whole of Europe should become a totalitarian state; we are not the world.

It is not impossible that we might see the whole world succumb to a totalitarian and atheistic regime. Even so, it would still not be the end. In that case we, the spies of God, would have to draw up large-scale maps of every city and every village. There, in such and such a street, behind the café, at the crossroads in the town of X, in the fifteenth house on the right, there is a cellar, and in this cellar a child, playing, has traced a clumsy cross on the plaster wall . . .

Permit me to close with a story which I once intended to write — a fantasy in a melodramatic vein, which takes place in the distant future, say two centuries from now, when the whole world is governed by a single party and organized with an efficiency undreamt of today. The curtain rises on a sordid little hotel in London or New York, it doesn't matter which. It is late at night. An old man, tired, down-hearted, nondescript, wearing a shabby raincoat and carrying a battered suitcase, comes up to the reception desk and asks for a room. He signs the register and disappears wearily up the stairs (the hotel is too poor to have an elevator). The house detective looks at the register and says to the clerk:

'Did you see who that was?'

'No.'

'It's the Pope.'

'The Pope? Who's that?'

Catholicism has been successfully stamped out. Only the Pope survives, elected thirty years before at the last conclave (a secret conclave, its members believed, though in reality monitored by an even more secret police), and doomed to rule over a Church which has virtually ceased to exist. After the conclave the cardinals had met the fate of the rest of the priests: a white wall and a firing squad. But the Pope was authorized to live. He even receives a small pension from the State because he is of use in demonstrating how dead the Church is, and because there is always the possibility that some survivor will betray himself by trying to get in touch with him. But there are no more survivors. Rome, naturally, has been renamed for over a century.

I was going to describe this little man, this little Pope, drifting miserably here and there, purposelessly, driven on by the vague hope that somewhere, some day, he might encounter a sign to show him that the Faith survived after all and he need no longer be haunted by the fear that what he had professed to be eternal might die with him. I won't bore you with the story of his useless wanderings and his deceptions, each duly recorded and filed at the headquarters of the World Police. In the end the World Dictator got tired of the game. He wanted to put an end to it in his own lifetime, for although he was only fifty while the Pope had long since passed seventy, accidents happen to dictators and he did not wish to surrender his place in history as the man who, with his own finger on the trigger of the revolver, had put an end to the Christian myth.

So at the end of this story which I never wrote, the Pope was brought by the police into the Dictator's secret room with its soundproof, bulletproof walls, and there, in the padded silence, the Dictator, after offering the Pope a cigarette, which he refused, and a glass of wine, which he accepted, told him he was going to die on the spot – the last Christian, the last man in the world who still believed. After dismissing the detectives the Dictator took a revolver out of his desk drawer. He granted the Pope a moment to pray (he had read in a book that this was customary), but he didn't listen to the prayer. Then he shot him in the left side of the chest and leaned forward over the body to give the coup de grâce. At that instant, in the second between the pressure on the trigger and the skull cracking, a thought crossed the Dictator's mind: 'Is it just possible that what this man believed is true?' Another Christian had been born.

An address given at Les Grandes Conférences Catholiques in Brussels (translation by Philip Stratford). The address closes with a story Greene wrote forty years later under the title 'The Last Word'
January 1948

John Gerard

'This last era of a declining and gasping world' – so Gerard describes in his modest preface the setting of his *Autobiography*. How strangely that phrase would have sounded to a Victorian ear, to the ear of Archdeacon Grantly or Mr Micawber – a phrase, it would have seemed to them, as outlandish as the details of Gerard's adventure (it would be more accurate, when we remember his narrow escapes, his disappointments and betrayals, the long terrible scene of his torture, to call it his Passion). This history would have been as remote from them as an historical novel, and as an historical novel they would have preferred *Esmond*, with its remote romanticism, the dandyism of snuff-box and cane. They would have been a little disturbed even by Gerard's love story, for this, when you come to think of it, is a love story, the story of a man who loved his fellows to the worst point of pain.

Outlandish, yes; but for a quarter of a century now we have been travelling slowly back towards those outlands of danger through which Gerard moved in his disguise of fashion, with his talk of the hunt and of cards. We can read the *Autobiography* like a contemporary document or perhaps as something still a little ahead of our time, as though in a dream we had been allowed to read an account of life in 1960: life as it is going to be lived.

This is what gives the book, in its excellent translation from the Latin, such a sense of excitement, of immediacy. Listen to the narrative of Gerard's arrival in his native country: the danger in the familiar lane, death lying in wait in all the peaceful countryside.

'After crossing the sea we sailed up the English coast. On the third day my companion and I saw what seemed a good place to put ashore in the ship's boat. As we thought it would be dangerous for all of us to land together, we asked God's guidance in prayer. Then we consulted our companions and ordered the ship to cast anchor off the point till nightfall. At the first watch of the night we were taken ashore in the boat and dropped there. The ship spread its canvas and sailed on.

'For a few moments we prayed and commended ourselves to the keeping of God, then we looked about for a path to take us as far inland as possible and put a good distance between us and the sea before dawn broke. But the night was dark and overcast, and we could not pick the path we wanted and get away into the open fields. Every track we took led up to a house – as we knew at once when the dogs started to bark. This happened two or three times. Afraid we might wake the people inside and be set on for attempting to burgle them, we decided to go off into a nearby wood and rest there till the morning. It was about the end of October, raining and wet, and we passed a sleepless night. Nor did we dare to talk, for the wood was close to a house. However, in little more than a whisper we held a conference. Would it be better to make for London together or separate so that if one of us was caught the other might get away safely? We discussed both courses thoroughly. In the end we decided to part company and each to go his own way.'

That homecoming has been enacted in many countries during our half-century since Father Pro landed at Vera Cruz in his bright cardigan and his striped tie and his brown shoes, but here, in Gerard's narrative, it is happening in our own Norfolk, to us.

Father Gerard's prose is plain, accurate, vivid. The act of writing is very like the act of sculpture: one is presented with a rude block of facts, out of which one has to cut the only details that matter. 'As exciting as a novel' – how often we have read that misleading phrase in a publisher's advertisement, and how seldom, in fact, is the novel exciting. How seldom do we find the novelist properly detaching his subject matter, his characters, his mood, his scene, from the preliminary stone as Gerard does.

We have seen in his account of his landing how quietly and almost modestly Gerard sets his scene, the mood of suspense and pursuit conveyed in the simplest terms – an overcast night, a strange house, the barking of dogs. One could have quoted more dramatic scenes – Father Southwell's Mass interrupted by the priest hunters, Gerard's own arrest and torture, his escape from the Tower. For his ability to draw character, quickly, in the running course of his narrative, there are many examples. Father Southwell who will be known to many readers only as the poet who wrote 'The Burning Babe', as much a lay figure as his fellow poets of the time of whom we know so little, comes alive in Gerard's narrative as he worries over the correct technical terms to maintain his superficial disguise as a country gentleman.

'When I got the opportunity I spoke about hunting and falconry, a thing no one could do in correct technical language unless he was familiar with the sports. It is an easy thing to trip up in one's terms, as Father Southwell used to complain. Frequently, as he was travelling about with me later, he would ask me to tell him the correct terms and worried because he couldn't remember and use them when need arose: for instance, when he fell in with Protestant gentlemen who had practically no other conversation except, perhaps, obscene subjects, or rant against the saints and the Catholic faith. On occasions like this there is often a chance of bringing the conversation round to some other topic simply by throwing out a remark about horses or hounds or the like.'

Was it some such experience as this that brought the metaphors of the hunt even into the poems of the Blessed Henry Walpole whose cell in the Tower Gerard was later to occupy?

> *The falkener seeks to see a flight*
> *the hunter beates to see his gamme*
> *Longe thou my soule to see that sight*
> *and labour to enjoy the same.*

Southwell is a major character in Gerard's story, but how easily he touches in even his anonymous figures, the warder who wept over his torture, or this convert, identified by Father Caraman as Sir Oliver Manners, sketched so vividly in the margin of the narrative that we seem to see him full length, the very cut of his doublet, the shape of his leg, the spread of the long Elizabethan fingers on his book, though Gerard has used not one phrase of physical description.

'You might see him in the court or in the Presence Chamber, as it is called, when it was crowded with courtiers and famous ladies, turning aside to a window and reading a chapter of Thomas à Kempis's *Imitation of Christ*. He knew the book from cover to cover. And after reading a little he would turn to the company, but his mind was elsewhere. He stood absorbed in his thoughts. People imagined that he was admiring some beautiful lady, or wondering how to climb to a higher position.'

Compared with these Topcliffe might be thought an easy character to draw, but the priest hunter has been the bogey man of so many stories that we feel a certain surprise at finding him start up here as evil in fact as in fiction, wearing a court dress with a sword hanging at his side 'old and hoary and a veteran in evil'. (It is rather as though Mr Hyde had stepped out of Stevenson's pages into the authentic Edinburgh streets.)

' "I will see that you are brought to me and placed in my power. I will hang you up in the air and will have no pity on you; and then I shall watch and see whether God will snatch you from my grasp." '

There is one portrait in this gallery one sadly misses. On 14 April 1597 five men reported on their examination of Gerard in the Tower: only two of them were known to Gerard, but one, we learn from Father Caraman, was Francis Bacon. For a moment one would like to imagine oneself a follower of the Baconian heresy and to believe that it was William Shakespeare who faced Gerard across the board, for isn't there one whole area of the Elizabethan scene that we miss even in Shakespeare's huge world of comedy and despair? The kings speak, the adventurers speak (so that we can imagine in Faulconbridge's rough tones the very language of Francis Drake), the madmen and the lovers, the soldiers and the poets, but the martyrs are quite silent – one might say that the Christians are silent except for the diplomatic tones of a Wolsey or Pandulpho or the sudden flash of conscience in Hamlet's uncle at prayers. What Franciscan ever resembled Friar Lawrence with his little moral apothegms, his tags of Latin and his herbs? One might have guessed from Shakespeare's plays that there was a vast vacuum where the Faith had been – the noise and bustle of pilgrimages have been stilled: we come out of the brisk world of Chaucer into the silence of Hamlet's court after the Prince's departure, out of the colours of Canterbury into the grey world of Lear's blasted heath. An old Rome has taken the place of the Christian Rome – the pagan philosophers and the pagan gods seem to have returned. Characters speak with the accent of stoics, they pay lip service to Venus and Bacchus. How far removed they are from the routine of the torture chamber.

'When the Lieutenant saw that I could speak he said: "Don't you see how much better for you it would be if you submitted to the Queen instead of dying like this?"

'God helped me and I was able to put more spirit into my answer than I had felt up to now.

' "No, no I don't!" I said. "I would prefer to die a thousand times rather than do as they suggest."

' "So you won't confess, then?"

' "No, I won't," I said. "And I won't as long as there is breath left in my body."

' "Very well, then, we must hang you up again now, and a second time after dinner."

'He spoke as though he were sorry to have to carry out his orders.

' "*Eamus in nomine Domini,*" I said. "I have only one life, but if I had several I would sacrifice them all for the same cause."

'I struggled to my feet and tried to walk over to the pillar but I had to be helped. I was very weak now and if I had any spirit left in me it was given by God and given to me, although most unworthy, because I shared the fellowship of the Society.

'I was hung up again. The pain was intense now, but I felt a great consolation of soul, which seemed to me to come from a desire of death. Whether it arose from a true love of suffering for Christ, or from a selfish longing to be with Christ, God knows best. But I thought then that I was going to die. And my heart filled with great gladness as I abandoned myself to His will and keeping and contemned the will of men.'

If Shakespeare had sat where Bacon had sat and given the orders for the torture, one wonders whether into the great plays which present on the inner side, however much on the outer Lear may rave or Antony lust, so smooth and ambiguous a surface, there would have crept a more profound doubt than Hamlet's, a sense of a love deeper than Romeo's.

Introduction to *The Autobiography of an Elizabethan* by John Gerard
1951

Indo-China:

France's Crown of Thorns

The Indo-Chinese front is only one sector of a long line which crosses Korea, touches the limits of a still peaceful Hong Kong, cuts across Tongking, avoids – for the moment – Siam, and continues into the jungles of Malaya. If Indo-China falls, Korea will be isolated, Siam can be invaded in twenty-four hours and Malaya may have to be abandoned. In Tongking the French hold one sector of this vast front, and in the six years they have held it, the French army has lost more men than the Americans in Korea. This is the simple truth: war can sometimes appear to be simple.

From the bell tower of the cathedral of Phat Diem, 120 kilometres south-east of Hanoi, I could contemplate a panorama of war that was truly classical, the kind that historians or war correspondents used to describe before the era of the camera. At a radius of 600 to 800 metres Phat Diem was encircled by rebel forces, but very peacefully; ahead of the parachutists, howitzer shells exploded in little clouds, hanging motionless for a moment in the calm air above the plain, as in a painting. On my left, above the profile of those strange mountains, sculptured and eroded by the elements, an aeroplane was supplying a small, isolated

French post with ammunition, and when night fell the flames rising from the burning market of Phat Diem grew more vivid, adding an almost comforting element of colour to the landscape in the biting cold of this December night. Yes, war seemed very simple from the height of the bell tower.

Clearly it was an illusion – the only illusion of simplicity possible to retain in the midst of this confused struggle conducted on both sides by regulars and irregulars, by illustrious French generals and medieval warlords – one of them a kind of Buddhist prophet, another a cannibal who eats the liver of his enemy to strengthen his own body; elsewhere, a Catholic Bishop who commands his own army and hates the French more than the Communists; a new kind of Pope who preaches a dogma of synthesis and incorporates in his clergy a college of female cardinals; and (last but not least) the chief of a Third Force who makes war on everyone and places high-explosive bombs in the very centre of Saigon in order to kill innocent civilians. Western slogans and all that talk the politicians retail about the necessity of containing Communism seem here to apply only to a very small part of the picture. And it is even more difficult to fit in the oriental dragons and the fabulous serpents, different parts of a puzzle which form no part of any familiar design.

Vietnam, a creation of Western powers confronting the thrust of nationalism as much as Communism, is made up of three states: the old French colony of Cochin China, where members of the liberal professions take pride in their French citizenship, and the two ex-protectorates of Annam in the centre, and Tongking in the north. The Vietnamese government, selected and appointed by the French administration, was until recently presided over by Mr Tran Van Huu, formerly chief accountant of the *Crédit foncier d'Indochine*. He was never, and still does not possess the authority of an elected government. There is no national assembly. Under the wily Tran Van Huu's presidency the government consisted of nothing but a group of appointed individuals whose worth can be graded from simple utility right up to the strictest and most capable executive of them all, Mr Nguyen Van Tam, Minister of Public Security, who lost two sons – and one of his own fingers – to the Viet Minh.

The Emperor Bao Dai, chief of state, has kept himself prudently in the background. Just past forty, educated in France, married to a Catholic (but the Empress lives in Cannes), he sometimes gives the impression of showing more interest in sports than in his somewhat nominal responsibilities. In fact, he is an intelligent and subtle man, resolved not to compromise himself, and to survive. Nevertheless, the death of General de Lattre seems to have given him the opportunity of reappearing on the scene, and the substitution of Mr Nguyen Van Tam for Mr Tran Van Huu reinforced his administration significantly. As chief of police, the new Prime Minister has been too involved in French policy to be able to adopt a very independent line, but at least several of his ministers have been selected from Tongking, the most independent state, and overtures have been made to members of the Dai-Viet Party. This is the nationalist party of the north; it has always refused to collaborate with Mr Tran Van Huu, but its members enjoy a reputation for integrity.

Their entry into the government will doubtless somewhat soften the memory of the comparison General de Lattre made on a visit to the United States between Vietnam in the French Union and Australia in the Commonwealth. This remark was not only erroneous, it lacked tact and served to irritate cultivated Vietnamese who realize, with bitterness, the factitious character of their independence. They might indeed ask if Great Britain maintains a police organization in Canberra to parallel the Australian; if the British Governor-General expels diplomatic representatives of foreign powers without consulting the Australian government; or whether visitors must possess an English as well as an Australian visa.

General de Lattre was completely sincere when he stated that a French victory in this war would be followed by the withdrawal of his troops, but the Vietnamese would possibly have found more acceptable the policy of the English in Malaysia, provided with the same guarantees of good faith that were given India and Pakistan. They would have been better able to accept a slow and continuous progress towards independence than a show of independence, a show which costs them very dear: an uncontrolled and notoriously cruel local police force, a President who has never been elected and whom the Emperor can replace only with the consent of France. Until recently, the Emperor and the President have avoided any hint of a consultative assembly, and in a recent radio broadcast the Emperor would go no further than to suggest the creation of an assembly half of whose members he would name himself.

Who is the enemy? That is difficult to define. (Even the term Viet Minh is disconcerting for a foreigner who produces a smile or becomes suspect when he speaks of his Viet Minh friends instead of his Vietnam friends.) The Viet Minh is the nationalist government which, under the apparent direction of Ho Chi Minh, controls the greater part of Tongking and Annam. One of the most widely discussed subjects is how much authority is in the hands of the Communists, and the extent of Ho Chi Minh's personal power. Ho Chi Minh was indoctrinated in Moscow around 1920, but that doesn't necessarily make him a Stalinist to the death. There are few survivors of those first days of the Communist regime. There is some reason to believe that when he went to France in 1946 to carry on negotiations as the recognized Vietnamese chief of state, the stage was set for a shift of power to the Commander-in-Chief, Vo Nguyen Giap, an ex-lecturer in philosophy at the University of Hanoi, who, in Ho's absence, secured for himself command of Tongking.

At that time, Ho Chi Minh obtained from France conditions which would be difficult to improve upon today. They included the concession of real independence to Vietnam and the progressive withdrawal of French forces. Today, after six years of exhausting struggle and the death of 30,000 men, these are not the kind of demands that could be formulated on the battlefield.

It is difficult to believe that with such an accord in his pocket and the nation almost unanimously behind him, Ho Chi Minh decided to put everything he had achieved once more into question in the hope of rapid victory by force of arms. It is more probable that his hand was forced by Giap and other Communist leaders. There were few French troops in the north, 5,000 in Hanoi, some few thousands more in Lang Son and Haiphong, but two years later there would have been even fewer of them. Today at Lang Son Ho Chi Minh rules over nothing but ruins, and 160,000 men of the French army (including Moroccans, Senegalese and Legionaries) plus a Vietnamese army of 200,000 stand between him and the Hanoi–Haiphong delta, the essential bastion in the defence of Siam and Malaysia.

If Ho Chi Minh is really only the nominal head of the Viet Minh, who has taken his place? At the time of the battle for Hanoi, Giap was the military chief, but today the impression one gathers from reports of refugees from the Viet Minh zone is that power – civil as well as military – is in the hands of Dang Xuan Khu (alias Truongh Trinh), Secretary General of the Communist Party of Indo-China. Certain lawyers and doctors, who are sincere nationalists, have also reported that the growing pressure of Communist doctrine makes life intolerable for intellectuals. The churches still operate (for the moment the Viet Minh is more discreet towards Catholics and Buddhists since the latter's pacifism and lack of internal organization makes them more vulnerable) but persecution lies in wait just down the road. The evolution of the Viet Minh in this regard seems to be the same as in China in the first days of Communism. But one must remember that the numerous Catholic population of Tongking is almost entirely rural. They don't read European newspapers; indeed, they don't read at all. Ho Chi Minh, their great leader, teaches them by radio that the duty of Catholics is to be nationalists: no report reaches them of priests killed and nuns imprisoned in China. Propaganda is a one-way street. They could see the prudent behaviour of the Viet Minh soldiers when they penetrated the enclosure of the cathedral at Phat Diem last December, and since then they cannot understand the military necessity of the slow advance of the parachutists along the canals which cross their fields and the ruins of their abandoned farms.

It is clear that an element of idealism exists in the Viet

Minh zone which is not at all Stalinist. Certain illusions still persist. A writer, taken prisoner and then released to teach literature in the schools, describes with nostalgia the life he led there. He and his pupils received the same rations as the troops. The daily distribution of rice was made with a simplicity and justice often absent in more developed countries. (Officers and their men were entitled to the same 600 grams of nourishment; a variance in treatment was only noticeable at the end of the month when wages were paid in money or in kind.) He spoke with regret of this school that moved with the troops. When they entered a village, they would select a big hut, a door taken off its hinges would make do for a desk, he and his pupils would sit down on the ground, their haversacks containing their daily rations slung across their shoulders. At the sound of a whistle announcing an air raid, they would take cover in a nearby forest. The weight of the haversack, the sound of the whistle, the feel of the improvised desk under the fingers, the flickers of the kitchen fires in the forest, such things can attach a man to a cause — until the weight of doctrine benumbs him with its monotony. Communism simplifies the war by eliminating the factors of pure nationalism.

I have written that Vietnam is composed of three states, but it would be more precise to say three countries, for the people of Cochin China differ much more from the Tongkinese than they do from the Siamese. Hanoi, the capital of Tongking, is a three-and-a-half-hour flight from Saigon, and one shivers in Hanoi when one swelters in the heat of Saigon.

Each state has its own kind of war. Cochin China, along with Saigon, capital of Vietnam, is mainly held by the French and their allies. There the forces of the Viet Minh are composed of partisans, and the war is a guerrilla war. All the roads leading out of Saigon are guarded by watchtowers erected at one-kilometre intervals. More in form than in solidity, these lookouts are reminiscent of the watchtowers of French châteaux or English castles. Every evening at six traffic is suspended, for when night falls the adjacent ricefields become a no man's land.

In this flat, marshy country, all tender green or faded gold, held partly by the French and partly by their strange and often doubtful allies, a war of ambush is carried on. Even in Saigon it is a war of random assassination, of grenades thrown into cafés, nightclubs and cinemas. Life goes on, however, despite the grenades, although some people prefer to drink in an upstairs bar or dine in a restaurant protected by an iron grill, but these things are not major preoccupations. Unless one is unlucky, all one hears of the war is the occasional small explosion in the distance which might just as well be an automobile backfiring.

Nevertheless, ever since a local girl blew herself up with a party of sailors from a warship anchored in the Saigon river, one finds it quite natural in the big hotels to be advised against taking a Cochin Chinese woman to your room.

Of all France's allies in Indo-China, the most astonishing are the Caodaists, members of a religious sect founded around 1920. Their capital, which they call 'The Holy See', is Tay Ninh, some 80 kilometres from Saigon, where their Pope lives surrounded by cardinals of both sexes. At the entrance to the fantastic, technicolour cathedral are hung the portraits of three minor saints of the Caodaist religion: Dr Sun Yat Sen, Trang Trinh, a primitive Vietnamese poet, and Victor Hugo, attired in the uniform of a member of the Académie Française with a halo round his tricorn hat.

In the nave of the cathedral, in the full Asiatic splendour of a Walt Disney fantasy, pastel dragons coil about the columns and pulpit; from every stained-glass window the great eye of God follows one, an enormous serpent forms the papal throne and high up under the arches are the effigies of the three major saints: Buddha, Confucius, and Christ displaying his Sacred Heart.

The saints, Victor Hugo in particular, still address the faithful through the medium of a pencil and a basket covered by a kind of movable ouija board; the religious ceremonies are intolerably long, and a vegetarian diet is rigorously imposed. One should not therefore be surprised to learn that missionaries have been sent to Los Angeles.

The memory one retains of all this is phantasmagorical: a chain-smoking Pope discoursing hour after hour on Atlantis and the common origin of all religions, but who in fact makes use of this religious façade with all its pomp to support a solid army of 20,000 men with its own primitive arsenal to guard against an eventual stoppage of supply of French arms (mortars are fabricated from old exhaust pipes which, after a year of use, are given to the peasants for local defence) . . . Under the protection of this army, the pacifist Caodaist sect numbers a million and a half adherents. As Victor Hugo revealed to the faithful on 20 April 1930 at one o'clock in the morning: 'Instruct the infidel by every available method.'

But last summer a split occurred in the Caodaist ranks: the chief of the general staff, Colonel Trinh Minh Thé, went underground with 2,000 men. (The first indications of this dissidence were perhaps the champagne breakfasts to which he treated visiting journalists.) General Thé – as he has now promoted himself – states that he is as much the enemy of the Communists as of the French, but until now his exploits – such as the assassination of General Chanson, one of the best young French generals, or setting off high-explosive bombs in Saigon – have all been directed against the latter. During a lunch at Tay Ninh last February, a Caodaist Colonel complained to me about the difficulties General Thé was causing.

'The French want us to capture him,' he said, 'but that is obviously impossible.'

'Why impossible?' I asked.

'Because he has not attacked any Caodaists!'

This seems to illustrate with subtlety and precision the nature of the alliance between the Caodaists and the Franco-Vietnamese administration. Since then General Trinh Minh Thé's headquarters has been attacked, but he succeeded in escaping, though severely wounded.

Another picturesque element among the French allies in South Vietnam is provided by the Hoa Haos, with a tougher army than the Caodaists, and also with its own form of religion founded on Buddhism. Their first prophet was a Viet Minh partisan but when he came under suspicion due to overweening ambition, he was assassinated and his disciples rallied to the French. Their present General, rumour has it, was a rickshaw driver in Saigon whose wife has established a women's army. (Its sole activity up to the present has been the 'liquidation' of some of the General's concubines.)

Nor should one fail to mention the Binh-Xuyen. In theory, the authority of its commander is limited to the periphery of Cholon, Saigon's Chinese district, but since he has the gambling monopoly and owns establishments like 'Le Grand Monde' with dancing, floor-shows, roulette and dice games, he has become, with the aid of his private police force, the real force responsible for keeping order in Cholon itself. (Cholon is no further from the centre of Saigon than Harlem from Fifth Avenue or Montmartre from the Champs-Elysées.) He runs a kind of Al Capone regime and last November the French were forced to send armoured cars to Cholon to dislodge him. Rumours circulated that de Lattre was anxious to get rid of the Binh-Xuyen. Grenade attacks immediately became more frequent (a warning, no doubt, to the French and Vietnamese Sûretés, to stay out of the territory). In any case, the Binh-Xuyen still retains firm control of Cholon and its environs, holding out against the French as well as the Viet Minh.

The most reliable and also the happiest of the warlords in Cochin China is Colonel Leroy, founder of the Military Union for the Defence of Christianity (MUDC). When I visited him in February 1951 with a view to seeing the newly pacified region under his control, we had to travel protected by the armour plating of a landing barge. In February 1952 we were able to drift gently down the current in his personal boat, without even a rifle on board, to the sound of a Vietnamese orchestra.

Thirty-two years old, half French, half Annamite, Colonel Leroy is a curious and imposing personality. He quotes Proudhon, reads Montesquieu, discusses Pascal and Jansenism. He received me to the tune of *The Third Man* theme in a villa built in the middle of his new artificial lake, and, surrounded by dancing girls, treated me to a cognac. As far as social questions are concerned, he is much bolder than his own government: he advocates breaking up the great estates and distributing them to the peasants. With American aid, he has set up ninety-four first-aid stations in the territory under his administration (there are a total of ninety-six in all of Cochin China). In defiance of the President's orders he has instituted a system of local elections to a consultative assembly. Nor has he neglected the entertainment factor: he has built a free zoo around his lake with elegant Chinese pavilions, a bar, and neon lights shining all night long. What an astonishing contrast between this gay and rather bizarre Catholic state and the sober diocese of Phat Diem.

Annam, where the central cities like Hué, the former imperial capital, are controlled by Franco-Vietnamese forces, is accessible only by sea or air. The back-country, a region of mountains and deep forests, is thinly populated and there the Viet Minh has established its bases. The highway and railroad which skirt the coast and link Saigon to Hanoi are cut off in the south by Quang-Ngai and in the north by Vinh. In these pockets the Viet Minh use certain sections of the railroad by night.

In the north, towards Hanoi, nothing remains but the trace of former tracks. In the Red River delta the road runs along the former railroad embankment but there is no longer even a sign of rails, although here and there you can still see an old station with its ticket-window, vaguely disguised as a farm building. At the edge of a rice paddy a signal raises its arm, permanently frozen; a water pipe swings gently to and fro like the trunk of an aged elephant. The magic of utter neglect has fallen over the line and one cannot imagine that trains will again run along its roadbed.

Further north, in Tongking, the war has become the business of armies. Here the population is physically more solid than in the south, the climate harsher, the clothing coarser, the women less pretty, and play is forbidden. People here still remember the great famines, like the one in 1944 which caused more than a million deaths: this is the country of Ho Chi Minh, the head of the Viet Minh.

If one sees Cochin China in colours of green and gold, one sees Tongking only in brown and black. Two-thirds of the country is held by the Viet Minh, and along the Chinese border the French have lost all their positions save one. Before the arrival of General de Lattre in December 1950, the entire Red River delta, with its capital Hanoi and its only port Haiphong, was seriously threatened.

There is no doubt that during this period of retreat General de Lattre fully earned his marshal's baton. He gave his troops their first tangible victory, and then dug them in. When I saw Tongking for the first time, in February 1951, two weeks after the victory of Vinh-Yen, a line of forts was being set up around the delta. By October 1951 it seemed impregnable; Hanoi was no longer besieged. Nevertheless, something had gone wrong. The enthusiasm raised by the arrival of the chief was seeping away. Still, one couldn't say morale was bad; the French continued to fight ferociously, tenaciously, without illusions.

I have noted that the French were losing more men in this war than the Americans in Korea. About a thousand officers, equal to two entire graduating classes from Saint-Cyr, had already been wiped out, among them many promising career officers and future five-star generals. De Lattre's son had been killed at Phat Diem; Leclerc's was a prisoner of war. Faith in a miracle had vanished. For a certain time after the General's arrival, the troops felt they were under proper leadership, and were able to believe in victory. They knew that the delta, so necessary to the strategic plans of the Europeans, could not fall – unless of course the Chinese intervened and Ho Chi Minh was supplied with aircraft and pilots – but they also felt that they could never again return to the Chinese frontier, and that it was perhaps unnecessary to hold it.

One could not even say they were fighting with their backs to the wall. There is a certain advantage in being able to get one's shoulders up against a wall. But behind that stubborn and heroic army was a hostile population and an irresponsible administration unworthy of trust. If free elections had been held in Tongking, the majority of French officials admitted that Ho Chi Minh would have received eighty per cent of the vote (in the Vietnamese Assembly perhaps seventy per cent). His face is the most familiar one in the whole of Indo-China (for one year de Lattre's was perhaps as well known). Without newspapers, billboards or books to broadcast it, the depreciated coins stamped with his effigy are alone enough to make him as familiar to everyone, peasant or intellectual, as Stalin or Churchill are in the West.

The Vietnamese military structure has for a long time been as unreliable as its political structure. Created by General de Lattre, it is treated neither to commendations or reviews and depends entirely for its training on French cadres. Ho Chi Minh's soldiers belong to the same race, but with them he has produced a courageous and disciplined force which possesses all the virtues of a revolutionary army: devotion to the cause (for most of its members, a nationalist rather than a Communist one), a beloved leader, officers who have moved up from the ranks (in the Vietnamese national army the indigenous officers are the sons of families of wealthy landowners who have no real affinity with the peasants they command: they speak French or Vietnamese with equal facility).

The national army's lack of depth was made apparent in disastrous fashion at the time of the spectacular and ill-fated offensive against Hoa-Binh last November. The capture of the city, some 50 kilometres south-west of Hanoi, was made without serious losses to either side, but it was the first time the French had broken the delta defence line, and for the next two terrible months Ho Chi Minh concerted all his efforts to drive them out. De Lattre's evident objective had been to cut the supply line between China and Annam, but last February, just as the French were preparing to evacuate their position, the Viet Minh put a new route into service. With insufficient equipment (only one helicopter was available, which in this mountainous and heavily wooded region meant that every seriously wounded man was condemned to death) and too few troops, it was an achievement for the French simply to hang on to the bitter fruit of this questionable offensive as long as possible. On the other hand, it was a moral victory for General Salan (whom one could only refuse to compare with his illustrious predecessor through ignorance or lack of generosity) to have had the sense to order the evacuation of Hoa-Binh before it was too late.

But while the French were sustaining one counter-attack after another, the interior of the delta was being stripped of reserves. A propaganda campaign was undertaken to disguise this necessity. General Salan announced that the inner defence of the delta would henceforth be entrusted to the Vietnamese army. That was when the Viet Minh infiltrations began. During periods of calm at Hoa-Binh, the troops could hear bombs and shells exploding in their rear.

The case of Phat Diem is one example among many

of an infiltration that almost succeeded. I choose it because it illustrates so well the bizarre and confused nature of this conflict. Phat Diem is a Catholic diocese situated on the delta plain not far from the sea, a vulnerable point at the outer limit of territory held by the Viet Minh in Annam.

Since its foundation around 1890 by Père Six, a Catholic Annamite priest who became the Emperor's regent (the same Emperor who had had him tortured during religious persecutions), Phat Diem has resembled nothing so much as a medieval episcopal principality. The Bishop conducts his own foreign policy and has his own army, and it was only after the Viet Minh attack of 19 June when it collapsed miserably and the city was saved by French parachutists that this militia was disbanded. Those of its members who had not fled were absorbed into the Vietnam army. The present Bishop is Monsignor Le Huu Tu, a former Trappist. He is an austere man with the face of a sad, meditative monkey. He lives in the same house built by Père Six and makes good use, one feels sure, of the same unusual works of theology, and a dusty skull contemplates him from the other side of his desk. What experience does he have of the outside world? He went to Europe once, but his visits were limited almost exclusively to Rome, Lourdes and Fátima – a name which later must have had a sad resonance in Phat Diem. He is a nationalist and his number-one enemy is the French, after which come the Communists. Even with a foreigner, he makes no mystery of this order of preference. He knows the French (they took his army from him, the army which he persists in believing saved Phat Diem). He knows almost nothing of the Communists, save that the position of his diocese on the edge of the Viet Minh zone makes certain neighbourly contacts inevitable: Ho Chi Minh's currency circulates in the Phat Diem market at a very low rate of exchange (5 Vietnamese piastres for 2,500 Ho Chi Minh piastres). If he needs bamboo for a building or a milk cow for his hospital, he has to get them as contraband from Viet Minh territory. Catholics make up one-quarter of the people under his authority, but they are quite ignorant of religious persecution in China or in Europe.

Flying into Phat Diem creates some very curious impressions. One leaves the land of pagodas and suddenly one seems to have arrived in Europe over the Netherlands. In the distance, the straight canals run off towards the sea: at regular intervals of some 100 metres they intersect villages; and in every village there rises up a church as big as a cathedral. From the plane you can count more than twenty of these big churches at the same time. In the flat landscapes they take the place of windmills, and in this climate they all seem very old, even though some were built less than ten years ago.

But Phat Diem is in the very centre of the Orient, and sometimes one might imagine oneself in Europe seven centuries ago: the cathedral erected by Père Six, with its huge columns formed out of single tree trunks; the straight, endless road running from one village to another and crossing over the canals, forming a single city. It was a city noisy and dirty and full of life when I first saw it in November, but under their mushroom-shaped hats the faces were gayer than in Hanoi. There was no electricity, no public transport, no cinema, and only one rudimentary hospital, but sometimes one saw the Prince-Bishop passing through the streets on his way to the seminary, or a procession with lights and censers flowing out of the cathedral precincts, and every now and then a performance would be given in the Bishop's fantastic theatre, with its Swiss statues at the entrance, its religious symbols on the pediment, and under the stage a low, dirty dungeon where Viet Minh prisoners were locked up last summer. Life there was curiously free of monotony, and until June 1951 no one thought much about the war. The June attack itself only involved the forward positions.

'How happy we are to have such a Bishop,' an old man said to me. 'His prayers have saved Phat Diem!'

But in December, while the French were preparing to face the first important Viet Minh counter-attack on Phat Diem, the Bishop's prayers proved to be without effect.

Since the Bishop's visit to Portugal, Our Lady of Fátima was the object of a special devotion at Phat Diem, and on 9 December, as a gesture of amity towards the Bishop, the French commandant announced his wish to take part in the ritual procession of Fátima. He acted from the best of intentions, but while he marched at the head of the procession, the Viet Minh vanguard entered the village at its rear. No one reported their arrival until the Colonel was awakened at 4.30 in the morning by the explosion of a bazooka shell which blew out the façade of the house where the officers were billeted. His radio post, set up in a room opening on to the courtyard, was destroyed and a field gun was put out of action in the courtyard itself. The house was attacked on three sides by small advance units of the battalion that were making their way into the city. All the nearby French posts were cut off and when the officers did succeed in driving the enemy from their own house, the Viet Minh were installed opposite it. Clearing the main street took twelve hours, and when I arrived in the city five hours later, the Viet Minh forces had only been driven back 600 metres, leaving small French outposts still isolated.

Under such circumstances, the French considered themselves lucky to have lost only one officer and twenty-five men killed in the course of the first attack. It is hard to assess the losses of the Viet Minh: here and there the canal was filled with a thick gruel, heads floating above the accumulation of bodies below. But my most striking memories were still of that long empty street leading to the cathedral, so recently noisy and animated, where now only a few soldiers on patrol in front of the deserted houses were finishing mopping-up operations; of the interior of the cathedral where the population of Phat Diem had assembled in the cold night with their furniture, their statuettes, their portable stoves   an enormous, sad fairground where not a face was smiling; of some cheap religious pictures hanging on the wall of an abandoned farm; and of the bodies of a woman and her small boy caught in a crossfire between the parachutists and the enemy. This mother and child suddenly lost their anonymity when I realized that their faith and mine were the same.

All that already belongs to the past, a past without importance, without urgency, beyond remedy: the names of a few more officers among those I knew added to the list of the thousand officers killed; that pleasant and cultivated administrative officer, who came to see me at Phat Diem on a calm November day to talk about old books and theology, dead of his wounds; Vandenburg, with his long, dangling arms, leader of a famous commando unit composed of Viet Minh prisoners, assassinated by his own men and his unit broken up. Hoa-Binh has been evacuated. The

French have returned to exactly where they were last year: the delta still holds.

While General de Lattre was alive, predictions were based on the possibility of a Chinese intervention. Most of the rumours concerning Chinese troop movements came from the Formosan intelligence service, the most suspect of all services of this type and one which, unfortunately, is too often taken seriously by – amongst others – American authorities. To break the French line in the Red River delta there is no need of Chinese volunteers, and they would be very badly received, for the traditional hostility of the Tongkinese towards China has been reinforced since 1945 by the behaviour of Chinese nationalist troops who occupied Tongking between the departure of the Japanese and the return of the French. All the Viet Minh needs is more aircraft and a better anti-aircraft system.

People speak less now of Chinese intervention than of the possibility of an armistice. Would it be possible, one speculates, to stabilize the front as in Korea, and even to recognize Ho Chi Minh's government, and also to secure the progressive withdrawal of French troops (as in the old Hanoi Convention of April 1946), and finally to protect the frontier with China under a UN guarantee?

France, with a population one-third of the United States, has for almost seven years, in addition to the enormous financial burden, sustained a war as costly in human lives as the war in Korea. Who could blame her for wanting someone else to take over?

In the beginning the war may very well have been a colonial war (even if the Viet Minh fired the first shots), but the young men who, with stubborn and ferocious determination, are doing the actual fighting in a hard climate against a savage and fanatical enemy, care little for the rubber plantations of Cochin China and Cambodia. They are fighting because France itself is at war and firmly determined not to let its allies down *as long as humanly possible*. If we have criticized certain aspects of French administration in Vietnam we have not criticized France itself. France is the young pilot in his little B26 bomber probing his way between a hostile mountain and a hostile jungle into a valley too narrow to permit him to alter course. France is the soldier up to his chest in a rice paddy, the nurse parachuted into an isolated post, and even the police superintendent knifed in his bed by his trusted native servant. As for the future, England and America ought to remember that every human possibility has its limits.

Once this important reservation has been made, there is no doubt that the French are firmly determined to hold on. One could even observe a kind of recovery of optimism after the retreat from Hoa-Binh (carried out brilliantly and with complete success, this was a much more difficult operation than the one at Vinh-Yen, whose victorious outcome caused so much boasting).

Europe has the most urgent need of the troops the French are maintaining in Indo-China; but their return depends in large part on the realization of a single hope: the Vietnamese army. The high command calculates that in a year's time French non-commissioned officers can be withdrawn (it is said that General Salan counts on repatriating 15,000 men between now and the end of the year), officers up to the rank of captain within two years perhaps, and in three years . . .

It is a stern and sad outlook and, when everything is considered, it represents for France the end of an empire.

The United States is exaggeratedly distrustful of empires, but we Europeans retain the memory of what we owe to Rome, just as Latin America knows what it owes to Spain. When the hour of evacuation sounds there will be many Vietnamese who will regret the loss of the language which put them in contact with the art and faith of the West. The injustices committed by men who were harassed, exhausted and ignorant will be forgotten and the names of a good number of Frenchmen, priests, soldiers and administrators, will remain engraved in the memory of the Vietnamese: a fort, a road intersection, a dilapidated church.

'Do you remember,' someone will say, 'the days before the Legions left?'

Paris Match
12 July 1952
(Translation by Alan Adamson)

The Return of Charlie Chaplin

An Open Letter

Dear Mr Chaplin,

I hope you will forgive an open letter: otherwise I would have added to that great pyramid of friendly letters that must be awaiting you in London. This is a letter of welcome not only to the screen's finest artist (the only man who writes, directs and acts his own pictures and even composes their music), but to one of the greatest liberals of our day. Your films have always been compassionate towards the weak and the underprivileged; they have always punctured the bully. To our pain and astonishment you paid the United States the highest compliment in your power by settling within her borders, and now we feel pain but not astonishment at the response – not from the American people in general, one is sure, but from those authorities who seem to take their orders from such men as McCarthy. When Russia was invaded you spoke out in her defence at a public meeting in San Francisco at the request of your President; it was not the occasion for saving clauses and double meanings, and your words were as plain as Churchill's and Roosevelt's. You even had the impudence, they say, to call your audience your comrades. That is their main accusation

171

against you. I wonder what McCarthy was doing in those days?

Remembering the days of Titus Oates and the terror in England, I would like to think that the Catholics of the United States, a powerful body, would give you their sympathy and support. Certainly one Catholic weekly in America is unlikely to be silent – I mean the *Commonweal*. But Cardinal Spellman? And the Hierarchy? I cannot help remembering an American flag that leant against a pulpit in an American Catholic church not far from your home, and I remember too that McCarthy is a Catholic. Have Catholics in the United States not yet suffered enough to stand firmly against this campaign of un-charity?

When you welcomed me the other day in your home, I suggested that Charlie should make one more appearance on the screen. In this would-be story Charlie lies neglected and forgotten in a New York attic. Suddenly he is summoned from obscurity to answer for his past before the Un-American Activities Committee at Washington – for that dubious occasion in a boxing ring, on the ice-skating rink, for mistaking that Senator's bald head for an ice pudding, for all the hidden significance of the dance with the bread rolls. Solemnly the members of the Committee watch Charlie's early pictures and take their damaging notes.

You laughed the suggestion away, and indeed I had thought of no climax. The Attorney-General of the United States has supplied that. For at the close of the hearing Charlie could surely admit to being in truth un-American and produce the passport of another country, a country which, lying rather closer to danger, is free from the ugly manifestations of fear.

The other day a set of Hollywood figures, some of them

rather out-moded (Mr Louis B. Mayer and Mr Adolf Menjou were among the names) set up a fund to support McCarthy's fight in Wisconsin – a form of Danegeld. Now Hollywood uses English stories and English actors, and I would like to see my fellow-countrymen refusing to sell a story or to appear in a film sponsored by any organization that includes these friends of the witch-hunter. Our action would be an expression of opinion only; it would not condemn them to the unemployment and slow starvation to which McCarthy has condemned some of their colleagues. They will say it is no business of ours. But the disgrace of an ally is our disgrace, and in attacking you the witch-hunters have emphasized that this is no national matter. Intolerance in any country wounds freedom throughout the world.

    Yours with admiration
        Graham Greene

New Statesman and Nation
27 September 1952

Character in Search of an Author

Colonel Fawcett stands there at the portals of his book (a collection of letters, log-books and records made by his surviving son) wearing leggings and reefer jacket and fur cap, staring us straight between the eyes with a look that demands obedience, integrity and a healthy body; he has a beard and fierce moustaches and he sucks at his pipe, fearless and incorruptible. One wonders what he would have said to the young Peter Fleming with his Isis manner and his bright debunking ways if the Brazilian Adventure had really come off and the dubious Major Pingle had led the young man successfully to the old lion's lair. 'It had been comedy that I looked for from Brazil,' Fleming wrote, and he had little sympathy with the lost cities and the white Indians of Fawcett's dream. But somehow the comedy now is a little thin and dated, and it is Fawcett's romanticism that remains excitingly alive.

One is glad to read that Fawcett knew Rider Haggard, who presented him with a black basalt image said to have come from one of the lost cities and described by a psychometrist to whom Fawcett submitted it as 'a maleficent possession to those not in affinity with it, and I should say it is dangerous to laugh at it . . .' When these two men, the novelist and the explorer, met, at least one character in search of an author had successfully completed his quest. Sir Henry Curtis, as far as I remember, had no son, and Allan Quatermain lost his at an early age, but surely if their author had been kinder to those two characters, this would have been the very way in which either of them would have planned his final expedition.

'My eldest son, Jack, will accompany me on the next trip, and the third member of the party will be his school friend, Raleigh Rimell, who at present is in Los Angeles, California. Raleigh I have not seen for a long time and therefore know little about his physical condition today, but Jack has the makings of the right sort. He is big, very powerful physically, and absolutely virgin in mind and body. He neither smokes nor drinks. Nor do I.'

One smiles a little at the traditional boy's-book style, but it is with the affection one accords to 'Ballantyne the brave'. 'Please accept a *copa of chicha, senores.*' 'A large sounder of peccary had come across the river, chased by a stealth of hungry jaguars.' The style is rich, romantic, loose, but somehow through the verbiage and the extravagant anecdotes emerges an impression – a sense of wild nature, mystery, fortitude and doom. Perhaps we should not quite have believed the whole story – of cannibals and buried treasures, poisoned arrows, strange lights burning for ever in old ruins, of serpents sixty feet long, and terrible barbarities in small frontier towns – we might sometimes have suspected exaggeration, if the truth of the narrative had not in a way been sealed and attested by death. The young Fleming made a joke out of the unreal dangers of the Brazilian jungle, the *piranas* that did not tear the flesh, the savages who never drew bow, but the silence of these three – the old lion and his virginal cubs – after they set out from Dead Horse Camp is more eloquent and more convincing.

I think no reader's imagination can fail to be touched by some part of this book – my own was touched by the constant appearance of those almost symbolic figures, the kindly hospitable Germans who seem always to crop up unexpectedly on the boundary of the wild; I have met them myself in Chiapas and Liberia – and I found very moving too Fawcett's account of the ghost city of Matto Grosso.

'When human beings are banned from a dwelling they inevitably leave behind some shreds of their own personalities; and a deserted city has a melancholy so powerful that the least sensitive visitor is impressed by it. Ancient ruined cities have lost much of it and do not impress in the same way. It is the places abandoned in the recent past that clutch most at the visitor's heart . . . In the debris of a church I found the remains of what had once been the Bishop's ceremonial chair.'

The objective of Fawcett's last expedition was Z – the great lost city reported by Francisco Raposo in the eighteenth century and never again discovered. To those who have visited Angkor, which was only found in the nineteenth century, a city of temples so vast that four days are insufficient to allow one to inspect it properly, there seems no particular reason to doubt that equal marvels may remain buried in the Brazilian jungle. Men have died for far more extravagant dreams. Was there more sense in the polar quests? One remembers Scott's last letter from his snowbound tent, and Fawcett's final words from Dead Horse Camp deserve to be remembered with it.

'Raleigh I am anxious about. He still has one leg in a bandage, but won't go back. So far we have plenty of food, and no need to walk, but I am not sure how long this will last. There may be so little for the animals to eat. I cannot hope to stand up to this journey better than Jack or Raleigh, but I had to do it. Years tell, in spite of the spirit of enthusiasm . . . You need have no fear of any failure.'

Review of *Exploration Fawcett* by Lieut. Col. P. H. Fawcett, edited by Brian Fawcett
New Statesman and Nation
2 May 1953

The Young Henry James

To a biographer the early formative years of a writer must always have a special fascination: the innocent eye dwelling frankly on a new unexplored world, the vistas of future experience at the end of the laurel walk, the voices of older people, like 'Viziers nodding together in some Arabian night', the strange accidents that seem to decide not only that this child shall be a writer but what kind of a writer this child shall be.

The eleven-year-old Conrad prepares his school work in the big old Cracow house where his father, the patriot Korzeniowski, lies dying:

'There, in a large drawing room, panelled and bare, with heavy cornices and a lofty ceiling, in a little oasis of light made by two candles in a desert of dusk, I sat at a little table to worry and ink myself all over till the task of my preparation was done. The table of my toil faced a tall white door, which was kept closed; now and then it would come ajar and a nun in a white coif would squeeze herself through the crack, glide across the room, and disappear. There were two of these noiseless nursing nuns. Their voices were seldom heard. For, indeed, what could they have had to say? When they did speak to me it was with their lips hardly moving, in a cloistral clear whisper. Our domestic matters were ordered by the elderly housekeeper of our emergency. She, too, spoke but seldom. She wore a black dress with a cross hanging by a chain on her ample bosom. And though when she spoke she moved her lips more than the nuns, she never let her voice rise above a peacefully murmuring note. The air around me was all piety, resignation and silence.'

Stevenson is scared into Calvinism at three years old by his nurse Cummy: 'I remember repeatedly awaking from a dream of Hell, clinging to the horizontal bar of my bed, with my knees and chin together, my soul shaken, my body convulsed with agony.'

The young James at thirteen finds himself 'overwhelmed and bewildered' in the great Galerie d'Apollon with its frescoes by Lebrun and the great mythological paintings of Delacroix.

'I shall never forget how – speaking, that is, for my own sense – they filled those vast halls with the influence rather of some complicated sound, diffused and reverberant, than of such visibilities as one could directly deal with. To distinguish among these, in the charged and coloured and confounding air, was difficult – it discouraged and defied; which was doubtless why my impression originally best entertained was that of those magnificent parts of the great gallery simply not inviting us to distinguish. They only arched over us in the wonder of their endless golden riot and relief, figured and flourished in perpetual revolution, breaking into great high-hung circles and symmetries of squandered picture, opening into deep outward embrasures that threw off the rest of monumental Paris somehow as a told story, a sort of wrought effect or bold ambiguity for a vista, and yet held it there, at every point, as a vast bright gage, even at moments a felt adventure, of experience.'

It is impossible not to hear in such memories the opening of the door: in some such moment of 'piety, resignation and silence' Conrad's brooding note of sombre dignity and laconic heroism was first struck, just as the Master of Ballantrae may have been buried alive in Stevenson's nightmare as years later in the Canadian wastes, while the great wide air of glory and possessions and 'bold ambiguity' was breathed into James like a holy ghost at Pentecost in the great Paris gallery, where the spoils of Poynton gathered round the schoolboy and Madame Vionnet bloomed from the ceiling, a naked Venus.

Mr Edel, in the first admirable volume of his three-volume biography, leaves James at the age of twenty-seven, the education over, the writing just begun. It is a testing volume, for here the greater part of the material has been supplied with incomparable glamour and cunning by the subject himself, in *A Small Boy and Others* and *Notes of a Son and Brother*. Mr Edel, with great scholarship and freedom from undue reverence, works his way in and out of this luminous smoke-screen: he never allows James to escape completely into the sense of glory. The grand old man of Lamb House has been shaped undoubtedly by these early years, but he was not a mere bundle of sensibilities, he was a man of great toughness, not unaware of the legend he was creating. A whole European visit of the James family must be eliminated from the autobiography, because it was one too many, an untidiness – it might have given an impression of a certain levity in the old Swedenborgian father. We are glad that Mr Edel digs it up, just as we are glad to be reminded, as the old James recalls the young James's ardent Oxford pilgrimage, among 'the perfect prose of the Gothic', which seemed to him (but did it at the time?) 'a kind of dim and sacred ideal of the Western intellect – a scholastic city, an appointed home of contemplation' – of less intellectual preoccupations: 'His constipation,' William writes to another brother, 'has been reduced to very manageable limits.'

The young James emerges from under Mr Edel's scrutiny more appealing, more honest even in his ambiguities, than the autobiographies let him appear. There was always a discrepancy between the James of the autobiographies and the James of the early letters – no doubt he *was* 'a passionate pilgrim' in this astonishing old feudal world of Europe, but he was also in his letters more young, vividly alive and irreverent than the old man later allowed for.

'To crown my day, on my way home, I met His Holiness in person – driving in prodigious state – sitting dim within the shadows of his coach with two uplifted benedictory fingers – like some dusty Hindu idol in the depths of its shrine . . . I have heard in the papal choir a strange old man sing in a shrill unpleasant soprano. I've seen troops of little tonsured neophytes clad in scarlet, marching and countermarching and ducking and flopping, like poor little raw recruits for the heavenly host.'

The character in *The Altar of the Dead,* with his rather stifling reverence for a faith he couldn't share, would never have dared to be so amusing. Strether would have been more cautious – perhaps Chad . . . but Chad had his Madame Vionnet. If only at this period of his life, one is tempted to exclaim, James had had one too! The sexual relationship has this enormous value, that a bed contains a woman, a human being and not a sense of glory. It is impossible to be vague in bed, it is even difficult to be ambiguous.

In these early years the heaviest smoke-screen has always surrounded the mysterious accident that happened to James, during 'twenty odious' minutes, when he was helping to work a pump at a small fire. (It was almost like filial imitation, for his father had lost his leg on a rather similar occasion.) Many absurd theories have been built upon this vague misfortune – some have even maintained that James was literally castrated. I remember many years ago being taken to task for suggesting that the accident was not in fact serious, but that its mystery and importance were deliberately inflated by James to explain his non-participation in the Civil War – in which his younger brothers behaved with exemplary gallantry. A sense of guilt may well have been responsible for James's exile in Europe – he had no wish to face the returned heroes or to watch their shabby future – and for his almost hysterical participation in the first world war. Mr Edel has organized a great deal of evidence to support this view – even James's own self-conscious words: 'To have trumped up a lameness at such a juncture could be made to pass in no light for graceful.' (The Old Pretender perhaps was trying to confuse us with an elaborate double bluff.) Within three days of the fire – so Mr Edel reveals – James was travelling and 'radiantly' visiting. Mr Edel's summing-up could not be bettered.

'The hurt is "horrid" but it is also "obscure". It is a "catastrophe" but it is in the very same phrase only a "difficulty". It is a passage of history "most entirely personal", yet apparently not too personal to be broadcast to the world in his memoirs, even though when it happened he kept it a secret and regretted the necessity of making it known. It is also "extraordinarily intimate" and at the same time "awkwardly irrelevant". This is perplexing enough. James compounds the mystery by giving no hint of the kind of hurt he suffered, although at various times during his life he complained of an early back injury, which he usually dated as of 1862. That he should have chosen to omit all specific reference to his back in his memoirs is significant; in some way he seems to have felt that by vagueness and circumlocution he might becloud the whole question of his non-participation in the Civil War. To the error of omission — "error" because of the consequences of his reticence — must be added the effect of his elaborate euphemisms: the use of the words *intimate, odious, horrid, catastrophe, obscure* and the phrase *most entirely personal*. These had an effect not unlike that of the unspecified "horrors" of *The Turn of the Screw*. His readers were ready to imagine the worst.'

There is a freedom and clarity in Mr Edel's first volume which promise well for the following volumes. The middle years are about to begin, and on these — apart from the letters, the unfinished autobiography and stray hints in the introductions to the novels — James himself has provided little material. Yet it was in these abandoned years behind the façade of the social figure, Half Moon Street breakfasts, dinners in Cadogan Place, memories of Mrs Greville and

Lady Waterford, 'my group of the fatuously fortunate' – that the greater ambiguities stand like the shapes of furniture in a great house shrouded in dust sheets. Now the lights are about to go on, a hand will twitch at the sheets, and James himself, who nosed with such sensitive curiosity around the secret in *The Sacred Fount,* would surely be the last to complain of a detective of such gravity and honesty, even if he should have to come to deal with what James might have considered the 'all but unspeakable'.

Review of *Henry James: The Untried Years – 1843–70* by Leon Edel
New Statesman and Nation
18 July 1953

Return to Indo-China

For the third time, and after two years, one was back. There seemed at first so little that had changed: in Saigon there were new traffic lights in the Rue Catina and rather more beer-bottle tops trodden into the asphalt outside the Continental Hotel and the Imperial Bar. *Le Journal d'Extrême Orient* reported the same operations in the north, around Nam Dinh and Thai-Binh, the same account of enemy losses, the same reticence about French Union losses.

In Hong Kong one had read the alarmist reports – the fall of Thakhek, the cutting in two of Annam and Laos, 'thousands of columns pouring south on the route to Saigon'. One knew then these reports were unreal – this grim shadow-boxing war will never end spectacularly for either side, and in Saigon I knew there would be little sign of war except the soldiers in the cafés, the landing-craft tied up outside the Majestic for repairs as noisy as road drills in a London summer – less now than ever for two years ago there still remained the evening hand-grenades, flung into cinemas and cafés, spreading a little local destruction and listed in a back-page column of the *Journal*. They had ceased with the shooting of some prisoners, and who could blame the executioners? Is it worse to shoot a prisoner than to maim a child?

The only people in Saigon who were thoroughly aware of war were the doctors, and they were aware of something the French were most of them inclined to forget. 'Until I became a doctor in a military hospital,' one said to me, 'I had not realized that nine out of every ten wounded were Vietnamese.'

And yes, there was another change. I noted that first evening in my journal, *'Is there any solution here the West can offer? But the bar tonight was loud with innocent American voices and that was the worst disquiet. There weren't so many Americans in 1951 and 1952.'* They were there, one couldn't help being aware, to protect an investment, but couldn't the investment have been avoided?

In 1945, after the fall of Japan, they had done their best to eliminate French influence in Tongking. M. Sainteny, the first post-war Commissioner in Hanoi, has told the sad ignoble story in his recent book, *Histoire d'une paix manquée* – aeroplanes forbidden to take off with their French passengers from China, couriers who never arrived, help withheld at moments of crisis. Now they had been forced to invest in a French victory.

I suggested to a member of the American Economic Mission that French participation in the war might be drawing to an end. 'Oh, no,' he said, 'they can't do that. They'd have to pay us back' – I cannot remember how many thousand million dollars.

It is possible, of course, to argue that America had reason in 1945; but, if their policy was right then, it should have been followed to the end – and the end could not have been more bitter than today's. The policy of our own representative in Hanoi, to whom M. Sainteny pays tribute, was to combine a wise sympathy for the new nationalism of Vietnam with a recognition that France was our ally who had special responsibilities and, more important perhaps, a special emotion after the years of defeat and occupation.

American hostility, humiliation at the hands of the defeated Japanese and the Chinese occupying forces, exposed French weakness and saw to it that Vietnamese intransigence should grow until in 1946 France could hardly have bought peace with less than total surrender.

I suppose in a war the safe areas are always the most depressing because there is time to brood not only on dead hopes, dead policies, but even on dead jokes. What on my first two visits had seemed gay and bizarre was now like a game that has gone on too long – I am thinking particularly of the religious sects of the south, the local armies and their barons to whom much of the defence of the Saigon delta is entrusted: the Buddhist Hoa Haos for instance.

Their general's wife has formed an Amazon army which is popularly believed to have eliminated some of the general's concubines. The French had originally appointed the Hoa Hao leader a 'one star' general, but when he came to the city to order his uniform he learned from the tailor that there was no such rank in the French army. Only a quick promotion to two stars prevented the general from leading his troops over to the Viet Minh.

The Caodaists, too, began by amusing – this new religious sect founded by a Cochin civil servant in the 1920s, with its amalgam of Confucianism, Buddhism and Christianity, its 'Pope', its Holy See, its female cardinals, its canonization of Victor Hugo, its prophecies by a kind of planchette. But that joke had palled, too; the Caodaist cathedral in the Walt Disney manner, full of snakes and dragons and staring eyes of God, seemed no longer naïve and charming but cunning and unreliable like a smart advertisement.

You cannot fight a war satisfactorily with allies like this. The Caodaists, by the military absorption of the surrounding country, number 2 million and have an army of 20,000. They have had to be courted, and the moment the courtship loses warmth the threat appears. They have been given no Ministerial appointment in the new Government of Prince Buu Loc, and no Minister went down to their great feast day last month that was supposed to commemorate the seventh anniversary of the Caodaist fight against Communism. Though messages were read from General Navarre and the Emperor Bao Dai, there were none from the Government. When the turn came for the Caodaist Commander-in-Chief to speak, his venom seemed directed as much at his Government as at the Communists – 'Who could foresee the treatment reserved for us, the suspicions of which we were to become the object?'

The 'Pope', in his Chu Chin Chow robes, smiled and smiled under his gleaming mushroom hat. In the cathedral the effigies of Confucius, Buddha and the Sacred Heart stared down the glittering pastel nave at the pythons coiled round the papal throne. It was all very tricky and it might well cost blood. I remembered how the Chief of Staff, Colonel Thé, had taken to the sacred mountain in 1951 with 2,000 men to make war on French and Communists alike.

There was a time when certain Americans, dreaming of a third force, showed an interest in Thé, which one hoped waned that morning in the square of Saigon when his 200-lb bombs exploded among the shopping crowds. Now he had kidnapped a cardinal, but the cardinal was rumoured to have offended the 'Pope', and the leader of yet another private army told me he could always arrange a meeting for me with the self-promoted General Thé in the Holy See itself. The eye of God watched the Caodaists from every window, but sharp human eyes were also very much required.

And then of course there was the leader who treated his faulty liver homoeopathically with the help of human livers supplied by his troops, and the Binh-Xuyen, the private army under General Bay Vien, who controlled the gambling joints and opium houses of Cholon, the Chinese city which is a suburb of Saigon itself. (He had cleaned the city of beggars by putting them all, one-legged, armless, broken-backed, in a grim concentration camp.)

These, and such as these, were the men at arms in the south, fighting haphazardly the guerrilla war in the Saigon delta, while the real troops drained north into Annam and Laos and Tongking, the Foreign Legion, the Moroccans, the Senegalese, and the Vietnam army itself under officers who had neither the money nor the influence to ensure their stay in the south.

One flies from the bizarre and complicated Cochin to the sadder and simpler north. In the plane to Hanoi I thought of what the doctor had told me; for in the plane were many crippled Tongkinese returning home after being patched in the south. One had seen just such faces, patient, gentle, expecting nothing, behind the water buffaloes ploughing the drowned paddy fields: it seemed wrong that war should have picked on them and lopped off a leg or an arm – war should belong to the brazen battalions, the ribboned commanders, the goose-step and the Guards' march.

Outside the air terminus at Hanoi the trishaw drivers waited for fares, and not one driver would lend a hand to help his crippled countrymen alight. A French officer shouted at them furiously to help, but they watched without interest or pity the shambling descent of the wounded. There, by the dusty rim of the street, lay the great problem – those men were not cruel, they were indifferent. This was not their war, and the men on the crutches were unhurt by their silence. They had not come home, like Europeans, as heroes, but as victims – this was not their war either.

One cannot escape the problem anywhere, in the office of a general, the hut of a priest, at an Annamite tea party. Vietnam cannot be held without the Vietnamese, and the Vietnamese army, not yet two years old, cannot, except here and there stiffened by French officers, stand up against their fellow countrymen trained by Giap since 1945.

Last year General Cogny made the brave experiment inside the delta defences of entrusting the region of Bui-Chu purely to Vietnamese troops. It seemed a favourable place for the experiment since the region is almost entirely Catholic, and the Catholics, however nationalist, are absolute opponents of Viet Minh. But Giap's intelligence was good: he loosed on these troops one of his crack regiments and two battalions deserted with their arms. A third of Bui-Chu with its villages and ricefields passed under Viet Minh control. One could match this, of course, in European armies – inexperience can look like cowardice – but perhaps the cause in this case was neither.

The repeated argument of the Vietnamese is: 'How can we fight until we have real independence – we have nothing to fight for?' They recognize that their present army without the French could not stand up against the revolutionary regiments of Giap's for a fortnight. They cannot expect full independence until their army is capable of resistance, and their army cannot fight with proper heart until they have achieved it. The result is frustration and bewilderment.

The frustration and repetitiveness of this war – running hard like Alice to remain on the same square – lead inevitably to day-dreams. In time of despair people await a miracle, hopes become irrational.

One propaganda offensive is matched by another. Both sides perform before a European audience and gain inexpensive tactical successes. Giap seizes for a while Thakhek and the world's Press takes note – its recapture, like the denial of a newspaper report, figures very small. The French stage 'Operation Atlante' on the coast of Annam, reclaiming an area of impressive size that had been administered by the Viet Minh since 1946 – an easy offensive, for there were hardly more soldiers in the area than administrators. But troops were needed to guard the new territory, so that Giap was enabled to attack on the high plateau above and the fall of Kontum stole the news value.

So the war goes drearily on its way. Dien Bien Phu takes the place of Na-Sam in the news: the 1953 attack on Luang Prabang is repeated in 1954 and stops again within a few miles of the Laotian capital. Lunching at Nam Dinh, I was asked by the general commanding whether I had ever had so good a *soufflé* before to the sound of gunfire. I could have replied that I had – two years before, at the same table, to the sound of the same guns.

Everybody knows now on both sides that the fate of Vietnam does not rest with the armies. It would be hard for either army to lose the war, and certainly neither can win it. However much material the Americans and Chinese pour in they can only keep the pot hot, they will never make it boil.

Two years ago men believed in the possibility of military defeat or victory: now they know the war will be decided elsewhere by men who have never waded waist-deep in fields of paddy, struggled up mountain sides, been involved in the muddle of attack or the long boredom of waiting.

Sunday Times
21 March 1954

Last Cards in Indo-China

After all, in Vietnam, during the last two years, there had been a change more important than the traffic lights in Saigon. Until General de Lattre left for Paris and death at the end of 1951, the war could be regarded as military. France was magnificently on the defensive – under de Lattre's predecessor she had come so close to defeat and demoralization that the defensive by itself was a kind of military victory.

Early in 1951 I listened to de Lattre opening a club for veterans of the First Army. 'We will never evacuate Hanoi,' he told the members. 'I have left my beloved wife here as a proof.' A few months before, women and children were being officially evacuated, and his words were as decisive as a victory. Now no one believes in the military capture of Hanoi any more than in the military defeat of the Viet Minh General Giap, the ex-professor of history and geography who has demonstrated again to the world the value of an amateur soldier in a revolutionary army. The war has become political.

Revolution can be conquered only by a revolutionary spirit. The Vietnamese will not have the heart for a hard civil war until they feel they have gained independence and are fighting to preserve their liberty.

Under de Lattre, Vietnam took a step towards the kind of independence that might easily have been attained in 1946 at Fontainebleau before the Constitution of the French Union had hardened. Ho Chi Minh, who remains the only leader with a popular following in Vietnam, seems to have been genuinely anxious to retain a measure of French influence. M. Sainteny, who compares him with Gandhi in his reluctance to use force, who negotiated with him in Hanoi and accompanied him to Fontainebleau, writes:

'He is disposed to concede to France the care of those things which she holds most dear: her economic and cultural interests.'

He quotes Ho Chi Minh as saying:

'If we wish to administer our own country, and if I ask you to withdraw your administrators, on the other hand I shall need your professors, your engineers and your capital to build a strong and independent Vietnam.'

After more than seven years of war one wonders whether there is a single Frenchman who would not accept that definition of independence: but what is acceptable now to France has become unacceptable to the Viet Minh and the United States.

De Lattre was completely sincere when he spoke of independence, but he was a soldier and not a diplomat, and the natural suspicion the Vietnamese feel for the French was not allayed by an ill-phrased speech of his in America, nor by his appointment of the police chief, Mr Nguyen Van Tam, as President.

The Vietnamese could even then have been rallied by some striking symbol of independence – there is a time for symbolic acts to relieve the tedium of slow constitutional progress. The unfortunate National Congress was no such symbol, but a personal disaster for the Emperor who had demanded it, for the President who had unwillingly followed instructions and for the French who were politically exposed by it.

We in the West are dominated by the idea of adult suffrage, but adult suffrage means chaos or corruption in a country like Vietnam with no political traditions, a majority of illiterate peasants and no political parties, as we know the term. Political parties in Vietnam, apart from the religious sects – the Caodaists, the Hoa Haos, the Catholics – have no platforms, no records of membership, no contact with the working class: even the nationalist Dai-Viet Party of the north, whose leader is now the Governor of Tongking, is less a party than a group of men who supply funds and under a Dai-Viet Governor receive the fruits of office. In power the party consists of Civil Servants, out of power of men waiting to be Civil Servants.

The weakness until recently of the central Government has been threefold: the necessity to give Ministerial posts to each group that calls itself a party and to each sect, the necessity of compromising with the French authorities, and the necessity of satisfying, perhaps sometimes by inactivity, the Chief of State, the Emperor Bao Dai.

The French choice in 1946 of what was known as 'la solution Bao Dai' may well prove disastrous; for the Emperor, linked by education and self-interest to France, has absolute power to dismiss the President and Government. There is no appeal, and every Government is aware of the influences exercised behind the scenes, not only by the French authorities, but also by such prominent foreign visitors as Mr Nixon, the Vice-President of the United States. Any Government with a genuine programme of reform faces a blank wall, a time-limit, the knowledge that beyond a certain point lies the wilderness. If independence is to be secured by Vietnam peacefully and not by Viet Minh violently, one is forced to the conclusion that the country needs a genuine President rather than an Emperor of doubtful qualifications.

Even in Annam, the traditional home of the Emperors, loyalty to Bao Dai has waned during the last few years, and his popularity in that State has never equalled Ho Chi Minh's. It must be remembered that no great divinity hedges this sovereign. As an Emperor, he was hand-picked – a former Emperor in retirement died last week, and his true heir, a young man of outstanding ability, had been killed in a plane crash on his way back to the country. Bao Dai abdicated once in 1945 (to become chief adviser to Ho Chi Minh, under the name of M. Vinh Thuy), and perhaps that position accords better with the constitutional progress of Vietnam.

Prince Buu Loc's Government is the first since the war with the strength and incorruptibility to establish a genuine concordat with the French. In Europe, a strong Government is one with popular support: here, without elections and without real parties, a strong Government is a group of individuals with a common aim and determination, free from corruption and free from the necessity of clinging to office for the sake of the perquisites. Never before in Vietnam has there been a Government with a common aim; for every previous Government has included the sects, and there is little in common between the Caodaists, the Hoa Haos and the Catholics. One doubts, too, if there has ever before been a Government free from serious corruption, and certainly none where the chief Ministers were indifferent to the fruits of office.

At its inception Prince Buu Loc's Government was criticized because many of the leading personalities, including the President himself, knew Paris better than Vietnam, but one doubts whether any previous President, whether ex-accountant or ex-police chief, had a profound knowledge of the peoples of Cochin China, Annam and Tongking.

The new Ministers have one enormous advantage over former Administrations – they do not depend on politics for a living, they can pack up and return to France and the work they left from motives of patriotism. (The Minister for Foreign Affairs, for instance, is Professor of International Law at Toulouse University.) They are nearly all young men, and they have exceptional opportunities for political blackmail – 'unless we can reach agreement you can find another Government'. The French respect them as they may not always have respected more pliable Ministries.

But the problem of the Emperor remains – does he really desire the independence of his country if independence threatens the security of the royal domains and interests? Certainly there is a suspicion that the old dowager Empress at Hué is not without power. It may have been imagination, but one seemed to detect a certain disillusionment among Ministers after a month of office, as though they had begun to discover where so many tracks led: to the palace of Dalat, the hunting lodge of Ban Mé Thuot, the palace at Hué built in imitation of the Forbidden City of Peking.

They had taken office with gaiety and enthusiasm, their austerity rules were smiled at (orange juice instead of champagne at official receptions), but they were a symbol that de Lattre would have approved, and the appointment of a new Ministry of Democratization, vague though its functions were, promised relief from the old bureaucracy. Yet after a month was there a first rift between those prepared to have a raid, however brief, behind the lines of privilege, and those who began to lose confidence in ever successfully battling against the great amorphous Boyg? Whatever the outcome, no Vietnamese Government has taken office with purer motives.

The possibilities of blackmail have been vividly shown by King Norodom of Cambodia. French propagandists have drawn the picture of a playboy king, making and acting in his own films, leading a phoney army on a phoney operation. But one should judge by results. The King's impulsive departure to Siam and his brief exile won from the French more concessions than Bao Dai has ever gained by his more hidden tactics, and the military operation led to the surrender of two out of three guerrilla leaders, who were satisfied that the King was winning independence for his people.

Nor has the King yet exhausted his powers of blackmail. If this tiny State should choose to leave the French Union, economic sanctions are all that could be applied and bankruptcy would be less serious to Cambodia than the effect of her action to France in Africa. The lesson of Cambodia is presumably being studied in Saigon.

There is a race now in Vietnam between independence and war-weariness. French policy is no longer a problem – never has there been less suspicion of French intentions. The great French companies have decided to quit, they are moving their assets, even the Banque de l'Indo-Chine is shifting her massive weight. Without the Emperor, Prince

Buu Loc's Government might quickly reach an agreement with France.

If no agreement is reached, weariness and division may well suggest quack remedies. The possibility of surrendering Annam and Tongking and establishing a Cochin China Republic becomes again the subject of dinner-table discussion. The pipe-dream of substituting American for French Union troops might lead to a disastrous temporary peace which would abandon many non-Communist Nationalists to the mercy of Viet Minh – in particular the Catholic populations of the north, Thai-Binh, Bui-Chu and Phat Diem.

Will independence come too late? Has the control of the Viet Minh movement passed irrevocably into the hands of the Communists? Has Ho Chi Minh been converted to the solution by violence which he so long opposed, or is he a virtual prisoner in Communist hands?

My own rational answers would be uniformly pessimistic. I believe the moment of independence has been delayed too long. I believe in no solution for this unhappy country except what is dictated around the counsel tables of Geneva, Washington, Peking and Moscow. I do not believe that ever again will one see the strange sunsets falling on the Baie d'Along, the lamp glowing on the cook's face as he prepares the opium pipe. The last performance has begun: a country one has loved is about to retire behind the curtain.

But because a game is nearly lost, there is no point in not playing the last card of any value (one cannot do more than lose), and that card is complete independence.

And even now one can experience fleetingly a little hope, however illusory. During January I spent three days in Bui-Chu, the scene of the surrender of the Vietnamese battalions. New Vietnamese troops had been sent with a new commandant; only one small artillery post on the perimeter flew the French flag; this small pocket of Vietnam, under its courageous Annamite bishop, was to all intents independent. The commandant was Buddhist, but he felt behind him a population united by their Christianity – not the Christianity of new converts, but of men and women whose great-grandparents had survived the Emperor's persecution a hundred years ago, when to shelter a missionary entailed death under the elephant's hoof.

Gunfire was almost continuous, but under that mantle of sound new converts were baptized, a new church dedicated. Last summer the Viet Minh attacked the seminary (kidnapping almost the only foreign priest) and shot down four Vietnamese sisters in the chapel. 'Then,' an old priest said to me, 'I began to learn French.' In the school, small girls in silk trousers and blue jackets sang for me what they called a song of peace, weaving their tiny fingers that might at any moment break into flower at the tips. 'We want only peace, to live quietly in friendship, but if the Communists come, we will fight them and kill them . . .'

'If all villages were like Thui-Nhai,' the commandant said, 'there would be no problem in the delta.' This village guarded by its own militia had defeated nine attacks between August and 30 December. The militia consisted of the whole population – from old men to girls of twelve. They paraded before the church gay with Vietnamese flags – the small girls carried knives and wore hand-grenades on their belts. A maze of mud walls, rifle emplacements in the church itself, a mortar built out of any old junk, this was indeed total war. A Vietnamese priest described the young leader: 'He is a commandant without rank or pay, who eats his mother's rice in return for fighting his father's enemies.'

I thought in contrast of the cripples scrambling from the Hanoi bus, the exhaustion and the indifference. Of course one cannot put one's hope of a country on a single village and a home-made mortar, and yet, as the sound of the evening guns flapped over the ricefields in the late golden light, one thought how in the break-up of a world there was no point in anything but irrational hope, 'to hope till Hope creates/From its own wreck the thing it contemplates'. I noted in my journal, 'Yesterday the commandant of the 46th Viet Minh Regiment came in to surrender, carrying with him plans for the capture of Bui-Chu . . .'

Sunday Times
28 March 1954

Before the Attack

At the military airport at Hanoi at 7 a.m. to wait for a plane on the shuttle service to Dien Bien Phu, the great entrenched camp on the Laos border, which is meant to guard the road to Luang Prabang, the capital of Laos. There is a daily fog over the camp which lies in a plain surrounded by Viet-held mountains. At 11 a.m. we got away. Among the passengers two photographers in camouflaged uniforms. They seem to me comparable to those men who go hunting big game with cameras alone.

I always have a sense of guilt when I am a civilian tourist in the regions of death: after all one does not visit a disaster except to give aid – one feels a *voyeur* of violence, as I felt during the attack two years ago on Phat Diem. There violence had already arrived: it was there in the burning market, the smashed houses, the long street empty for fear of snipers. It was very present in the canal so laden with bodies that they overlapped and a punt of parachutists stuck on a reef of them: and it came suddenly home on patrol when two shots killed a mother and child who found them-selves between the opposing forces. What panic had they felt? I felt a little of it myself when for a few moments I lost my companions and found myself stumbling between the Viet Minh and the Foreign Legion. I told myself then that I hated war, and yet here I was back – an old *voyeur* at his tricks again.

Violence had not yet come to Dien Bien Phu, except in the smashed and bulldozed plain which three weeks ago had been a Thai village and a forest of trees and ricefields among the stilted houses. Giap's men were known to be all round, perhaps two divisions strong, and heavier artillery and anti-aircraft than they had yet employed were on the way. With coolie labour it was being brought down from the Chinese frontier. The French are waiting and hoping for an attack, the air is noisy with planes building up supplies, and primrose parachutes come wavering down like the seeds of some wild plant on a windy day.

In the mess at lunch there was a big blonde woman over for the day to see whether the Social Services could be of assistance to the camp. Colonel de Castries (his neat dark histrionic features reminded me of Mr Ernest Milton in *King John*) teased her unmercifully. The time, he told her, had not yet come for sweets. He had '*autres objectifs*'. She became angry and rather pitiful, this big woman with her desire to help among a lot of amused and uninterested men who did not want her feminine care.

Then the Colonel in turn lost his temper with two of his brother officers who insisted on discussing Na–Sam, the strong defensive post in the north evacuated last year by the French. He said he would not have another word spoken about Na–Sam. Na–Sam had nothing in common with Dien Bien Phu. 'This is not a defensive post, this is a post from which to counterattack. I will not have Na–Sam mentioned in the mess.' His chief of staff hastily asked me if I had seen

Claudel's *Christophe Colombe* when I was last in Paris.

Before dark fell the mortars tried out their range. The evening star came out to the noise of the shells. I had a sense of unreality. There the Viet Minh were, able to observe the arrival of every plane, every movement in the camp from the encircling hills. They knew our strength better than we knew theirs. We were like actors in an arena.

The French had so planned their defences that if the Viet attacked – and the most likely hours were between four and ten in the morning when the heavy morning fog began to lift – they would have to pass down between three small fortified hills that stood like sentries at the entrance to the plain. They would be enfiladed here, they would be enfiladed there, but I just couldn't believe that anything was even going to happen.

Slept after an admirable dinner in a dug-out shared with the intelligence officer.

6 January

Before lunch visited the camp of the Thai partisans. A delightful domestic scene. Up to the present they had been allowed to keep their families with them. Small boys were playing in and out of the emplacements and dug-outs. A woman suckled her baby while her husband in a steel helmet stood admiringly by: a small girl returned with green vegetables from market: a group of women gathered round a cooking pot. War momentarily seemed charming and domestic, but if a shell were to burst here, how far worse than any man's war.

After the camp a Thai village outside the lines. The Thai women, from the moment they walk, wear the same elegant close-buttoned costume, the same hat like an elaborately folded napkin; in the same dress they toddle beside their mother and stumble as an old woman towards the grave. They have more open faces than the Vietnamese: in old age their features are almost European, so that you could easily mistake them for weather-worn Breton women in their national costume. In one village lived the mission priest in a hut that was chapel and dispensary as well as home. He had a long sharp nose and a long narrow beard and eyes full of the amusement of life. One hand was bent and crooked – he had been tortured by the Japanese, and he carried also the scar of a Viet Minh wound. His business was not conversion, there were practically no Catholics among the Thais: he was there to serve the Mass for himself and to serve the Thais with medicine and friendship.

In the afternoon caught a military plane back to Hanoi in time to wash and dine with an old friend. It was good to lie down and relax after dinner and smoke and talk as two years ago. His opium was the best I had smoked since I was in Hanoi last.

Spectator
16 April 1954

Catholics at War

8 January

At 9.50 I took a plane from Hanoi to Nam Dinh. Here, two years ago, I had stayed with Colonel Sezaire. From here I had slipped into burning, besieged Phat Diem in a French landing craft carrying Vandenburg and his black-clothed Commando of ex-Viet Minh prisoners – Vandenburg, with his animal face and dangling hangman's hands (a few weeks later he was murdered by his own Commando before they deserted). Nothing in the delta ever seems to change – not even the gunfire.

I was on my way to Bui-Chu, the Annamite bishopric on the edge of Phat Diem – the first region to be handed over by the French to the Vietnam forces, a premature decision, for two battalions deserted to the enemy with their new American weapons, and the French had temporarily to return to clean up the mess.

Some hours had to be passed before my plane to Bui-Chu and these I spent with a French colonel, who took me to a performance of *Le Cid*, in French, given by the equivalent of ENSA to the students and teachers of the Nam Dinh schools. It was not such an odd choice as might appear, for the Vietnamese theatre, too, is heroic and the costumes were less alien to the Vietnamese idea of theatre than contemporary ones would have been. All the same, there was a continuous ripple of laughter – perhaps some of it was caused by the dialogue, which it is difficult for even an Englishman to appreciate (*honneur* and *gloire* sounding regularly like the tolling of a bell), but probably more was caused by the presence of real women on the stage (as unknown in the Eastern theatre as it was in Elizabethan England) and by the abrupt and exaggerated changes of gesture and tone. When a man actually knelt at a woman's feet the laughter rose higher than ever.

At 3.50 I caught my plane to Bui-Chu – ten minutes by plane but six hours by road if the road had been open, because of the loops of the Red River. The Bishop of Bui-Chu was a very different character from the neighbouring Bishop of Phat Diem, younger, with a greater knowledge of the world outside than the former Trappist monk. The Bishop of Phat Diem was only interested in building more and more churches (for which he hadn't the priests): the conditions of the market, the lack of a hospital – this meant little to him, and he was interested in education only in so far as it produced priests. I did not find him a vain man, but his position was that of a medieval Bishop – the temporal ruler of his diocese. When he drove in his jeep down the long narrow street of Phat Diem, his fingers raised in benediction, impassive as a statue, he reminded me of an ancient mural, in which only the significant lines have escaped the destruction of time, the raised fingers, the tassel on the episcopal hat. The Bishop of Bui-Chu belonged to our day and world – and our day and world includes the pockmark of bullets on the seminary wall which the Viet Minh attacked in June. They broke in at night and carried away four priests (two of them Belgian, whom I remembered meeting in 1952 and with whom I discussed English literature). They fired, too, into the sisters' chapel and killed four sisters – one falling dead under the statue of Our Lady (the wall still bore the mark of the bullets).

There is a terrible squalor about war in these days; men emerging from holes, bearded, dirty, wearing the chevrons of their rank wherever is most convenient; the little forgotten hospitals like those of Bui-Chu, served by a few priests and sisters, without enough bandages; the wounded women; the men with their feet gashed on the bamboo points of the Viet Minh defences. Four wounded had come in today and two had died. It was part of the day's work, but there was no clean room for doctor and nurse to retire to, no bath, no easy chair, no change from the smell of wounds.

One of the priests, a young man with a squint, pale gums and several gold teeth, took me to his room and gave me tiny glasses of sweet altar wine. He had been learning English from one of the Belgian fathers who was kidnapped and he was anxious to practise. He was suffering, he said, from '*faiblesse générale*', and could do little work. He was my constant companion for two days, giggling and trying to copy my English pronunciation, carrying on his lessons up to the last possible moment, in the jeep on the landing ground.

9 January

Mass in the cathedral at 6.45, after being woken by gunfire before daybreak. It was strange and moving, in the big cathedral, to be the only European. The grace of the Annamite priest and his vestments, everything the same and yet all the faces so different. The Church seemed to give a model for the politicians – Christianity can survive without Europe. Why not trust the people?

After Mass I was pulled away before I could get my breakfast by two priests who wished to be given a small lesson in English.

During the morning visited the refugee camp – six hundred people who had been evacuated from the villages captured in June by the Viet Minh. In one hut were five families separated by hangings. In one tiny compartment hung a picture of Our Lady, with a bleeding heart, and Bao Dai.

The commandant in charge of the troops in the Bui-Chu area. A Vietnamese with a tough, sympathetic face, full of confidence, a Buddhist. Under his leadership, to all intents Bui-Chu was independent. Only one French artillery post remained, otherwise not only the troops but the Church was Vietnamian. Could they fight? To answer that question they brought me to the fortified village of Thui-nhai.

One approached it by a jeep along the narrow causeways between the canals. The commandant thought of sending ahead of us a mine-detecting patrol, and a few minutes before we arrived they found a mine, enclosed in a wooden box with a piece of wood over the detonator. A mine of Chinese manufacture with the instructions printed in Chinese. Why is it one is not more thankful for life? The commander of the patrol went, later, to the Bishop's residence to receive his thanks for saving the life of his guest, but it is too difficult to thank God with any sincerity for this gift of life.

The fortified village of Thui-nhai was the most impressive thing I have seen in the Indo-China war. Here was a popular Dien Bien Phu made with the spades and pickaxes of local men: a maze of mud walls and firing emplacements that extended right into the church itself, mud ramps standing in the aisle for the last stand. Since August the village, with no aid from proper troops, had beaten off nine night attacks by the Viet Minh, the last on 30 December. Everyone who could walk was in the militia. The church was gay with yellow Vietnam flags, and in the Square, for my inspection, in orderly ranks, stood the whole village: small girls of twelve carried knives and wore hand-grenades in their belts. One home-made mortar, a Bren gun, a few Stens – for the rest they had to fight with old rifles and knives and grenades – there were plenty of these. The commandant was young, smart, imaginative. He had organized his own information office: the village Roll of Honour, charts of organization, photographs. As we sat with him at tea, the squinting priest said to me, 'He is a commandant without rank or pay, who eats his mother's rice in return for fighting his father's enemies.' If all villages were as homogeneous as this and as well organized, there would be no problem in the delta, but here was the enormous advantage that every soul in the village was Catholic. They felt a personal threat.

I think that the loss of the two battalions had been good for Bui-Chu. It brought the threat home and killed complacency. Catholicism had not been enough. Now they were being encouraged again. The commandant of the 46th Viet Minh Regiment had come in the day before to surrender, carrying with him plans for the capture of Bui-Chu. He was surprised to find himself received by a Vietnam commandant and a Vietnam captain (a young intelligence officer with a kind of fanatical smartness, who had once been a Franciscan). The major was following one of his own captains who had surrendered three weeks before. Both men were Communists – not nationalists caught up in the Viet Minh camp and disillusioned. Something was badly wrong with the 46th Regiment, and nobody knew what. Had these men offended the political commissars attached to each battalion? We are too apt to forget the strain in the enemy's camp, seeing only our own tensions and doubts.

After lunch, I flew round the Bui-Chu defences in a Morane plane piloted by a young medical student called up from Hanoi University. Only one post of artillery flew a French flag with the Vietnamese – a bird's-eye view of independence. When I returned, the Bishop put his head into my room and asked whether I would like 'a small promenade'. The promenade turned out to be the consecration of a new church in a village which had become entirely Catholic a year ago. As the Bishop moved around the walls scattering holy water, while the guns grumbled like an aching tooth, one was aware that the political or material motive here for becoming Catholic was very small.

After that, tea with the *Chef de Provence*, and the awful tiredness that comes from hospitality – the strain of politeness and friendliness in the absence of companionship. Then one longs most to be with the people one loves, the people with whom it is possible to be silent.

10 January

The conversions certainly go on. Before Mass this morning, in the Bishop's chapel, there were fifteen baptisms, thirteen of them in one family. It was the patronal feast, and a Mass more gay than any I have seen outside Vienna. The Bishop was robed to the music of violins, gay tinkly music like an eighteenth-century gavotte. The altar boys carried the vestments with a ballet grace: even the candles on the altar seemed to dance. One was worlds away from the dull bourgeois Masses of France and England, the best clothes and the beadle, and the joyless faces and the Gregorian chants. This was a Mass to be enjoyed, and why not? The sacrament is too serious for us to compete in seriousness. Under the enormous shadow of the cross it is better to be gay.

Later, the school children performed a long heroic play in verse as incomprehensible to me as *The Cid* had been to the Vietnamese, and then there was a banquet for all the priests and schoolmasters and officers. I had to leave in the middle of it to catch my plane back to Hanoi, and the squinting priest went with me, learning English to the last.

Tablet
17 April 1954

A Memory of Indo-China

It was December 1952. For hours I had played at iron bowls in the airport at Haiphong, waiting for a mission. The weather was overcast and the planes stood about and nobody had anything to do. At last I went into town and drank brandy and soda in the mess of the Gascogne Squadron. Officially, I suppose, I was at the front, but it was hardly enough: if one is writing about war, self-respect demands that occasionally one shares a very small portion of the risk.

That was not so easy since orders had come down from the État Major in Hanoi that I was to be allowed only on a horizontal raid. In this Indo-China war horizontal raids were as safe as a journey by bus. One flew above the range of the enemy's heavy machine-guns; one was safe from anything but a pilot's error or a fault in the engine. One went out by timetable and came home by timetable: the cargoes of bombs sailed diagonally down and a spatter of smoke blew up from the road junction or the bridge and then one cruised back for the hour of the *apéritif* and drove the iron bowls across the gravel.

But that afternoon, as I drank brandy and soda in the mess, orders for a mission came in. 'Like to come?' I said yes. Even a horizontal raid would be a way of killing time. Driving out to the airport the officer remarked: 'This is a vertical raid.' I said, 'I thought you were forbidden . . .' 'So long as you write nothing about it,' he said. 'It will show you a piece of country near the Chinese border you will not have seen before. Near Lai Chau.'

'But I thought all was quiet there and in French hands?'

'It was. They captured this place two days ago. Our parachutists are only a few hours away. We want to keep the Viets head down in their holes until we have recaptured the post. It means low diving, and machine-gunning. We can only spare two planes – one's on the job now. Ever dive-bombed before?'

'No.'

'It is a little uncomfortable when you are not used to it.'

The Gascogne Squadron possessed only small B26 bombers, prostitutes the French call them, because with their small wing-span they have no visible means of support. I was crammed on to a little metal pad the size of a bicycle seat with my knees against the navigator's back. We came up the Red River, slowly climbing, and the Red River at this hour was actually red. It was as though one had gone far back in time, and saw it with the old geographer's eyes who had named it first, at just such an hour, when the late sun filled it from bank to bank. Then we turned away at 9,000 feet towards the Black River, and it was really black, full of shadows, missing the angle of the light: and the huge, majestic scenery of gorge and cliff and jungle wheeled round and stood upright below us. You could have dropped a squadron into those fields of green and grey and left no more trace than a few coins in a harvest field. Far ahead of us a small plane moved like a midge. We were taking over.

We circled twice above the tower and the green-encircled village, then corkscrewed up into the dazzling air. The pilot turned to me and winked: on his wheel were the studs that controlled the gun and the bomb chamber: I had that loosening of the bowels as we came into position for the dive that accompanies any new experience – the first dance, the first dinner-party, the first love. I was reminded of the Great Racer in the Festival Gardens when it comes to the top of the rise – there is no way to get out: you are trapped with your experience. On the dial I had just time to read 3,000 metres when we drove down.

Now all was feeling, nothing was sight. I was forced up against the navigator's back: it was as though something of enormous weight were pressing on my chest. I was not aware of the moment when the bombs were released; then the gun chattered and the cockpit was full of the smell of cordite, and the weight was off my chest as we rose. And it was the stomach that fell away, spiralling down like a suicide to the ground we had left. For forty seconds no worries had existed: even loneliness hadn't existed. As we climbed in a great arc I could see the smoke through the side window pointing at me. Before the second dive I felt fear – fear of humiliation, fear of vomiting over the navigator's back, fear that middle-aged lungs would not stand the pressure. After the tenth dive I was aware only of irritation – the affair had gone on too long, it was time to go home.

And again we shot steeply up out of machine-gun range and swerved away and the smoke pointed. The village was surrounded on all sides but one by mountains. Every time we had to make the same approach, through the same gap. There was no way to vary our attack. As we dived for the fourteenth time I thought, now that I was free from the fear of physical humiliation, 'they have only to fix one machine-gun in position'. We lifted our nose again into the safe air – perhaps they didn't even have a gun. The forty minutes of the patrol had seemed interminable, but it had been free from the discomfort of personal thought. The sun was sinking as we turned for home: the geographer's moment had passed: the Black River was no longer black, and the Red River was only gold.

Down we went again, away from the gnarled and fissured forest towards the river, flattening out over the neglected ricefields, aimed like a bullet at one small sampan on the yellow stream. The gun gave a single burst of tracer, and the sampan blew apart in a shower of sparks; we didn't even wait to see our victims struggling to survive, but climbed and made for home. I thought again, as I had thought when I saw a dead child in a ditch at Phat Diem, 'I hate war'. There had been something so shocking in our fortuitous choice of a prey – we had just happened to be passing, one burst only was required, there was no one to return our fire, we were gone again, adding our little quota to the world's dead.

I put on my earphones for the pilot to speak to me. He said, 'We will make a little detour. The sunset is wonderful on the Calcaire. You must not miss it,' he added kindly, like a host who is showing the beauty of his estate; and for a hundred miles we trailed the sunset over the Baie d'Along.

The helmeted Martian face looked wistfully down on the golden groves, among the huge humps and arches of porous stone, and the wound of murder ceased to bleed.

Listener
15 September 1955

Catholic Temper in Poland

The ancient editor-in-chief of *L'Humanité* was leaving Warsaw; they put flowers on him as you put flowers on a tomb. The smooth managerial types stood around and kissed the nicotinous yellow cheeks, and then they shoved him on board the plane. One pushed from behind, another lugged from in front, another took the hat off his long white locks, another caught his flowers: the Communist editor-in-chief went aboard.

My own fellow passenger was young, with a blue-gray puffy face; and when he took off his hat, you saw a shaven skull; he too had been seen off, and by his country's representative, who had succeeded after seven years in fishing him out of a Polish prison where he was serving fifteen years for espionage. He wouldn't talk, for another of his countrymen still lay in the same jail, but he ate – how he ate! There was more thick bread than anything else in our meal, but his tray was empty before I had eaten more than one sandwich, so he cleared my tray as well and emptied my briefcase of all the cookies and chocolates and sandwiches with which kind friends had stuffed it. The night before, he had eaten two kilograms of sausage, he told me, but he hadn't been able to sleep a wink in the comfortable legation bed.

Monsieur Cachin, the oldest French Deputy, dozed in his seat out of touch with the problems of *L'Humanité,* and I couldn't help smiling to think of the many readers who have asked me why I sometimes write thrillers, as though a writer chooses his subject instead of the subject choosing him. It sometimes seems as though our whole planet had swung into the fog belt of melodrama, but perhaps, if one doesn't ask questions, one can escape the knowledge of the route we are on. A venerable old man with long white hair and long white mustaches says good-by to his warm-hearted friends, and after life's fitful fever he sleeps well; a young man, as young men should, has a healthy appetite. The world is still the world our fathers knew.

It might even be possible so to regard Poland. In Warsaw the Old Town has risen like a phoenix: if we stand in the main square we find it almost impossible to believe that a few years past there was nothing here but a heap of rubble. Every house has been faithfully reconstructed: each bit of molding is exactly as it was.

At first I was inclined to praise the poetic sense of the Communist government. Hitler had said Warsaw was to be erased, and here it stands again: the fifteenth- and sixteenth-century houses, the little Apotheke, the old café. Faced with an eliminated town and the terrible problems of housing, one would have expected a Communist government to rear great tenement flats with perhaps another Palace of Art and Culture nearly (but not quite, for the Poles have taste) as hideous as the gift palace from Moscow that shoots up its useless tiers like a gangster's wedding cake in the center of the city. Poetic, imaginative, a little 'reactionary', how charming to be able to praise a Communist government for these qualities.

But then a doubt niggles at the brain. The Old Town was destroyed in the insurrection of 1944, one of the bravest and foolhardiest episodes in all Polish history, when men armed with homemade grenades and a few pistols held out for two months against a German army already on the spot, seeing their city destroyed house by house rather than surrender, while the Russian generals halted their advance to allow Hitler time to eliminate these men and women who had wanted to liberate themselves. Officially the insurrection never took place; there is no record of it – so I was told – in the Museum of War, and soon there will not even be any broken bricks to show that the Old Town had ever been destroyed. We know how Trotsky has been excluded from the history of the Revolution. Perhaps history now has to be rewritten architecturally, too.

A blinkered traveler can certainly find much that seems unchanged: the wide gray windy square of Cracow with its stone market colonnade fall of toys and gay peasants' clothes and the apple women sitting in black shawls by the piles of bright apples; in Czestochowa the trumpets' wail as the silver curtain descends at the last Mass over the most convincing portrait ever painted of Our Lady, with the Swedish lance-thrust in her cheek – 'Help of the half-defeated'; the old streets of Lublin; the little fifteenth-century wooden church at Dembo with the relics of Sobieski in a vestry hardly larger than a confessional box; the humor and lightheartedness of Warsaw. (Let us give the Communist government the credit for being the source of so much humor; it was they who prevented for some while the publication of the dogma of the Assumption because they thought the date of the feast – which had been celebrated since the ninth century – was somehow connected with the defeat of the Russians by Pilsudski after the First World War.)

In the countryside there are still native craftsmen carving wooden saints and Stations of the Cross as though Byzantium had not fallen to the Turks; at a wedding in snowy Zacopane the carriages waited, the drivers in the tight trousers of the Tatra mountains, while the inviters to the feast rode to and fro in their bright jackets, and the bride was drawn from the church by two men, and the bridegroom by two girls who held his arms, and the singing began as the carriages wheeled away.

The traditional storytellers still fix you with an Ancient Mariner's eye, and little touches of modernity only give life to the old fables. When we picked our way through the freezing mud of one village an old man told his tale of how he had visited the United States, where a Mr Frick possessed two piles of gold and silver so large it would have taken twelve men to shift them. A friend of the storyteller had been invited to go and see the piles, but when he got there, Mr Frick commanded him to add twenty-five dollars in gold and twenty-five dollars in silver to each pile. Oh, he had been properly caught, his friend had been. But when the old man was invited to visit the piles, he got the better of Mr Frick, telling him, through his interpreter, 'If there were seven million fools in the world, you could climb to heaven on your piles of gold and silver.'

In the same way it would be possible to pass through Poland, as it was possible for many tourists to pass through Mexico in the 1930s, and see no sign of tension between Church and State. But the State has learned wisdom since the experience of Mexico, and here in Poland, where the Church really represents the country, the Communist has to tread with care. The Church represented the nation against Russia in the days of the Tsar, it represented the nation against Hitler, and now it represents the nation, in the eyes of the nation, far more than the group of men who rule it in the interests of Russia.

Even the workers in Nowa Hutta, the new industrial city built out of nothing in three years on the plain outside Cracow, fill the churches – not always for religious motives, but as a little gesture of independence where the opportunities for independence are few. Nevertheless the number of communicants (and a man will not go to communion as a political act) has grown enormously. Only since the Revolution has the Pole, I believe, changed his habit of communicating on certain major feast days only.

But turn the stone and the position is not so happy.

The old independent Catholic press is dead. *Tygodnik powszechny*, a Catholic weekly whose circulation ran into six figures, was closed down because the editor refused to prejudge one of those clerical trials in which the government unwisely indulged before it realized the strength of Catholic feeling. For some months there ceased to be a Catholic press, but this, too, did not suit the government, which needed the façade of religious toleration. *Tygodnik* was started again, though no member of the old staff consented to work for it, and it was put into the hands of the Pax movement.

The Pax movement is perhaps the most ambiguous feature of Polish life today. The leader, Mr Boleslaw Piasecki, was before the war a nationalist and an anti-Semite; during the war he was a partisan leader who fought courageously both the Germans and the Russians (he lost his first wife in the Warsaw insurrection). He surrendered to the Russians and was condemned to death. However, he was spared and taken to Moscow, whence to the astonishment of many Poles he returned to Warsaw with permission to start the Pax publishing firm and the Pax movement which forms a keystone of the so-called Clerical Lay Catholic National Front Activists.

Pax is a cadre consisting of only about 350 members, all laymen, and round that cadre, which reminds one a little of the Communist Party, there are a great many fellow travelers – many of genuine sincerity – including several thousand priests. Their ostensible aim is to support the social and economic changes in Poland – many of which were both necessary and admirable – and to prove, as it were, the 'progressiveness' of Catholics.

They are allowed to publish a certain number of books from the West (and one can give a great deal of praise to this activity, though the Catechism, which has been printed in hundreds of thousands, contains phrases of political significance unknown to our 'penny' version). They have two weekly papers – the new *Tygodnik* with a circulation which has fallen to 30,000, and the *Dzis i jutro,* a more ideological weekly with a circulation of about 5,000. *Dzis i jutro* has been put on the Roman Index, but, in spite of this, publication has been continued.

The opponents of Pax (who are the vast majority of Catholics in Poland) sometimes claim that the movement is Russian-inspired and was a clever attempt to divide the Church. One uses the past tense; for, if that was the intention of the Pax leaders, they have dismally failed. Pax has very little importance in the Catholic life of Poland.

Conventions are held: a vicar-general appears on the platform, priests with humorless and uneasy faces help to fill the big halls in Cracow and Warsaw; Viet Minh priests (as the Eastern custom is) clap delightedly their own speeches, and Mr Piasecki orates on the subject of the aggressive Atlantic powers in true Marxist terms. But the Church goes on without them, and congregations prefer for Mass or confession the churches which are served by a priest who is not a Patriot.

Peace, Democracy, Patriot – these words when spelled with a capital have been taken over in a special sense in Eastern Europe. Certainly among the fellow travelers of Pax there are many sincere patriots (without the capital letter) who wish to take part in the social reform of their country; and if a debt has to be paid by their Catholicism, they try to pay it in the smallest possible coinage.

It is too easy for us to condemn them. We have no Auschwitz to remember. The girl we entertain to dinner has no prison number tattooed upon her arm. Every visitor to Poland should be made to visit this camp of death where the prison blocks have been turned into a museum. One long corridor of glass contains behind it nothing but 20,000 tons of women's hair; another window forming a whole wall contains a hill of tiny shoes.

In Warsaw, on every waste patch, there are rough stovepipe crosses which are the people's memory of murder. No single Lidice is remembered – there were too many of them. The Katyn massacre fades into insignificance against six million dead. German rearmament to these people – Catholics as well as Communists – is a betrayal. No crimes have been committed by Communists equal to what Poland has suffered from Germany.

But the crucial question which I found no follower of Pax ready to answer with directness or simplicity is: 'Where is your point of resistance? At what point will you warn the government that if they go farther you will cease your collaboration and close down your presses? You exist. Therefore you must be of value. Therefore you have the possibility of blackmail.'

Apparently that point was not reached with the arrest of Cardinal Wyszynski, and the Cardinal's integrity lies on the conscience of many followers of Pax, but less, I think, on the conscience of their leaders. The Cardinal has now been released from prison and is confined in a convent at Komancza near Sanok, not far from the USSR and Czech borders.

Officially he can see whom he pleases, and many a Pax follower emphasizes the salubrity and natural beauty of the region where he dwells. I presented Mr Piasccki with an open letter addressed to the Cardinal, begging the favor of an audience and promising I would make no mention of our meeting in the press. I asked to receive even a refusal in his own hand, but no reply came.

I think it probable that the government regret the arrest of the Cardinal; they have gone too far, however, to withdraw, unless they can represent his return to Warsaw as part of a bargain. Such a bargain is not impossible, but the outsider is mystified, as so often, by the present policy of the Vatican. At the moment, Vatican policy seems directed as much against the Catholic people of Poland as against the Communist government.

No one in Poland today – except perhaps some old lady dreaming of the past in her denuded apartment – wants the return of an *émigré* government, and yet the Vatican recognizes an *émigré* ambassador. It is as if the Pope still received as the ambassador of Russia some White Russian grand duke from the days of Nicholas II. Nor are any Poles prepared to consider the return of the Western Territories to a Germany responsible for such immeasurable suffering; yet when the bishopric of Breslau fell vacant a German cleric was appointed who now lives in the comfort and security of Western Germany.

Most Catholics in Poland feel a pinprick to their pride when letters to administrators in the Western Territories are addressed by the Roman Curia to 'Germania', and pray for the day when the realities of the situation shall be recognized by the Vatican, and perhaps – in that case who knows? – the Cardinal they love may come back to his diocese in the capital of Poland.

Atlantic Monthly
March 1956

The Price of Faith

I cannot imagine a reader who will not be interested by this book, though serious Protestants may find its levities shocking – they are apt to consider it unfair that Catholics should combine an authoritarian Church with freedom of speech and freedom of criticism. Perhaps they may be inclined to complain that I have the character of Mr Facing-Both-Ways if I quote with pleasure some of Mr Wall's amusing excavations from the Eternal City: the standing joke in Rome that the letters of the Pontifical Registration number SCV (*Stato della Città del Vaticano*) stand for '*Se Crista Vedesse*' (if Christ were to see); Pio Nono's fondness for billiards (he once had supper on the roof of St Peter's and was reputed to possess the evil eye); and Mr Wall's nostalgic reminder of Alexander VI and his mistress:

'Vasari said that the Madonna with child was a portrait of the Pope's beautiful mistress, Giulia Farnese, whose career was the beginning of the great Farnese fortunes: the girl the Pope adored in his later years when his children were already growing up around him, the girl who caused him so many pangs of jealousy that, on one occasion, when Alexander feared she might go back to her husband to whom he had married her for cover, he threatened her with Apostolic excommunication . . . Giulia Farnese or not, she is certainly the *femme fatale* for the exasperated sensuality of a strong man in late middle age.'

But I would not like to give the impression that Mr Wall's book is merely a journalist's light compilation. Always easy to read, almost always informative, it can sometimes conceal under its light manner a seriousness that deserves to be called deadly. There is his criticism, for example, of the renewed wealth of the Religious Orders:

'the Religious Orders are once again enormous property-owners. In Ireland they have for long been buying up the great country houses that private families can no longer afford to keep up, thus reversing the development that happened with the Reformation. But by and large in the English-speaking countries, this aspect of religious life is unknown. In Italy, especially in the poorer parts, it can become astonishing and paradoxical. In Rome huge new buildings are going up all the time for seminaries, monasteries and convents. They cost a fortune to build and they are by no means sparing in amenities – other than aesthetic ones. So one gets people vowed to perpetual poverty living in incomparably better surroundings than the ordinary poor of the country, with better food, better clothes, and so on. The real poor are still living half a dozen in a room in huts that let in the wind and rain in winter, and are like furnaces in summer, without bedding, without drains and without any material hope.'

We mustn't let our amusement with the picturesque – or the droll (such as the dictionary published by Monsignor

Bucci, Secretary of Briefs to Princes, of 'new Latin Words for modern inventions, such as telephones, motors and various kinds of explosives') blind us to the temporary and temporal faults of this huge organization whose only real purpose is the propagation and preservation of Christ's teaching. Because we believe the essential has never been lost, we can be amused up to a point by the faults of conservatism, the elaborations of ceremonial, the small immoralities and dishonesties belonging to any organization; we can always turn away from Rome to some dry mountainside where a stigmataed priest spends hour upon hour in the confessional attending with kindness and insight to the worries of the poor. Magna Carta has the great resounding clause 'To none will we sell, deny or delay right and justice', and this formula is applicable to the Church. In these days – of greater efficiency and greater honesty and far less temptation – there is little danger of justice being sold or deliberately denied, but it can very easily be delayed. Some feel it was so delayed in the case of the worker-priests and of the Jesuit teachers of Lyons: others may think the gift of faith may be delayed by the hearty materialism of the Church in North America. Mr Wall writes:

'A Catholic of my acquaintance confessed to a priest that she feared she was "lacking in Faith, Hope and Charity". The priest, who had a strong brogue, said: "I'm not interested in these airy-fairy things; have you eaten meat on Friday, now?" '

Most Catholic writers, I suppose, receive a good many letters from would-be Catholics or from lapsed Catholics who have got into the hands of just such unthinking men. The price of faith as well as liberty is eternal vigilance.

Review of *Report on the Vatican* by Bernard Wall
New Statesman and Nation
7 July 1956

Spies

I doubt whether I have known more than a dozen spies in my life, and I am still uncertain about two of them – a certain Swiss business man whose notebook I borrowed for a few hours many years ago (strangely it contained the address of a friend of mine two thousand miles away who died a year later in a Nazi concentration camp), and another man of rather indeterminate origin with whom I planned to spend a Christmas holiday in the Banana Islands, in the company of two African blind dates – malaria robbed me of that holiday, somebody else's malaria, which made it worse. Of one spy, however, I have reason to be certain: he had hardly the qualifications of the others, for he was illiterate, he couldn't count above ten, and the only point of the compass he knew was the East, because he was a Mohammedan. I was reminded of him in recent years by the report of a divorce case in which the judge expressed severe criticisms of a private detective. The detective was also illiterate, he rode to his work on a bicycle and dictated his reports to his landlady who was stone deaf. Life is strange.

How very strange life is the readers of this anthology will certainly learn if they have not learned the lesson already. I wonder how many would be able to detect truth from fiction in this anthology if the editors had not printed the names of the contributors. Does Cicero's visit to the German Embassy in Ankara seem more or less fictional than Hannay's to the headquarters of the British Secret Service? Could the reader really tell which was fiction, between Mr Dennis Wheatley's spy trapped in a bathroom at the Ritz, and Colonel Lawrence's misadventure in Arabia? Of the two I find Mr Wheatley's style a shade more convincing, for I cannot help wondering how Lawrence, bent by his captors over a bench, could observe on his own body the marks of the Circassian whip. A good spy should not embroider – it is Colonel Lawrence's apparent embroidery which makes me, unwilling as I am to side with Mr Aldington under any circumstances, distrust the texture of his report. For in this strange funny nightmare world we welcome the prosaic. An intimate friend of mine once received simultaneously from two spies a report on the contents of a concrete shed on an African airfield – one spy said that it sheltered a tank, the other old boots. How could my friend help being biased in favour of the old boots? So I can believe in Mr Ambler's fictional Colonel Haki and his ambition to write a detective story, while I find it hard to believe in the real Colonel Baden-Powell on a butterfly-hunt in Dalmatia incorporating the plans of fortifications into the pattern of his butterfly's wings. Bond's travelling equipment imagined by Mr Ian Fleming is certainly no more fantastic than the furnishings of Herr Schellenberg's private office. This is true, that is untrue, take your pick.

For the characters in one section, *A Gaggle of Suspects*, I feel a personal sympathy, for there was an uncomfortable month during the winter of 1951 in Indo-China when I too found myself under suspicion. (Little did I realize that I was in such distinguished company – Wordsworth and

Lawrence, Gauguin and Thomas Mann.) Some days passed before I realized what lay behind the literary interests of a member of the Sûreté stationed in Hanoi. Day by day he combed the bookshops for copies of my novels, and in the evening he would present himself with his little pile of books, seeking *dédicaces* for himself, for his wife, for his friends. At last I realized he was not the 'fan' I had been vain enough to believe: he was trying inconspicuously to carry out the directions of the Commander-in-Chief, General de Lattre, who had on one embarrassing occasion and at his own dinner-table accused me of espionage. I was able after that to save M. 'Dupont' further trouble. We arranged to meet in the evenings for a drink and a game of *quatre-cent-vingt-et-un* at the Café de la Paix where I would tell him what I had been doing during the day. The courtesy of the Sûreté demanded that the guest – and suspect – should always win: the courtesy of the suspect demanded that the drinks should be equally divided. Unfortunately my police agent was unaccustomed to anything stronger than vermouth-cassis, and his wife refused to believe it was only duty which kept him up late and sent him home under so unaccustomed an influence. I still feel a sense of guilt towards my friendly watcher when I remember that sad tired bloodhound face, apparently sprung from some spiritual liaison between M. Fernandel and Mrs Browning, lifted from the glass he didn't want to drink, to listen to the story he didn't want to hear, apprehensive and reproachful. How merciless one can be when right is on one's side. He had a weak heart and there was an occasion when he passed completely out. Perhaps it was to quiet the memory of that kindly ineffective ghost that I have joined with my brother to compile *The Spy's*

Bedside Book and to evoke figures far more absurd and improbable.

Introduction to *The Spy's Bedside Book*, edited by Graham Greene and Hugh Greene
1957

The Novelist and the Cinema

A Personal Experience

A memorial article should be free from bitterness, and now that the day of the film-story is over and, if the cinema should happen to survive, it is likely to be as a kind of circus-show presenting such enormous wide-screen features as *Around the World in 80 Days* or *War and Peace*, we can remember that once there were prizes for the writer, not so glittering as the popular journalists like to make out, but prizes none the less that helped many writers to survive through the lean sad years of the thirties — for working men the years of the dole and for the writer the years of the gramophone which could not be paid for, the life-insurance that had to be surrendered, of sleepless anxious nights.

How lean those years were the young writer may not realize who was launched by his publisher during the book-boom of the forties when every novel sold and it was only a question of how much paper should be allotted to this writer or to that. The position was not realized even at the time by the unreliable chroniclers of the popular press, and some of us found it ironic in 1939 to be regarded by journalists as best-sellers and to know what in fact our publisher's accounts showed. I can only take my own case and record that after eleven years and eleven books the numbers of my first edition had increased by 500 – from 2,500 printed of my first book to 3,000 printed of my eleventh. In those years neither the BBC nor the Central Office of Information had become the patrons of a young author or, in my age-group, of the not-so-young. His chance of surviving a little above the lean standard of the weekly reviewer (with all *that* entailed of deadening reading – so many books a week that were clearly food for worms) lay in the cinema – the small chance of winning a kind of Irish Sweep, of receiving money for the outright sale of work already done, or a little later the less desirable prize of employment for six weeks at £50 a week as a script-writer (and how difficult it was to realize that the £50 would cease and leave one committed to this expense or that at one's normal income of £12 a week). I won my first Irish Sweep in 1932, when my American agent sold a novel *Stamboul Train* to 20th Century-Fox. It was my fourth novel, I was down to £30 in the bank, a child was on the way, I had been refused the job of sub-editor on the *Catholic Herald* because my qualifications were held to be 'too good', and I had no prospects. The amount was not high by the standards of the publicity agent – I think £1,500 – but it enabled me to go on writing without seeking other employment until a second prize came my way in 1934, when Paramount bought *A Gun for Sale* for, I think, £2,500. It wasn't – in spite of the figures the journalists gave – possible to make a fortune by films, but they enabled one to live, and I feel glad to have been able to survive by such outright sales as these of work done for another purpose, rather than by taking employment in a Government department or a broadcasting corporation as would be the case now.

So my first feeling towards the films is one of gratitude. I suspect there are better writers than myself who have the same cause for gratitude, William Faulkner, Hemingway . . .

Now when you sell a book to Hollywood you sell it outright. The long Hollywood contracts – sheet after closely printed sheet as long as the first treatment of the novel which is for sale – ensure that you have no 'author's rights'. The film producer can alter anything. He can turn your tragedy of East End Jewry into a musical comedy at Palm Springs if he wishes. He need not even retain your title, though that is usually almost the only thing he wishes to retain. *The Power and the Glory*, a story I wrote in 1938 of a drunken Mexican priest with an illegitimate child who carries on his vocation stumblingly, sometimes with cowardice, during the religious persecution of the early thirties, became, as *The Fugitive*, the story of a pious and heroic priest: the drunkenness had been drained away and the illegitimate child (I believe this is so, for I never saw Mr John Ford's film) became the bastard of the police-officer who pursued the priest. One gets used to these things (like the strange intrusion of a girl conjuror into *This Gun for Hire*) and it is a waste of time to resent them. You take the money, you can go on writing for another year or two, you have no just ground of complaint. And the smile in the long run will be on your face. For the book has the longer life.

The most extreme changes I have seen in any book of mine were in *The Quiet American*; one could almost believe that the film was made deliberately to attack the book and the author, but the book was based on a closer knowledge of the Indo-China war than the American director possessed and I am vain enough to believe that the book will survive a few years longer than Mr Mankiewicz's incoherent picture. Again, why should one complain? He has enabled one to go on writing.

I repeat that I am grateful to the cinema. It made twenty years of life easier and now, if the inferior medium of television kills it, I wonder whether television will do as much for the author. At least the cinema, like a psychiatrist, has enabled one to do without it.

But that last sentence which slipped unthinkingly off the pen has a certain sadness. Am I the same character who in the 1920s read *Close-up* and the latest book on montage by Pudovkin with so much enthusiasm, who felt in *Mother, The Gold Rush*, in *Rien que les heures, Souvenirs d'automne, Warning Shadows*, even in such popular Hollywood films as *Hotel Imperial* and *Foolish Wives*, the possibility of a new kind of art? of a picture as formal in design as a painting, but a design which moved? The 'talkies' were a set-back, but a temporary one. Quite quickly – even in so early a film as *The Perfect Alibi*, they too began to show here and there, in isolated scenes more often than in complete films, a selectivity of sound which promised to become as formal as the warning shadow – and they had a special interest to the writer. He was no longer merely the spectator or the critic of the screen. Suddenly the cinema needed him: pictures required words as well as images.

Thus another prize was offered to the writer in those lean thirties – employment. This was more dangerous to him, for a writer should not be employed by anyone but himself. If you are using words in one craft, it is impossible not to corrupt them by employing them in another medium under direction. (Proust found even conversation dangerous – the more intelligent the more dangerous, 'since it falsifies the life of the mind by getting mixed up in it'.) This is the side of my association with films that I most regret and would most like to avoid in future if taxation allows me to.

My first script – about 1937 – was a terrible affair and typical in one way of the cinema-world. I had to adapt a story of John Galsworthy – a sensational tale of a murderer who killed himself and an innocent man who was hanged for the suicide's crime. If the story had any force at all it lay in its extreme sensationalism, but as the sensation was impossible under the rules of the British Board of Film Censors, who forbade suicide and forbade a failure of English justice, there was little of Galsworthy's plot left when I had finished. This unfortunate first effort was suffered with good-humoured nonchalance by Laurence Olivier and Vivien Leigh. I decided after that never to adapt another man's work and I have only broken that rule once in the case of *Saint Joan* – the critics will say another deplorable adaptation, though I would myself defend the script for retaining, however rearranged, Shaw's epilogue and for keeping a sense of responsibility to the author while reducing a play of three and a half hours to a film of less than two hours.

I have a more deplorable confession – a film-story directed by Mr William Cameron Menzies called *The Green Cockatoo* starring Mr John Mills – perhaps it preceded the Galsworthy (the Freudian Censor is at work here). The script of *Brighton Rock* I am ready to defend. There were good scenes, but the Boulting Brothers were too generous in giving an apprentice his rope, and the film censor as usual was absurd – the script was slashed to pieces by the Mr Watkyn of his day. There followed two halcyon years with Carol Reed, and I began to believe that I was learning the craft with *The Fallen Idol* and *The Third Man*, but it was an illusion. No craft had been learnt, there had only been the luck of working with a fine director who could control his actors and his production.

If you sell a novel outright you accept no responsibility; but write your own script and you will observe what can happen on the floor to your words, your continuity, your idea, the extra dialogue inserted during production (for which you bear the critics' blame), the influence of an actor who is only concerned with the appearance he wants to create before his fans . . . Perhaps, you will come to think, there may be a solution if the author takes a hand in the production.

I thought that myself, and I do retain the happy memory of one unsuccessful film, *The Stranger's Hand*: days at Venice drinking grappa with Mario Soldati, running races down the Giudecca with Trevor Howard, the friendliness of the Italian unit. It encouraged me to go further along this road in a film which shall be nameless. To be a co-producer is no job for a writer. One becomes involved with the producer's monetary troubles: one has to accept actors who are miscast because another man's money is involved. As a writer one hasn't the blind optimism of the film-maker who believes against all evidence that somehow the wrong actors, the wrong director, the wrong cameraman, the wrong art-director, the wrong colour-process, will all come together and produce a lucky accident.

It isn't the way that books are made. We have to learn our craft more painfully, more meticulously, than these actors, directors and cameramen who are paid, and paid handsomely, whatever the result. They can always put the blame for a disaster elsewhere which no novelist can. So the author – turned co-producer – shrugs his shoulders and gives up while the game is only half through. He knows what the result will be. Why go through the unpopular motions of fighting every battle lost at the start? He knows that even if a script be followed word by word there are those gaps of silence which can be filled with the banal embrace, irony can be turned into sentiment by some romantic boob of an actor . . . No, it is better to sell outright and not to connive any further than you have to at a massacre. Selling outright you have at least saved yourself that ambiguous toil of using words for a cause you don't believe in – words which should be respected, for they are your livelihood, perhaps they are even your main motive for living at all.

Included in *International Film Annual* (2), edited by William Whitebait
1958

Lines on the Liberation of Cuba

Prince of Las Vegas, Cuba calls;
Your seat is reserved on the gangster plane:
Fruit machines back in Hilton halls
And at the Blue Moon girls again.

The Times
28 April 1961

Letter to a West German Friend

What a relief it is sometimes to find oneself on a material frontier, a frontier visible to the eyes, tangible – even when in Berlin it is a wall. For most of us have all our lives in this unhappy century carried an invisible frontier around with us, political, religious, moral . . . Nearly forty years ago I stepped across such a frontier when I became a Catholic, but the frontier did not cease to exist for me because I had crossed it. Often I have returned and looked over it with nostalgia, like the little groups on either side of the Brandenburg Gate who on holidays stare across at each other trying to recognize a friend.

I was reminded of my invisible frontier when I stayed with you in West Berlin. Up at night in the roof-garden of the Hilton Hotel – a garden where vari-coloured bottles take the place of flowers – you pointed out to me the great arc of lights around the West, and the deep space of darkness beyond, broken only by occasional short chains of yellow beads. 'You can see,' you said, 'where the East lies'; yet it is the mark of frontiers – the evil of frontiers perhaps – that things look quite different when you pass them. Four days later, driving into East Berlin from Dresden and Potsdam, I was not particularly aware of darkness – not at any rate a greater darkness than you will find in the industrial quarter of any large city at ten o'clock at night. It was true there was no Kurfürstendamm, though that name conveys now none of the gay associations of the twenties. The big new restaurant in the Unter den Linden was still bright with lights; the shop windows too were lit and there was an elegance in the window-dressing which you do not find in Moscow. Alone of Communist cities Moscow seems to frown on the allure of consumer-goods – she makes the worst of what she has, while in East Berlin and Bucharest and Warsaw they make the most.

We left the Hilton bar, you remember, and drove to Bernauerstrasse, where the wall shows itself, especially at night, in its most uncompromising form; shoddily built, the colour of mud and rust, protected on the eastern side by a depth of wire-entanglement, it is all the uglier for its pettiness; it stands little higher than a man's head between the blind houses on one side of the street. The eastern windows have been bricked up, and at night the houses near the wall bear the obvious dark sign of evacuation. Here and there a light . shines from fifty yards behind. A church has lost its only entrance, the wall running slap across the doorway. Upon the western side the dark crosses and perpetual wreaths are like the memorials on alpine roads where a man has plunged to death.

This wall, and the check-points where foreigners and West Germans can visit East Berlin for the day, represent the great difficulty of Communism. For a possible convert they stand there more impassably than any dogma or historical fact. I find no difficulties in the economic dogmas of proletarian democracy, and what happened in Budapest, after all, happened less than half a century ago in Dublin. Official atheism I am able, perhaps mistakenly, to regard as a passing phase (I prefer in any case atheism to agnosticism under the guise of official Christianity), and the comparison of living standards is an unreliable and unpleasing argument. What of the standards of living in rich Venezuela? Do we have a better car than the man next door? I remember a young West German friend saying, 'How glad I shall be when butter and meat cost the same on both sides of the wall. Then we can argue about things that matter.' You would think from the photographs of daily visitors that it rained only in East Berlin, and that the rain fell on nothing but ruins in the East – missing the new apartment-buildings and the new stores.

There is a wall neurosis: the visitor is more aware of it in the West than in the East because there the wall is geographically inescapable. Take a drive in the evening as we did in the little patch of country still belonging to West Berlin: the road is packed with cars, driven by people seeking the illusion of space and air, until suddenly there the wall is again, not of brick or cement this time, but of wire and water, the water divided by buoys and patrolled by eastern police boats.

Belief, like it or not, is a magnet. Even what seem the extravagant claims of a belief are magnetic. In a commercial world of profit and loss man is hungry often for the irrational. I do not believe that the little knots of people who gather near Check-point Charlie are there to demonstrate repugnance, as do the bus loads at the Brandenburg Gate. Part of Berlin has become a foreign land and they are staring into the strangeness, some with enmity, others with apprehension, but all with a certain fascination. Behind them lies the new city, the smart hotels, the laden stores; but capitalism is not a belief, and so it is not a magnet. It is only a way of life to which one has grown accustomed.

To take the few steps beyond Check-point Charlie can be compared with the acceptance of the last difficult dogma – say the infallibility of the Pope. There are moments when the possible convert is in a state of rebellion; he can see the wall and nothing but the wall. There are moments when he will gladly stretch his faith to the furthest limits. Perhaps there is always one moment when he shuts his eyes and walks into the wide ruined spaces beyond the check-point. He looks back over his shoulder and the dogma has suddenly changed. What had been a threat can even appear like a protection.

You were unable to accompany me for obvious reasons beyond the check-point, but you have asked me to tell you what I noticed there. You reminded me how my character Fowler in *The Quiet American* claimed proudly to be a reporter and not a leader-writer and you recommended me to be the same. But for a reportage one requires more than the two and a half days I had in the East, and one requires to speak the language however roughly. The reporter can deal in this case only with himself; he can report only his own evanescent impressions. Of course, I could write to you about the magnificent Leda of Rubens at Dresden, at Pilnitz the magnificent Gauguin and the Toulouse-Lautrec brothel scene, curiously described in the catalogue as a scene in the artist's *atelier* (puritanism or innocence?); I could describe the ruins left by the great blitz, a war crime worse than that of Hiroshima; I could note the big changes since three years ago in East Berlin, the new apartments on either side of the Karl Marx Allee where I remembered desolation, a shop of new designs in furniture and ceramics which would do credit to our English Heal's, in the poorer older streets which have survived bombardment not too bad a selection of consumer-goods – at least they are purchasable in a variety of small shops: one is not subjected to the crowds and ennui of the gigantic GOUM.

The more expensive clothes-shops have style – they were also full of clients with enough money to spend. Wine is chiefly Bulgarian. Food is simpler and less varied than in West Berlin, but it is not expensive. I judge not from the big restaurants, but the small country inn where I lunched, well off the autobahn, on the way to Dresden, and the people's restaurant where I dined in Potsdam. The hotel in Dresden was a luxury hotel with show-cases of champagne, perfume, and women's clothes (well designed). I have a feeling that these are not the details you want.

I have spoken of the wall as a protection. Naturally this was the way it was presented to me by the young officer at the Brandenburg Gate in a speech too long, too prepared and too innocently propagandist: a protection from spies, saboteurs and black marketeers. His stories of deaths along the wall almost too carefully duplicated the circumstances of deaths on the western side. Crosses and wreaths are a popular expression, and though they may be as misleading as photographs, they are a great deal more convincing. It was not from this officer that one gained the sense of the wall as protection, nor from the booklet purporting to give the names, addresses and telephone numbers of the CIA staff in West Berlin, beginning with a Mr Harry Grant of 15 Taylorstrasse and ending with a Miss Jane Rowlay of 17 Stuartstrasse (telephone 76-49-87). There were private tragedies of divided families *before* the wall was built as well as after – families divided by the temptations of the West.

The West is too inclined to attach heroic motives to all

those who escape across or through the wall. Courage they certainly have, but how many are 'choosing freedom' for romantic motives, love of a girl, of a family, of a way of life, and how many are merely tempted by a standard which includes transistor radio-sets, American blue jeans and leather jackets? As long as living standards differ, there'll always be motives less than noble.

You may think I was conditioned by the friends I made on the other side of the wall, for true it is, when I passed Check-point Charlie returning west, I felt as if I were leaving something simple behind me and coming out again into the complex world of Bonn. In a few more minutes I would be talking again with my western friends about the case of *Der Spiegel*, about the wiles of the old Chancellor, about Doenitz's school speech in defence of the Nazis and the headmaster's suicide; I would be asking about the record of General Spiedel and the latest Nazi scandal in the government of Bonn.

There have been scandals, of course, on the other side, but they have been ruthlessly cured: the sore does not continue to run there indefinitely. In West Germany one hesitates to probe the past of any man in his fifties or sixties. I felt no such hesitation in the East. Of four friends I made there two were old Communists who had spent the war in a refugee camp in Shanghai; one had served in the British Army, landing with a Scottish regiment in Normandy; one, having fought with the International Brigade in Spain, saw the war out in South America. Perhaps the old Catholic convert has something in common with the old Communist convert which makes it easy for the two to get on terms – he has lived through the period of enthusiasm and now recognizes the differing regions of acceptance and doubt.

One Communist, who had been an orthodox Jew, said to me, 'I gave up my faith when I was eighteen and joined the party. Now at fifty one realizes that everything is not known.' There's a funny story – told in the East. Khrushchev has been asked by the Central Committee to visit the Pope and try to reduce the tension of the Cold War. He reports to the Committee when he returns: 'I have reached a compromise with the Pope.' (The members express uneasiness at the very idea of compromise.) 'I have agreed that the world was made in seven days.' (A tumult follows.) 'Yes, but listen to what the Pope has agreed – that it was made under the leadership of the Communist Party.'

On this side of the wall we are apt to believe that we have a monopoly of laughter and self-mockery. Brigitte Bardot is playing in the East . . .

New Statesman
31 May 1963

Return to Cuba

There are only three ways now into beleaguered Cuba, by Prague, Madrid (curiously enough) and Mexico. I chose Mexico, which I had not seen for a quarter of a century, and I remained glad of my choice, even after my pockets had been rifled of pounds and dollars within ten minutes of landing. For Mexico is a warning to revolutionaries: it presents a remarkable tableau of a revolution which has failed.

Failure was beginning, as I remember it, twenty-five years ago: in the south there were the closed and ruined churches and the abandoned and resentful Indians; in San Luis Potosí a bandit-general who controlled the city's water and shut it off to irrigate his farm, and everywhere there were the politicians and the pistoleros, leaning from the balconies of their city halls and spitting down on to the poverty below.

Now, driving around the rich new suburb of Pedrigal, built on volcanic lava by a speculator who bought the arid land for a few dollars a hectare, one is aware that private wealth is again in full flood: the ingenious modern bungalows of steel, glass and wood (clinics for living in), gardens raised on the black lava base at enormous cost, swimming-pools which flow below the houses so that the lazy man can dive straight from his bed into the water. It is astonishing how many ultra-rich a poor country can support. 'Money speaks,' my driver said, 'but it shouts in Mexico', as he pointed out to me the estate of the ex-Commissioner of Police.

Here in Mexico, he told me, as one item of cost led to another, a girl in a good house costs sixteen dollars, but in the suburb of San Angel, with its cobbles and balconies and seventeenth-century elegance, you pay a hundred dollars, an inclusive charge. 'The girls are swimming in a pool,' the driver said, as though that were a speciality new to an Englishman. 'You can have what you want, any girls, any drinks, no extras.' He added reasonably, 'But you would do better with sixteen dollars, for a man cannot drink more than one bottle of whisky or two bottles of champagne, and one girl is surely sufficient for most men. With a hundred dollars you are paying only for an illusion.' The driver's name was Jesus and the conversation reminded me of many conversations in the old Havana.

Upon *this* revolution the United States never closed the frontier; assets were never frozen nor was trade discontinued. The Danaë of revolution was softened by the golden shower. It might so easily have happened the same way in Cuba.

The attitude of Mexico to Cuba has the ambivalence of guilt. Jove who sent the golden shower must be propitiated, but in the memory of those living there *was* something called the Mexican Revolution. Was it not celebrated in a film by Eisenstein? It had artists – the sentimental Rivera, Orozco, the savage Siqueiros (but Siqueiros is now in gaol – he did not realize in time that the revolution was over; it's safer now to do murals, like O'Gorman's, of Mexico's Aztec past).

To satisfy the ghost of revolution Cubana Airlines must be allowed to maintain a skeleton-service to and from

Mexico; to please the United States the passengers must be made as uncomfortable as possible. Their photographs are taken for police records and presumably for the FBI – even diplomats are photographed every time they carry a bag to or from Havana. Transit visas only are granted to passengers from Havana and the delay at the airport is prolonged beyond the limits of plausibility. I was lucky when I returned; I was cleared in a mere two and a half hours (the passenger list numbered sixty). Mexican customs regulations are very lenient – most travellers will find their wants adequately covered by the long and detailed list of duty-free goods: 'Eighteen pieces of underwear . . . Fifteen pairs of socks . . . Six shoes . . . One pair riding boots . . . One umbrella . . . Two fine tie-clips, and two inexpensive tie-clips . . . Fifty books . . .' But every book that comes out of Havana is closely regarded – even my *Pickwick Papers* – and on a counter the pile of confiscated material rose to a height of two feet.

In Mexico one saw the American blockade in action. In the streets of Havana one saw the result. No Socialist country which I have visited has shown such a poverty of consumer-goods; photographs of Batista atrocities take the place of goods in the windows. One bar is full – another empty: this indicates the temporary presence in one of soda-water or ginger-ale to help the rum down. In the Floridita, which was one of the great restaurants of the world, daiquiris may give out any day for lack of limes. I notice in my diary of 1957 that on 11 November I had for lunch there crayfish *an gratin* containing white truffles, asparagus and small peas. Now in 1963 I had some bean soup, tinned langouste and rice, one bottle of beer (served only with meals and never more than one), coffee – this meal cost me $6.80.

All the same the Floridita is crowded, and by a new class of customer, who is neither rich nor old. A lot of money is chasing too few goods. In the old town it is almost impossible to find a taxi free, for if there is nothing much else to buy, a taxi-ride is always welcome. Your best policy is to find a taxi that has broken down and then stay beside it. As there are no spare parts at the garages it will be mended somehow, in time, and your patience will be rewarded. The driver borrows a knife from a man in a jockey cap who lounges all day in the square. Somehow he has procured, too, the sole of an old shoe. He cuts and carves and stamps a hole and presently the spare part is finished. His cheerfulness is unabated – it is impossible not to love this country.

A long queue stretching round a whole block is for a sudden release of basket balls (food-queues, except for bread, are not very evident: rations are staggered, so that it is only when your own number goes up in the store-window that you fetch your ration). Of course there is a lot to irritate – bureaucracy is a constant danger, and for a country in need of dollars, they make it unnecessarily difficult to change American Express cheques. There must be times when the men from the mountains look back with nostalgia to the simple days of fighting before the days of forms. Bureaucracy, like Hemingway's battlefield, is strewn with paper.

The Havana of which I have longer memories was the Havana of Batista; of that sad time only the big hotels on the Malecon – the great motorway along the bay of Mexico – survive and the smart respectable night-clubs of Vedado. Havana then was a great open city for the bachelor on the loose. The Mambo, the brothel which greeted the incoming tourist on the road from the airport, is a restaurant now:

the Blue Moon is closed: the discreet superior establishment on the Malecon also; Superman no longer goes through his nocturnal ritual – perhaps he is a refugee in Miami. The Shanghai Theatre is shut and moulders away. There for $1.25 you could have seen a nude show with three blue films a night, and there was a pornographic bookshop in the foyer for those yet unsatisfied.

The roulette-tables too are gone from the hotels, and the fruit-machines – these like the brothels had been controlled in Batista's day by the members of Murder Incorporated. Anastasia's death on the waterfront of New York had its echo in Havana. For Havana was not a colony of America – it was a colony of Las Vegas, and with the departure of the gangsters the police have departed too. In 1958 they offered protection in the Chicago sense of the term; they were omnipresent, at every street corner and in every bar, and in every hotel entrance, in every casino. Now you would have to search a whole morning to find one uniformed policeman.

Let me jot down quickly a few other changes which catch the eye. When you drive out to the Country Club you pass the homes of the millionaires. Washing hangs from the balconies; the garage doors are open and classes of peasants sit before blackboards. (Seventy thousand are being educated in Havana.) In the Country Club itself the portrait of the founder, Mr Snope, still hangs in an unused drawing-room full of expensive tasteless furniture – Mr Snope wears white riding-breeches and a plaque records how he gave this park 'for the well-being and happiness of the people' (the yearly subscription of 'the people' ran into four figures). Now the children of the dramatic school are eating a free lunch on the terrace and the new schools of music, ballet, folk-dancing, and of the plastic arts rise among the soft, green slopes, once a golf-course. The schools of painting, sculpture and murals, designed by the young architect Ricardo Porro, resemble an African village built in brick. Each school has a roof like a kraal, little lanes wind intricately from one school to another, fountains unexpectedly play, every vista at every turn is different. It is like a village hidden among the hills and it reminds the visitor that Cuba is African as much as it is Spanish, and that the African has at last been freed — segregation is over.

For the problem today in Cuba is not a problem of freedom. The huge crowd that gathered before the monument to Marti to hear Castro's three-hour speech on 26 July was not the regimented or hypnotized crowd that used to greet Hitler.

This was a cheerful Bank Holiday crowd that had come to take part in an amusing show — Castro's speech was like a continuous movie: some came for an hour and moved away and others came. There were interludes of song, interludes of comedy, interludes of farce — a young man in front of me went down on all fours to make pig-noises when the invasion was referred to. Nor was the speech an exercise in empty rhetoric — in all Castro's speeches there is a sense of a man thinking aloud. He explains his course of action, he admits mistakes, he explains difficulties — one has the sense that he respects the intelligence of his audience, and if he makes every point three times it is to clarify it to himself.

There is a touch of ancient Athens about Havana today; the Republic is small enough for the people to meet in the *agora*. Castro walks unexpectedly into the hotels and starts a discussion; he stops at a café where foreign students are gathered and is interrogated on Khrushchev's view of art.

'Khrushchev is not a man of extremes. He is critical of everything, but I have never heard him criticize himself.' Lorry-loads of small farmers come up from the country to lodge in the great hotels and discuss the new agricultural policy. They meet Castro – he is more accessible than Mr Macmillan.

This availability, this continuing debate, is one answer to the problem: how to keep the sense of glory? For a revolution which began like a heroic fable with twelve men in the mountains pitted against an army and an air force is in danger from the growth of *ennui*. Guevara rules his Ministry on strict Marxist lines, the tide of paper rises, but Fidel (not even his opponents call this man by his surname) fights his personal crusade to maintain the sense of glory and the sense of the unexpected. The arts have never been so encouraged (Socialist realism is a joke and not a threat); there is small danger of a Pasternak case with the State publishing house directed by a novelist of world-reputation, Alejo Carpentier; Marxism here seems to be shedding much of its nineteenth-century philosophy.

There is no inherent opposition between Marxist economics and Catholicism, and in Cuba co-existence with the Church has proved easier than in Poland (Cuba is less strictly Catholic than Poland, just as Marxism here is less philosophical). On a recent anniversary of the attack on Batista's palace by a handful of young men led by José Antonio Echeverría the chairman read out the political testament of the dead leader and omitted a sentence:

'We are confident that the purity of our intentions will bring us the favour of God, to achieve a reign of justice in our land.' Castro leapt on the omission and based his whole speech upon it. 'Can we be so cowardly, so mentally

256

crippled, that we have the moral poverty to suppress three lines? What kind of concept is this of history? Can such cowardice be called "the dialectical concept of history"? Can such a manner of thinking be called Marxism? We know that a revolutionary can have a religious belief. The Revolution does not force men, it does not intrude into their personal beliefs. It does not exclude anyone.'

These are not empty words. When the Nuncio was celebrating the coronation of the new Pope last July Castro paid him a courtesy call which lasted for an hour and a half. Seven priests had been in prison (four had been taken in the company of armed rebels); all have now been released. The churches are open; catechism classes are taking place in Havana for 2,000 small children; in Santiago there has been a retreat for parents.

But through the radio the Church in America continues to poison the wells. 'Send your children to catechism to prove you are counter-revolutionary,' they broadcast after the event. 'Attend retreats and show that you are against the Government.' An American priest who accompanied the body of a dead American student back to Miami and gave a truthful interview to the Press found himself rebuked by the Archbishop ('Confine yourself in future to the subject of brain-washing and leave the Catholic Church alone'). Bishop Fulton Sheean in a broadcast declared that the Church in Cuba was persecuted in the same way as the Church in China. Invincible ignorance? Perhaps, but laymen are warned by theologians not to rely on that plea. Perhaps it is a fortunate thing for the world that Fidel Castro was educated as a Catholic and knows that the voice of the American hierarchy is not the voice of the Church. It is too often the voice of the Cold War.

I write 'fortunate for the world', for here in Cuba it is possible to conceive a first breach in Marxist philosophy (not in Marxist economics) – that philosophy as dry as Bentham and as outdated as Ingersoll.

'Let us speak of the comrade who received the order to skip the phrase. He is a poet. He has written a little book of poems and among his poems there is one called: "Prayer to the Anonymous God". First he told me about his religious beliefs, and later he told me that now he has a complex! How can he not have a complex, when he comes here and they tell him to skip that word? What does the Revolution become? A yoke. And that is not a Revolution. What does the Revolution become? A school of domesticated animals. And that is not Revolution.'

This is a new voice in the Communist world.

Sunday Telegraph
22 September 1963

Nightmare Republic

After the drum-beats which continued for an hour or more, after the saints' banners and the chanting and the Latin prayers, came the priest swinging his censer. But the censer was a live cock, and after the priest had incensed the congregation, he put the head in his mouth and crunched through the neck. Then, using the neck like a tube of red-brown paint, he made his mystic designs upon the earth-floor.

I remember this ceremony from nine years ago, and the long service which followed: the novices borne in like mummies wrapped in white sheets with only a hand protruding, a hand which was held in a live flame by the attendants while the drums beat to cover the cries; the arrival of the god of war, Ogoun Ferraille, who took possession of one of the peasants and sent him careering around the temple with a naked sword. You find the ceremonies reflected in many Haitian paintings, especially in those of Hector Hyppolite, who was a Voodoo priest. Even around the mural of the Marriage at Cana in the Episcopalian Cathedral the drummers play and a dead pig has the appearance of a ritual slaughter.

Some strange curse descended on the liberated slaves of Hispaniola. The unconscious of this people is filled with nightmares; they live in the world of Hieronymus Bosch. Perhaps it is wrong to speak of the unconscious, for here the Ego and the Id seem joined in unholy matrimony. Baron Samedi, in his top hat and tails, who haunts the cemeteries smoking a cigar and wearing dark glasses, spends the days, so some believe, in the Presidential Palace, and his other name is Dr Duvalier.

A reign of terror has often about it the atmosphere of farce. The irresponsible is in control. The banana-skin is a deadly one, but it remains a banana-skin. From the moment you land from an aeroplane in Port-au-Prince – that city of ruined elegance where the houses belong to the world of Charles Addams and the door may well be opened to you by a Boris Karloff – you are in the hands of the unpredictable.

You reach your hotel, symbolically enough, in darkness, for the plane touches down around 5.30, and between 6.30 and 7.30, and again from 8.30 to 9.30, the lights are all out. In the hotel you may find yourself the only guest (the tourists fled last spring and never returned). There were three others in my hotel and the owner calculated with wry insouciance that he could break even with five of us (his wages bill used to be $1,500 a month and is now $100).

While you wait for the lights to go on, you sit around oil-lamps exchanging rumours – the rebels are only twenty-four hours from Port-au-Prince, one optimist declares; the army has suffered a hundred casualties (it is always a hundred when an optimist speaks); a military plane has been shot down. Someone has heard on the Voice of America . . . On the way to the hotel one night when I was stopped at a road-block, the man who searched me for arms, patting the hips, the thighs, laying a hand under the testicles, asked my companion in Creole, 'Is there any news?'

But there is no such thing as news any more. (The stories which appear in the *New York Times* or the *New York Tribune* as a rule have a Santo Domingo dateline and reflect the hopes of the exiles.) The President's daughter is said to be on hunger-strike to induce her father to leave; the President's wife has abandoned him and is in America . . . The Spanish Ambassador came home the other night to find a black dog in the Embassy, but none of his staff would touch it because it might house the spirit of Clément Barbot, the President's deadly enemy, shot down a few weeks back on the edge of Port-au-Prince by the Tontons Macoute, the evil militia founded by himself. The Ambassador (the story grows and grows) had to put the dog in his car himself and drive it away. He tried to turn it out in the great square by the Presidential Palace, but it refused to move – the dog was too close to Dr Duvalier. Only when he reached the cathedral did he consent to budge, trotting off into the dark to seek another sanctuary. Of course there was no truth in the story, but it seemed probable enough in this city without news and, between certain hours, without light.

A few minutes from the hotel one can see the blackened ruins of Benoit's house. Benoit, one of Haiti's prize marksmen, was suspected of having been concerned in the attempted kidnapping of the President's children earlier in the year. He took refuge in an Embassy and his house was set ablaze with petrol by the Tontons Macoute, who machine-gunned the flames. Mme Benoit escaped, but no one knows whether her child is alive, nor how many servants were shot or burnt to death.

Anything may happen, any time, anywhere. One night a

man came running up the steps of the hotel, under the impression that it was an Embassy, seeking refuge. He was probably a madman, for surely everyone knows for his own safety the position of each Embassy, but what dark experience had driven him mad? Was he one of the sixty-two army officers who were so suddenly dismissed this year? Some have disappeared, some have taken sanctuary; the Chief of Staff who signed their dismissal walked next day into a South American Embassy for refuge. The British Chargé finds his car abandoned on a street – the chauffeur has been taken to the police station to be interrogated about his master's movements, and there is no redress.

The diplomats have watched the slow disintegration of the American Military Aid Mission, after the head of the Mission objected to the arms for the army going to the Tontons. In the last weeks of its existence pilots were not allowed to visit their planes, even to service them, and Marines were separated from their ship. No one makes a stand. It is as though the diplomatic missions – with the honourable exception of the British Ambassador – had been hypnotized by the dark glasses of Baron Samedi (they are the uniform also of the Tontons Macoute).

In the cathedral, on the national day, when the excommunicated President puts in his one appearance at Mass, the Tontons arrive armed with sub-machine-guns and search, even behind the altar. Then they take up their position in the cathedral with their guns covering the diplomatic corps, while in the choir rifles dominate the congregation. The bishops of Haiti and Gonaïves have been driven into exile, the Nuncio has departed. (A kind of evil farce enters even into the religious conflict. The Bishop of Gonaïves had tried to suppress Voodoo and required of his communicants that they should surrender their Voodoo charms — he was accused of robbing the country of archaeological treasures.)

There have been many reigns of terror in the course of history. Sometimes they have been prompted by a warped idealism like Robespierre's, sometimes they have been directed fanatically against a class or a race and supported by some twisted philosophy; surely never has terror had so bare and ignoble an object as here — the protection of a few tough men's pockets, the pockets of Gracia Jacques, Colonel Athi, Colonel Desiré, the leaders of the Tontons Macoute, of the police and of the Presidential guard — and in the centre of the ring, of course, in his black evening suit, his heavy glasses, his halting walk and halting speech, the cruel and absurd Doctor.

Everyone is in some sort a prisoner in Port-au-Prince. The exit visa for a foreigner is twice the price of the entry. For a Haitian a passport costs $100 and the visa (controlled personally by the Doctor) another five. You pay your money, but it is dubious whether you will ever see your passport.

Travel on the island is almost at a standstill. The roads were always a deterrent, but now there are road-blocks round Port-au-Prince to the north and controls at every small town to the south. Within a circuit of a few kilometres from Port-au-Prince I was searched four times, and it took me two days at the police station, where the portrait of the Doctor is flanked by snapshots of the machine-gunned bodies of Barbot and his companions, to gain a two-day permit for the south. The north, because of the raids from the Dominican Republic, was forbidden altogether.

All trade which does not offer a rake-off is at a standstill. A whole nation can die of starvation so long as the Doctor's non-fiscal account is safe. The public revenue of Haiti in a reasonable year should be around $28 million, but the non-fiscal account which is paid directly into the President's pocket amounts to between $8 million and $12 million. On all the main commodities, sugar, flour, oil, tyres, cement, a special tax is levied which never goes into the general account. The export of cement is forbidden because the world price would not admit this extra tax. The export would aid Haiti, but not the ring.

The President has, of course, other less traditional sources of revenue. The British Ambassador was expelled because he protested at the levies which the Tontons Macoute were exacting illegally from all businessmen. An arbitrary figure was named and if the sum were not forthcoming the man would be beaten up in his home by the Tontons Macoute, during the hours of darkness.

Tolls are enforced on all cars between the rich suburb of Petionville and Port-au-Prince. These particular sums go to the only project in Haiti visible to the naked eye. This project is the new town of Duvalierville, forty miles out of Port-au-Prince. The Doctor has obviously read accounts of Brasilia and in the absurd little tourist houses with roofs like wind-wrecked butterflies one can detect Brasilia's influence. There is no beach, and the town, if it is ever finished, is supposed to house 2,000 peasants in little one-roomed houses, so that it is difficult to see why any tourist should stay there. The only building finished in Duvalierville is the cock-fight stadium. In the meanwhile the peasants' homes have been destroyed and they have been driven from the area to live with relatives. Many people believe that the town if finished will become a Tontons garrison.

As with most major constructions in Haiti, since the Emperor Christophe built his fantastic citadel on a mountain-top, the cement used is cruelty and injustice. Labour on the project is controlled by the Tontons Macoute. One young labourer was taken off his job because a Tonton wanted it for another. The labourer tried to appeal to him, 'Please I am hungry. I have no work', and the Tonton promptly shot him through the head, the cheek and the body. He now survives in Port-au-Prince, paralysed.

It is impossible to exaggerate the poverty of Haiti. One has the sense that even the machine of tyranny is running down. The levies on businesses have ceased because there is no money to exact. The army has received no pay for two months (but the President has seen to it that the army is powerless), nor have the civil servants nor the priests.

Port-au-Prince has always been a city of beggars who make their headquarters around and in the Post Office, but even they feel the pinch now that the tourists have departed, and there may well be truth in those hollow voices that pursue you even within the grounds of the hotels: 'Master, I'm bad. I'm real bad. I'm hungry.' These are the professionals. Who knows what has happened to the hundreds of workers abandoned by the tourist trade? They are starving invisibly behind the decaying mud walls of the Port-au-Prince slums. Meanwhile an officer of the Tontons Macoute is building a large ice-skating rink up at Kenscoff, the mountain village above Port-au-Prince.

What hopes are there for this poor, beautiful and bedevilled country? Optimists point out that Duvalier has no supporters (apart from the police and the Tontons). Even Voodoo is a doubtful ally; the priest, the *houngan*, is a luxury which only the more prosperous parts of the country can afford. Voodoo hardly exists in the poor south, but perhaps the Doctor for one reason may be content to see it wither. He is himself almost certainly a believer (he has declared 'Je suis immatériel'), but oddly enough it is his excommunication by the Church which prevents him from practising his religion, since a Voodoo worshipper must receive Holy Communion if he is to be accepted by the *houngan*.

The shooting of Clément Barbot has taken away the only real threat to Duvalier in the capital. Rebels may make raids in the north, but it hardly affects the inhabitants of Port-au-Prince. A few brave youths the other day attacked the police station at Kenscoff, and slaughtered a couple of Tontons and a couple of policemen. Three of them held out in a cave in the mountains for more than twenty-four hours against several hundred police, and they killed more than twenty of their pursuers ('a hundred' says the optimist) before they were burnt out with flame-throwers.

Did they hope the peasants would rise? That hope was killed for ever after the small Cuban invasion of 1959, when Barbot — then still head of the Tontons — massacred with machine-guns in a town square every peasant of the region where the men had landed. The peasants now will never rise until photographs of the President's dead body are nailed like Barbot's photo on the walls of every police station.

The refugees in Santo Domingo, like the Cubans in Miami, are divided among themselves. The last presidential candidate, Louis Dejoie, plays a vain, loquacious role in the restaurants of Santo Domingo while he denounces the few men who cross the border to fight. Intervention by the Dominican forces is out of the question. Haitians remember Trujillo's slaughter of unarmed Haitian labourers at the frontier-river now called Massacre, and Haitian pride cannot be exaggerated; it is a quality noble and absurd and comforting for the persecutors. Even a man released from the torture chamber under the palace who had been beaten almost to the point of death would not admit that he had been touched. The great-great-grandchild of slaves is never beaten. (A whip hangs on the central pillar of every Voodoo temple as a reminder of the past.)

Santo Domingo is fifty minutes from Port-au-Prince by air, but the distance separating the two places must be judged not in miles but in centuries. In Santo Domingo businessmen and politicians feel at home among the fruit-machines and the swimming-pools; on their belt a little leather purse has taken the place of a revolver holster. The talk at the next table in the luxury hotel is all of dollars and percentages, but neither business nor politics has any relevance in Haiti. Haiti produces painters, poets, heroes – and in that spiritual region it is natural to find a devil too. The electric sign which winks out every night across the public garden has a certain truth. JE SUIS LE DRAPEAU HAITIEN, UNI INDIVISIBLE. FRANÇOIS DUVALIER.

Sunday Telegraph
29 September 1963

Goa the Unique

At night, lying on the verandah of a village house in Anjuna, watching the constellations wheel out of view across the great arc of sky with what seemed the speed of satellites, I found it possible to forget the poverty of Bombay, 400 miles away, the mutilated beggars, the lepers squatting near the Pro-Cathedral.

The silver stubble of the paddy fields, squared off by trees and hills, lay in a strong wash of moonlight; at five in the morning a church bell woke me, sounding twice with a short interval between – the first notes urging men to pray against the evil spirits abroad at night (perhaps in the form of a sow followed by her litter trotting through the dark), the second to summon men to work.

At the close of night, just before the first colours of the sunrise, a pack of jackals would course back across the stubble to the hills, raising a cry like that of a crowd at a ball game – 'Rah, rah, rah.' Ox-carts began to creak invisibly, a few figures passed across the paddy carrying torches of coconut fronds, the red and yellow trickled like coloured water along the horizon behind the banyans, the mango trees, the cashews. Someone watching from an aeroplane would have seen in every direction white churches appear like splinters of moonlight on the landscape: the uniqueness of Goa.

Outside Goa one is aware all the time of the interminable repetition of the ramshackle, the enormous pressure of poverty, flowing, branching, extending like flood-water. This is not a question of religion: the Goan Hindu village can be distinguished as easily from the Hindu village of India as the Christian, and there is little need to drive the point home at the boundary with placards. The houses in the Goan village were built with piety to last.

There are few extremes of poverty and affluence: most houses, however small, are constructed of laterite blocks with brown tiles of great beauty. They were built by Goans not by Portuguese (for the Portuguese lived only in the towns), often by Goans in exile, in Aden or in Africa, who hoped to return one day, for the far-ranging Goan has a loyalty to his village you seldom find elsewhere. It seemed the first thing one Goan asked another – not in what city he worked but from what village he came, and in distant Bombay every Goan village has its club of exiles – 350 clubs.

In the first Indian village outside Goa on the road to Bombay you are back to the mud huts and broken thatch which are almost a sign of affluence compared with the horrible little cabins made out of palm fronds and bits of canvas and any piece of old metal on the outskirts of Bombay. These are dwellings to escape from; how can their inhabitants feel loyalty to Maharashtra – the huge amorphous member-State of the Indian Union neighbouring Goa, into which Goa must almost certainly be sooner or later submerged?

No wonder that in villages like Anjuna you find sad old men sitting in almost empty rooms on carved Goan chairs regretting the past – the green and red wines of Portugal, the Scotch whisky at thirteen rupees a bottle which will cost now, if you are lucky to find a bottle, fifty or sixty.

There is prohibition in Maharashtra State – in Goa there is only prohibition by price, which leaves the raw Indian gins and whiskies relatively cheap, with what effect on the health of the drinker cannot yet be known. A certain bitterness too remains after 'liberation', a word which began to alter its meaning in 1944 and is now as soiled as 'democracy'. There were military casualties, not many for these days, but there were also cases of rape and looting in Panjim, the capital of Goa, for in the last 'colonial' years Goa had known a mining boom and the luxury goods which came in with every boat from Lisbon fetched good profits across the border. A postman in those days received higher wages than a professor does now in India.

The last Portuguese Governor has left friendly memories (he is said to be in disgrace for having disobeyed Salazar's orders to destroy Panjim – it would have been no great architectural loss perhaps, though one would regret the dramatic statue of the Abbé Ferrias pouncing like a great black eagle on his mesmerized female patient). Nor do you hear anywhere a word against the Portuguese as individuals.

And yet in December the majority of votes by a small margin went to the party which favoured merging with Maharashtra. It was a communal vote – nearly all Catholics voted for a separate State and nearly all Hindus for a merger, but watching the face of my Hindu driver, as he saw for the first time ragged out-of-heels Poona and then the squalid outskirts of Bombay, I wondered whether his opinions were changing already after leaving the tidy streets and the great clean river at Panjim.

As for the Congress Party – it was nowhere. It fought as the party of 'the liberation', which did not count in its favour, and perhaps creditably, but suicidally, the party tried to keep the question of merger out of the election, as something which would be solved in the course of time. The Congress view now seems likely to prevail and Goa to remain a territory administered by India for at least another five years.

Perhaps in some minds there is a hope left that at the end of that period, after industrialization, with the growth of tourism, Goa may prove financially capable of becoming a separate State in the union, while Congress has an equal hope that in the course of time Goan Catholics may see the advantages of government from Bombay, Maharashtra's capital.

I doubt whether it is the closed Catholicism of Goa (the Patriarch in exile and little communication held with the Catholics of Bombay) which will decide the issue. Panjim, the capital, was celebrating Christmas, when I arrived, in Capriote rather than Indian style. Cars drove in procession around the streets on the way to Midnight Mass decorated with greenery, the passengers playing snatches of music and flinging firecrackers into the street. A little tidy provincial town with whitewashed eighteenth-century buildings, Panjim is by no means the 'God-forgotten place' that Lady Burton described a hundred years ago.

Indeed, there is more than a hint of the worldly Babylon which shocked Camoens. Serenaders played their guitars at night to a young woman who had arrived in town for Christmas, at a party I found myself handed as a matter of course a benzedrine tablet at four in the morning, naked bathing parties take place at a secluded beach, and who sleeps with whom is known to all Panjim.

Up in Old Goa all is silence and desolation. The huge

square, 250 yards across, once lined with palace, prison, churches, is overgrown, and only a small stone like that on a child's grave marks the site of the dreaded Inquisition. On Christmas Eve a pig running before the footlights seemed at first the only living thing up there beside ourselves. But in the cathedral there was a congregation of perhaps a dozen people sitting in a gloom the candles could not penetrate, while a choir of old Canons sang the Mass – elongated, emaciated El Greco figures in dingy scarlet dickies, half starved on thirty rupees a month (a little more than two pounds in our currency), and up near the invisible roof the bats twittered as loudly as their voices. At the High Altar the sacrament was not reserved for fear of robbers, and after Mass Communion was given by the light of one candle at a little side-chapel reluctantly unlocked for the purpose.

I had a sense that I was attending one of the last ceremonies of Christianity. This might well be St Peter's 300 years hence if the door on to the world is not kept open, and I was reminded later of the old tattered monseigneurs by the relics of another Raj in my shabby hotel at Poona, where the waiter was dressed in what remained of the semi-military uniform which his English employer had given him thirty years ago. 'No bacon,' he said sadly when I tried to order an English breakfast. 'No one asks for bacon now.'

It seemed a grim apocalyptic place, Old Goa, with the shrinking body of St Francis Xavier in the great church of Bom Jesus, built in 1594, the toe that a lady bit off preserved in a reliquary, and the silver crucifix on his tomb twisted awry by a Catholic thief a week before; in a cupboard of the same church were the skulls of martyrs, and other dubious portions preserved in bottles of spirits which reminded me of those you see in the windows of Chinese specialists in Kuala Lumpur advertising cures for piles.

In the convent of Santa Monica, where Burton tried to abduct an orphan and picked up the Lady Abbess by mistake, there is a weeping crucifix, and in Bom Jesus tucked obscurely away is the cross found on a hillside which miraculously grew, so that it had to be shortened to enter the church. The headpiece was strengthened by metal to prevent it shooting up farther – a sagacious measure which needless to say had complete success.

Catholic Goa is divided into two halves by the great Mandovi river – on the right bank lies Franciscan Goa, on the left Jesuit Goa, and as you might expect Catholicism is richer and superficially stronger on the left bank. Here are the iron ore mines, Margao with its elegant square lined with great houses, and on the outskirts the monstrosities of the new rich built like plastic soap dishes.

In the villages of this region Goan families still maintain their State. In the façade of one house I counted sixteen great windows in a row, and the salon was thirty-six paces long. In another house I saw in the granary a great wooden storage chest larger than the biggest barrels of Oporto, far larger than the cabins in which whole families live on the outskirts of Bombay. (Here there was even a flush lavatory in place of the usual hole in a laterite block above a trough where a pig stands honking to receive your droppings.)

In the big houses too are private altars of carved Goan wood, with tier on tier of little figures surrounded by artificial flowers, and in every spare space examples of china from Macao. The cellar will still contain a few last bottles of green and red wine, port, some liqueurs, even a little

Scotch. They will be assembled for your choice: Goan hospitality will not cease till the cellar is empty.

Here emotional stories may be told you of the last Portuguese days. 'There are still three seats on the plane, the Governor said to me. Come with us. You will be recompensed for all you lose here. I tell you there were tears in the Governor's eyes when he embraced me.'

This Jesuit Goa will find it harder to accept merger in Maharashtra, though it shares with India one evil characteristic against which Gandhi unsuccessfully fought – the hierarchy of caste. The early Jesuit missionaries worked closely with the Brahmins, and the Brahmins remain all-important around Margao. Caste has even been extended by Christianity, for Catholics consider themselves superior to Hindus, and Hindu Brahmins accept the superiority of Catholic Brahmins.

But in the village of Anjuna I was in Franciscan Goa, a poorer but surely a happier region, where the merger with Hinduism has already begun. Horoscopes are consulted, and even a Goan finds it hard to say which superstition is of Hindu, which of Catholic origin. A silver crucifix is buried under the lintel of every new house – that is Catholic, but what of the navel cords of children born there which are tucked under the floor or into the walls or even into a pillow?

On walls and houses are signs to keep away the evil eye: a skull will be hung on a mango tree which has a rich crop in case one looks at it with envy: on gateposts are lions to preserve the houses from evil – are these signs Catholic or Hindu – who cares?

Both Catholics and Hindus practise the same ceremony for removing the evil eye with the help of a wise woman: the sprinkling of salt, four or five chillies cast into a fire – if an explosion occurs all is well. Until recently at midnight the ghost of a woman who had drowned herself would walk across the paddy fields in front of my friend's house. She was not seen: she was only heard – jangling the bangles on her arm that all brides must wear (a Hindu or a Catholic custom?). A man in the village across the fields laughed at the sound – 'She does not frighten me', so she came and rattled the bangles by his head and he never spoke again. A year later he was dead.

My friend's aunt had many such stories to tell one night, speaking in Konkano, the Goan language. There was a solitary tree standing above the paddy where no other tree grew – an odd tree: one could not say what was its highest common factor, for many kinds of tree had grafted themselves on to the main trunk. It was an unhealthy spot to pass at night. You might be 'carried away' – this seemed a speciality of the spirits of Bardez where Anjuna lies. When you wake you find yourself up a coconut palm. 'It happened to your aunt. She had heard mangoes falling in the night, and she went out at the first strokes of the clock to gather them when she should have been praying for the evil spirits to pass. She was carried right away all over the rocks by the seashore, and put up a coconut palm. She was sitting there when the fishermen came down in the morning.'

This is what I will remember chiefly of Goa – the voice in Konkano telling of strange events, the cry of the jackals coming down from the hills, the golden evening light across the paddy, the sense of deep country peace.

Industrialization is bound to come, a tourist department has opened in Panjim, and there are great beaches waiting for great hotels, while just over the hills lies the enormous poverty of the subcontinent, ready to spread along the seaboard as soon as the fragile barriers are raised.

275

Portugal helped to form the special character of Goa and Goa's character may survive Portugal for a year or two. But you cannot hang a skull at the entrance of Goa as you can on a mango tree to avert the envious eye. No wonder that even in the great houses of Jesuit Goa you have a sense of impermanence. Dust lies on the furniture, in the best bedroom suitcases are piled on the floor with an overnight bag on top. It is as though the family has not had time to unpack properly, and yet already it is nearly the hour to leave.

Sunday Times
1 March 1964

The Rude Mechanicals

As I read Mr Ludovic Kennedy's admirable account of the trial of Stephen Ward, I was irritated at intervals by his references to 'the rude mechanicals', the jury. They were always, in his eyes, so easily deceivable – by prosecuting counsel, by police evidence, by the intonations of the judge. I share his view that the trial of Stephen Ward represented the worst that British justice can do – it belongs to a period of Conservative rule tarnished by the naïve figure of Mr Brooke as Home Secretary (how often as an undergraduate at Balliol I used to study that Humpty Dumpty face opposite me at breakfast and wonder how it had ever earned a scholar's gown), a period which has included yet another suicide, that of Mr Soblen, the still unexplained death of Mr Woolf, not to speak of all the half bricks belonging to the W1 police station. All the same I feel Mr Kennedy underrates 'the rude mechanicals', and I was not surprised, when, towards the end of the book, he admitted that he had never served on a jury.

I have the advantage over Mr Kennedy there; I have served once. We had no cases to catch the headlines and perhaps it was for that reason we felt carefree each time we adjourned, without the responsibilities of a murder or of a political case like that of Stephen Ward. Indeed I gained the impression that, if I had committed a murder, it was at this moment of time I would have the best opportunity to escape punishment. For we had, all of us, read detective stories, and we had a built-in conviction that the obvious culprit was innocent, that the police were not so clever as an amateur, and as for the judge – he was an old man, he belonged inevitably to the non-criminal classes, he regarded the police with less cynicism than we.

The first case we heard concerned the theft of lead by two men from a church roof. The police evidence was reasonably complete, although it included a witness, I think, who was an informer. The judge summed up unmistakably against the two prisoners. We adjourned.

I am not a fanatic for punishment – I may even have a prejudice in favour of the criminal classes if they confine their activities to stealing from those who are richer than themselves. I was not the foreman. I had no responsibility. There was a long pause, after the foreman had asked for our opinions, and at last someone spoke up. He said: 'I think they've got the wrong men.' We went ahead from there.

'The police witness – do you really believe what he said?'
'My opinion is the witness was really the guilty man.'
'The judge said . . .'
No one paid any attention to that.
'I certainly didn't like the face of that witness.'
'I'm certain he did it himself.'
Was there one voice raised in favour of the judge's summing-up? I can't remember it. Personally I played no part. Surely if my fellow jurymen felt there was a reasonable doubt, there must be a reasonable doubt. I was no more anxious than they were to find anybody guilty. The case was thrown out. I heard later from a policeman that the

men had been convicted many times before for stealing lead, but I don't regret our decision.

During the course of that carefree week we found everyone innocent, whatever the judge said. We even succeeded in stopping one case without hearing the evidence for the defence – a doctor who was accused of being drunk in charge of a car which had collided with a military lorry. The police evidence rested on a sergeant-major who resented his word being questioned, and none of us were very military-minded, and a police doctor – a foreign refugee – who had examined the accused and asked him various questions. He had asked him what year and what month George VI had died. I was probably the only juryman who could even roughly remember, and that was because of a night in Saigon when a strange Vietnamese had run after me in the street, while I was on the way to take a few pipes of opium with a French friend, and said to me, '*Mes condoléances.*'

'*Pourquoi?*'

'*Votre roi est mort.*'

Even the judge was surprised. He said: 'I'm not sure that I remember the date exactly myself . . . Why did you choose . . .?'

'I thought,' the doctor said in a heavy moral accent, 'that every Englishman would remember a date like that.'

Yet the rude mechanicals, I can assure Mr Kennedy, threw the case out – and this time without the disapproval of the judge.

I was a little anxious because I had a date in Paris at the weekend. The clerk of the court had assured me that the cases would be finished by Thursday or Friday at latest, but somehow in spite of all my efforts they weren't. There was, for me, an anxious moment in court when the clerk spoke to the judge. The judge said: 'I understand that one juryman claims he has important business next week.' He turned to me and said: 'Where is your business, Mr Greene?'

With a little hesitation I said: 'Paris, my lord.'

There was a titter in court, and the judge made a little pause. Then he went on: 'If counsel are prepared to do so, we will sit in court on Saturday morning.'

I thought it was a generous gesture since we had found everyone innocent in spite of all his summings-up. Because of our independence I don't like Mr Kennedy calling us so often in the course of his book 'rude mechanicals'. Not for one moment had we regarded *our* judge as 'an oracle, mouthpiece of wisdom, purveyor of uncontaminated truth'. We hadn't really thought about him much at all.

New Statesman
1 May 1964

The Outsider: On the Death of Adlai Stevenson

after a Press Conference in London
on the Vietnam War

Tiredness can resemble dishonesty,
and when he spoke to us,
it was only a matter of minutes
before the tired heart stopped.

So we were amazed by the words he used –
'We shall always fight against an outsider
imposing his will,' he said.
'Who is the outsider?' we demanded,
but he gave us no reply.
For tiredness can resemble dishonesty,
and you must be very tired when you die.

The outsider was waiting,
on the Embassy steps, in Grosvenor Square –
the outsider who is always finally there,
even though you begin
with an advantage in tanks & guns

and a 7th Day Adventist fleet;
the defences fall & the outsider steps within
and death resembles defeat.

Unpublished
July 1965

Ghosts of Possible Adventure

The first London restaurant I ever knew was the Florence in Rupert Street which has long disappeared. As a child I was impressed by the rich robes of the negro who served Turkish coffee. Here, every year, my parents brought their children to lunch before *Peter Pan*, and it was here, I think, that I was given my twenty-first birthday dinner. I have an idea that this was the only restaurant in London that my parents knew; they did not visit London often together, and my father had his club. But by 1925 I had my own haunts and the Café Royal was one of them.

I seldom in the twenties had a meal in the Café. The Grill Room, gay with caryatids, which is to me now what his club was to my father, was far beyond my means, and even the brasserie, which alas! has disappeared to make room for the restaurant, was for rather special occasions. A five-course meal then cost three and sixpence, and, though it was much less enticing, the five-course meal at Pinoli's was only half a crown, the same price as the very substantial dinner at the Salisbury in St Martin's Lane. So the brasserie for me in the early twenties was a rendezvous for drinks more than for meals; it was possible to spend hours there over a glass of lager at one of the marble-topped tables which occupied a half of the room.

I don't know why, but some ghosts from the nineties seemed to be there, conveying a suggestion of possible adventure. Perhaps the presence of Epstein and his latest model helped. All I know is that I never found an adventure, but the draught lager was excellent, as it still is. (Odd the sexual myths of the very young. I remember a story firmly believed at my school that in a certain famous hotel not far from the Café it was possible to obtain the services of a chambermaid by tying a face-towel to the exterior handle of one's bedroom door. I began to save up my money – the price of a workman's ticket to London and back, three and sixpence for a good dinner at the Café to put me in the right mood, with another three shillings for wine, eight and sixpence for bed and breakfast at the hotel, and then the face-towel tied around the knob. The dinner, I am sure, was worth the trip, but the chambermaid never appeared, though the footsteps of other inmates kept me awake with expectation till the early hours.)

If I could have chosen my life I would have been a young man (with money of course) at the *Pink 'Un* period of English history when the Café Royal had a serious rival in Romano's. I would have joined Colonel Newnham-Davis at the Café for dinner and perhaps we could have robbed Romano's for the evening of Bessie Bellwood. Or, like Lewis Seymour (the creation of the young George Moore), I might have found my adventure conveniently close by at the Royal Academy on the day of the private view and have taken her on by cab to the Café.

' "There are even occasions when it is unpleasant to be well known," said Lewis, as he followed Mrs Ward into a cab, and told the driver to go to the Café Royal. There was a side door, he assured her, in one of the back streets, a little back passage, the most convenient thing in the world, not a particle of risk.

'After some difficulty this luxury of modern life was explained to the dull-headed coachman, and five minutes after Lewis Seymour and Mrs Campbell Ward, these two representatives of fashion and art, were passing up a black back-stair, smelling of beer and grease.

' "It's dirty but safe," said Lewis, referring to the back way as they were ushered into a private room – a snug little nook with a glaring look of public vice. There was a chair and a divan, both covered with red velvet, and the table was laid for two. The ceremonious Swiss waiter closed the window, and took the order for lamb cutlets and a bottle of champagne. When he left the room there was a slight hesitation, but, taking Mrs Ward's hand, Lewis said: "And when shall I see these beautiful arms in a Greek dress?" '

Included in *Parnassus near Piccadilly, an Anthology: The Café Royal Centenary Book,* edited by Leslie Frewin 1965

Shadow and Sunlight in Cuba

Always my first day in Havana, whatever the cost, I have taken a meal in the Floridita, one of the prettiest restaurants in the world, which once used to be among the best. Three years ago, though many of the old waiters were still there whom I had known over ten years, the restaurant was no more than a dream of the past with little to eat but tunny fish and eggs and even the famous daiquiris unobtainable more often than not. Like a dream, too, there were incongruous details, such as the socialist-realist picture behind the beautiful Victorian bar of Fidel leading his men ashore from the *Granma*: not so ugly though as the gilded bust of Hemingway. The bust of Hemingway, alas!, remains (there is an official cult of Hemingway in Cuba which many young writers resent), but socialist-realism has withered in the bud – in the new flats built for slum-dwellers in Santiago I saw reproductions of Klee and Juan Gris, Wifredo Lam has a great gallery all to himself in the Museum of Fine Arts, pictures of Milián and Portocarrero hang in the Palace of the Revolution. And the bar of the Floridita is itself again, elegant, Victorian – the restaurant too, but at a price.

Here is what two of us ate my first day (steak at 7 pesos each we could not face): two excellent shrimp cocktails, two grilled red snappers, two bottles of beer, two cups of coffee. The price was 13 pesos 60 cents, and the peso equals 7s. 6d. In the National Hotel a ham omelette costs £1 12s. Little wonder that the restaurants have always a table free except at weekends when families escape, even at this price, from their rations. A bottle of very light beer costs 6s. in a restaurant. Wine is out of the question – Chilean at £3 10s., a poor Tokay at £5 12s.

But the restaurants are beautifully decorated, the service is excellent – a friend with pardonable exaggeration said to me, 'A rich man can live here as well as anywhere in the world', though he would pay a steep tax for his escape into an illusion of the past. For the prices of the meals are a form of taxation, and in fairness one should remember that the income tax is only two shillings in the pound and there are very few consumer goods to spend your money on. The illusion for the conservative would however be incomplete, even though in the Monseigneur they demand a jacket and tie for dinner, for there is one enormous change for the better. Havana under the rule of the Las Vegas bosses was a segregated city: every smart bar and restaurant was called a club so that a negro could be legally excluded. The name club continues, but the meaning has gone: integration is all but complete and apparently painless.

Rationing is severe because of the American blockade and the devastation wrought by Hurricane Flora in 1964 (poor Cuba, she has now suffered the onslaught of Inez). Almost everything is on the rationed list: three quarters of a pound of meat per head a week, one litre of milk, and I forget the quantity of fish, bread, rice, potatoes, coffee. Clothes and shoes are rationed too, though material is not. If a woman can afford the price of the material, she will not lack dresses nor her husband shirts. For a family, food rationing is eased considerably since the children will get a good midday meal at school and older students, in secondary schools and technical colleges, have free canteens.

It is men like my taxi-driver of pre-revolutionary days who suffer the worst, with a salary of £48 a month and a wife who cannot go out to work because of two small children; although in England his salary would escape income tax, in Cuba he must pay his ten per cent. Even the meat ration is a problem without a refrigerator: it means a daily queue for a block of ice at 2s. 6d. and the block is not always obtainable. As a taxi-driver in the days of the great brothelley good-time city he was well off, but his taxi fell to pieces beyond repair in 1962. He joined the army for three years and now he works in an office and trains to be an accountant. None the less he is not against the revolution. He feels a new social freedom. Nothing can exclude him from the smartest club or restaurant except the absence of cash. He is any man's equal except for the vacuum in his hip pocket. He was the first to admit that some of the hardship is due to the odd eating habits of the Cuban people. Fish is a supplementary ration, but the people, he said, don't much care for fish (how many meals were crunched under the wheels of our car one night on the road to Trinidad as the great yellow crabs crossed the road — not so good as the famous Morro crabs but good all the same); eggs are off the ration, but people are unused to eating eggs, especially eggs with white shells; vegetables and fruit in their season often rot away in the shops. With the school meals the Government are trying to change the eating habits of a nation.

All in all things have much improved since 1963.

Distribution is better, and in the country people fare better than in Havana (we bought unrationed Chinese shirts in Trinidad – coarse blue shirts at 2 pesos). This is partly due to official policy, for Havana is an unloved city, exploited in the past as an American playground (the tall hotels, only one air-conditioned at a time, stand around like bourgeois tombs); partly it is due to the near presence in the country of the peasant farmer who can own and cultivate for himself up to sixty hectares of land.

The attempt in 1959 to industrialize Cuba at the expense of sugar cane was a bad error, and now agronomy is the principal study in the new technical schools. Already there are six million head of cattle, and the meat, when you can afford it, is of first-class quality – I've never eaten such tender steaks of such a full flavour even in the best restaurants of Europe. On an experimental farm they are attempting for the first time to grow strawberries, asparagus, apples. Sugar cane, of course, remains the basic crop and the basic problem, for the Russian machinery for cutting proved suitable only for cane grown at a uniform height, eight per cent of the crop at most. Now efforts are directed towards mechanizing the cleaning of the cane – a harder human labour than cutting – by means of giant fans. Cuba, it is accepted now, will always depend on sugar, meat and coffee; industrialization, except where it is concerned with agriculture and housing, has been abandoned.

People grumble, of course, and people grumble at the grumblers – some negroes who have never known so good a time even yearn towards the States in spite of the daily photographs in *Granma* of coloured men beaten up by white police; and the real poor, who for the first time have money to spare, complain that there is nothing to buy. The complaints are superficial: the country reacts at once to any threat from outside; and one thousand counter-revolutionaries in the Escambray mountains failed where twelve Fidelists in the Sierra Maestre succeeded.

Some would include among the shadows of the revolution the separation of families, inevitable in a civil war of ideologies. I am not sure, remembering a girl who came to drink with me. She was celebrating her 'day of liberation' – that was how she described it. Her parents had left that day for America and she was free at last to live her own life. Nor are the children blamed for the faults of their fathers. I met one young woman working for the Ministry of External Affairs who had both parents in America while her brother was in prison as a counter-revolutionary.

But one dark shadow there is worse than blockade or rationing or hit-and-run raids, UMAP – a word which sounds like something from science fiction (as though humanity were somewhere buried in it). The initials stand for the forced labour camps controlled by the army. In theory there is not much wrong with them – a man unsuited for military service does his three years on the land, but the practice differs from the theory, for there is no leave or visits from his family. (Even the counter-revolutionary in the gloomy Batista-built prison on the Isle of Pines has his monthly visit.) Rumour says there are three categories liable to conscription – the vicious (who include the homosexual), the *lumpen* or layabouts, and the priests – three priests are in the camps now. The attack on the homosexuals, when it began to affect the arts, was taken up vigorously by a group of writers, and a number of actors who had been summoned to report at a camp were told by a leading member of the Government to ignore the order. In the case of a well-known actress who had been taken to a police station and interrogated there on the details of her sexual life, President Dorticos intervened, and Fidel himself drove to her home and apologized – an act of typical generosity. There seems to have been a struggle somewhere in higher circles between the intention and the practice.

> Between the conception
> And the creation . . .
> Falls the Shadow.

There are rumours that disciplinary measures have been taken against brutal officials in the camps; Fidel himself in his speech of 29 August made a statement which people hope applied to the camps: 'Do people want to turn this country into a concentration camp? When a new plan arises all they can think of is the use of prisoners surrounded by a barbed wire fence. The Revolution does not mean slave labour.' Often enough Fidel has admitted mistakes of policy and this one is more serious than a mistake over industrialization. A moral mistake is more dangerous than a tactical because it compromises the revolution. Only the revolution can kill the revolution.

I don't believe it will happen here because this is a revolution of the young, not of men grown old in the British Museum reading room: how young came home to me as I watched some members of the Government playing basket ball or rather fooling with a basket ball at two o'clock in the morning: Raul Castro, the head of the Armed Forces, Llanusa, the Minister of Education (at thirty-nine the oldest man there), the red-bearded chief of espionage and counter-espionage, the head of the Air Force, one of the Army *commandants* (major is the highest rank in the Cuban Army: the titles of colonel and general are associated with innumerable coups d'état in the ears of a Latin American). The young seem everywhere – couples embraced on the long sea wall at midnight, in the evening pouring out of the schools established in the abandoned rich houses of Miramar, talking in the gay ice-cream parlours at four in the morning. Someone said to me with disapproval, 'There has been a sexual explosion here. Why, the girls now simply make love for the pleasure of it.' There are statistically more young in Cuba in proportion to the old, I believe, than in any other country – figures helped by the fact that so many of the old have taken their seats in the American or Spanish planes.

There was some danger, so I thought in 1963, that the young to whom the heroic years belong to a childhood past, to whom Batista and his torturers are names only, would begin to resent restriction. It is valuable for that reason to have an enemy always in sight (on a clear day from the Havana front you can see the American ship with its listening devices on the horizon), and valuable too to possess a great field for further heroism in South America. I remember two small children, black and white, outside a tobacco factory in Las Villas: they were not more than twelve years old, but the little negro could just remember Camilo Cienfuegos, one of the most loved of the twelve, killed in a plane crash in 1959, crossing the road near the village on a white horse, and the other knew exactly where Che Guevara was – he was across the water 'helping our brothers', the catch-phrase of a school teacher, but for him a glimpse of adventure.

Next to defence and agriculture, education is the most important Ministry in Cuba. Llanusa imitates Fidel in his continual travels over the country, the unexpectedness of his visits. He sent a jeep for me at 2.30 in the morning to fetch me from Trinidad where I was sleeping into the Escambray mountains at Topes where 7,000 mixed students (the target is 15,000) who have graduated from the tougher primary school of Las Minas de Frio in the heart of the Sierra Maestre, train to be teachers. They combine practical and theoretical work. They have built their own classrooms and their own hospital to serve the region – they have even built a Greek theatre as large as Epidaurus. In Oriente too, at the foot of the Sierra Maestre, seven school 'towns' are being constructed with all the Cuban flair for colour and landscape gardening. Four thousand five hundred students are in occupation now, and the target is 20,000.

These are two examples only. The war against illiteracy is a genuine crusade with a heroic quality of its own. It has even produced its own pop music. One day before lunch in the Escambray the head of peasant and worker education, himself born a peasant, sang to his guitar, and this song, in the setting of mountain and forest where the counter-revolutionaries a few years ago murdered two students in an attempt to frighten the rest, was oddly touching.

> How many things
> I can tell you now
> Because I have learnt to write.
> Now I can tell you
> How I love you,
> Now I can tell you
> On the quiet stretches of the river,
> And in the trunk of the flamboyant tree
> I can write your name and mine.

It was a Sunday morning at Topes: there was a sense of happiness, freedom and achievement as the students, the children of peasants, played at cleaning the river or wandered, sometimes hand in hand, among the new woods they had planted themselves. We are too old and cynical now to echo Wordsworth, 'Bliss was it in that dawn to be alive', but I had been reading Hazlitt and these words came to my mind: 'We are in a state between sleeping and waking, and have indistinct but glorious glimpses of strange shapes, and there is always something to come better than what we see.'

Daily Telegraph Magazine
9 December 1966

The Mask Remover

The frontispiece to Mrs Cockburn's study, obsessively readable, of her husband Claud Cockburn and his hand-grenade, the *Week*, shows this subversive figure (at once proprietor, editor and usually sole contributor) muffled up to the eyes walking beside John Strachey in the park and listening to secret histories while a policeman peers around a tree to observe the two hunched furtive figures. The only thing wrong about James Fitton's admirable cartoon is that Cockburn would never have disguised himself even with a muffler, and that he shows unmistakable signs of fear – an emotion not easily associated with Cockburn. My memory has to go back some forty-five years to recall a Claud frightened and a Claud disguised.

We were, for obscure reasons which had nothing to do with politics, or even espionage, pushing a barrel-organ across Hertfordshire dressed as tramps. The first night we spent in a half-built house in a field outside Boxmoor – a drear December lodging, with a wind biting at us through the empty window spaces, so that we rose while it was still dark to escape the cold and found ourselves pursued the length of a long hedge by an invisible figure who coughed at us from the black field. Then – I can swear it – Claud as well as myself experienced fear until he realized that it was a cow which coughed. As for the disguise, while we passed through the town of Berkhamsted, where we were both known, we thought it better to wear Christmas masks, and these masks brought the tour to a premature close, each of us became so enraged by the other's false face. I know nothing of how I looked, but Claud's long lantern face was hidden under the swollen pink cheeks of Billy Bunter. The mask wore a perpetual toffee-fed grin, so that Claud's serious running-commentary on his life and times irritated me profoundly. Billy Bunter had no business to hold views about Stresemann's darker side, and I began to contradict every one of them behind my equally misleading mask, so that we would almost certainly have come to blows if we had not slipped in time behind a hedge at the entrance of Tring, taken off our false faces and changed our clothes. Then we abandoned the organ and parted, not quite such good friends for a while as we had been.

I like to imagine that it was on that occasion Claud learnt the danger of masks adopted even in play. Certainly the *Week*, those ugly cyclostyled sheets which have become a symbol of resistance in the thirties, did much in removing them – occasionally perhaps, for Claud Cockburn is a romantic, it came near to inventing a mask in order to remove it. Cockburn would often favour an interesting or amusing interpretation of events, being unwilling to accept the usual boring springs of political action. I notice in Mrs Cockburn's account no reference to that strange Affair of a Press Lord's Love Letters. Was this an occasion when Cockburn, the romantic, went astray?

The *Week* began with only seven subscribers; it became obligatory reading when an enraged Ramsay MacDonald attacked it at a special press conference to an audience which hadn't even known of the paper's existence; it died with the war – first suppressed as Communist and then revived for a few months, when the Soviet Union became our ally, in an unsuitable printed form, a premature resurrection which failed. Its ghost, of course, still lingers in certain pages of *Private Eye*, but while the *Week* survived without libel actions because there were no printers to prosecute and nothing to seize against the costs of an action but a second-hand shoelace, *Private Eye*, by becoming a valuable property, has made libel actions worth while. Behind the *Week* was one enthusiastic truth-diviner at the service of increasingly Communist beliefs. When Cockburn wrote that the king had no clothes, his opinion had to be treated with respect: one felt sure that more often than not he had good evidence for the king's nudity. But the comic pages of *Private Eye* clash with the inside news – Lord Gnome is necessarily a figure we cannot trust, and the statement in his pages that the king is naked may be only another Spike Milliganism. One doubts whether *Private Eye* could have so nearly played an important part in the Abdication crisis or been able to hound Howeson, the Tin King, into the Old Bailey dock (the editor of the *Week* was a little incongruously the European correspondent of Luce's *Fortune*). I have an uneasy feeling that under the same circumstances a small notice might have appeared in *Private Eye* regretting some minor inaccuracy in its report on the Tin King. I don't think the *Week* ever apologized to anyone. Success in journalism can be a form of failure. Freedom comes from lack of possessions. A truth-divulging paper must imitate the tramp and sleep under a hedge.

Serious though the *Week* was – sometimes a little too serious for one flippant reader, who would gladly skip a great deal of useful stodgy information about the TUC and related initials for the news it gave of King Carol's shy masseur forced to parade with crowned heads behind the hearse of King George V – no one will find a dull page in Mrs Cockburn's account of it. I find particularly exhilarating Cockburn's account of Ramsay MacDonald's 'invisible lack of health':

'On the occasion of his last big speech in the House on unemployment, he spoke disjointedly, kept peering over his shoulder while speaking. He stated afterwards to a member of the Cabinet that the strain of the circumstances had somehow translated itself into a curious impression that there was a man in the gallery aiming to shoot him in the back.'

Was the *Week* worth all the effort, Mrs Cockburn asks, and most of us would echo her conclusion that 'to tell the truth, or what one passionately believes to be the truth, must always be worthwhile'. Could the *Week* be revived in the conditions of the sixties? Perhaps there is more sincerity about today and society wears fewer masks, but a government which can solemnly appoint a Minister of Disarmament while it continues to import Polaris missiles has not altogether discarded their use. I once discussed with a former member of the French secret service the possibility – with the help of an old boys' network – of creating an international secret service which would publish all the information it obtained indiscriminately to all subscribers everywhere. Unfortunately my friend was murdered in mysterious circumstances in Morocco, so that our project never got off Fouquet's floor, but if fantasy had become fact, our journal would certainly have borne a family resemblance to the *Week*. The *Week* used an old boys' network of foreign correspondents, as ours was to have used ex-spies, and perhaps the only complaint I have against the *Week* is that it was never prosecuted under the Official Secrets Act.

A last memorial thought about the thirties: how odd that England in that decade contained two genuinely revolutionary figures who, not knowing each other, fought on the same side with methods wholly contradictory – Claud Cockburn, the mask remover, and Kim Philby, the mask wearer.

Review of *The Years of the Week* by Patricia Cockburn
New Statesman
31 May 1968

The Worm inside the Lotus Blossom

The empty house was beautiful. Colonial in style, it had a great tiled terrace, and they assured me (but we had no keys) that there was a 'marble bathroom'. The garden stretched out below us for some eighty yards – shadowy with orange trees – some in fruit and some in blossom, lemon trees, grapefruit, palms; there were roses and jasmine and a great flare of pink lapacha flowers. After a good lunch with my two writer friends at the village inn, and several glasses of *caña*, I had reached the hour for day-dreams.

'How much would this house cost?' I asked them. The smell of orange fought the smell of jasmine as it had done every day since I had landed from the river boat in the capital. It was to the smell of orange blossom I woke every morning in my hotel, which had once been the house of Martha Lynch, the mistress of the monstrous Lopez, and below my window a bush of jasmine grew blue and white flowers simultaneously.

One of my companions gave me the price in *guaranís*.

'About three thousand pounds,' I calculated. 'Or nearly that. But what a staff one would need.'

'Oh no, it could be run with one maid, a cook and a gardener.'

'And that would cost a small fortune?'

Again he gave me the price in *guaranís*. 'A week?'

'No, a month of course.'

'Forty dollars a month!'

Somebody rode by on a horse, silent on the dirt road: our car was the only one we had seen in the village, and the stillness of the universal siesta lay among the garden trees. A few days earlier on the main road to the south, more than half of it unpaved, I had made my statistics between two towns, Carmen and San Ignacio, 105 kilometres apart. We had seen 26 cars, 24 horsemen, and 16 carts pulled by horse or oxen. The cars had only just won.

The elderly, cheerful, alcoholic writer, who told me that he began to drink at 9.30 in the morning, said he would like to end his days here in this house – it was his pipe-dream . . . But the difficulties of a writer in this country were immense.

'And yet there's no income tax?'

'No income tax, no.'

'And no censorship?'

'Certain limits,' he said, 'are understood. One mustn't attack the President – or the United States, of course. But for a writer it is very difficult to save. We are a small country, there is much illiteracy.'

'You write in Spanish. There's all the Spanish world.'

'It is hard to find a publisher outside.'

In this river-bounded inland country one thinks of the world always as outside. Richard Burton called Paraguay 'the inland China', Cunninghame-Graham 'a lost Arcadia'. Now, of course, there are jet planes to the United States and Argentina, to supplement the railway built to the south by Englishmen in the 1860s with some of the old rolling stock still in use, and the river steamers which take four days and nights from Buenos Aires mounting against the current – the most suitable way to arrive, for on the wide Paraná river, between the low unchanging banks, one is gradually prepared.

It might seem daunting otherwise if one dropped down too quickly by jet from the noise and rush of Buenos Aires or New York into this land of deep tranquillity and the smell of flowers, where wind-blown oranges lie ungathered along the country roads. (They are three-a-penny in the market.) 'A land where all things always seem'd the same.'

What price is the lotus-eater prepared to pay for his tranquillity? Here he will pay not in dollars for a luxury suite with double windows against the traffic (there is no traffic), only with the half-closed eye and the prudent pen: to live here one would be charged in the quite small currency of the conscience.

One price, of course, is life under a military dictator, but in Paraguay there have always been dictators, civilian, military, ecclesiastical, the cruel and the kind. In the seventeenth century there was the benevolent Communist rule of the Jesuit missions who protected the Indians from the Spaniards, so that the native language, Guaraní, endures to this day and it is imprudent as well as useless to speak Spanish in the countryside.

The magnificent red baroque churches, the size of cathedrals, lie in ruins on both sides of the great Paraná river with their slitted watch-towers erected against Spanish slavers raiding from San Paulo and the wide colonnaded plazas where the Indian labourers lived in front of the church doors. Spain drove the Jesuits out, but more than the ruins attest their kindly influence now.

The later churches, built by Franciscans, still form one side of a great square facing the one-storied homes of the Indians; and the harp which played the labourers to work now joins with the guitar to play the Guaraní dances, the polka and the gallop. These are suitably Tennysonian names for a land which mingles with the seventeenth-century baroque a certain nineteenth-century romanticism – the railway station in Asunción belongs to the early railway age, an international college is built in neo-Gothic and looks like the home of Mr Rochester, a little white battlemented Baptist church bears the date 1822, and all the overgrown gardens of the crumbling houses are scented like Maud's with rose and jessamine.

The second dictatorship came after Independence when Doctor Francia cut Paraguay off from the world – the cruellest dictatorship of all, the dictatorship of El Supremo, an intellectual, a mathematician and astronomer, and an admirer of Voltaire and Rousseau, a crueller man even than Marshal Solano Lopez, who in his senseless war with Argentina, Brazil and Uruguay, reduced the male population to less than 30,000.

Paraguayan historians are busy now rehabilitating Lopez's name, perhaps because praise of a past dictator is a safe way of diminishing the stature of a present one. The bust of Lopez stands in front of the government building which he built like a *bon marché* Louvre, the military academy carries his name in large letters across its façade, and his body lies in the Heroes' Pantheon.

There is a covert admiration here for ruthlessness. All along the road to Encarnación in the south are little signs and crosses to the dead. 'Road accidents?' I asked my companion with some surprise, for we hadn't passed a car for many kilometres.

'Some of them,' he replied, 'but here there is not much respect for human life.'

The dead have more value than the living, they have more power, they may answer your prayers. A soldier was killed recently in an Asunción street and a rude cross now marks the spot and women pray there, 'though he was not exactly a saint', a priest said to me. Even the ghosts of the slavers still have power. In the country, peasants leave food at night in the clay ovens they use for cooking chipá to satisfy 'the little people' who arrive after dark to steal and sometimes rape a girl. You know when they are around because you can hear them whistling, but the trouble is that there is a spider which whistles, too.

Constitutional rule was never very successful; after the disastrous war of Marshal Lopez there were thirty-two presidents in Paraguay in sixty-two years; and in 1948, after six months' civil war, the Red Colorados (the Conservatives) became the only party. In the civil war it was the peasants and not the divided army, who had at least the excitement of action, that suffered most, and it was with relief they found themselves under a dictatorship again.

General Stroessner, who in August celebrated the beginning of his third period of power, has the air of a fleshy, good-humoured and astute owner of a beer cellar who knows his customers well and can manage them. In his third term he is able to relax. There are ugly stories of his early days, of opponents thrown from aeroplanes into the forest and bodies washed up with bound hands on the Argentine bank of the Paraná – the dead are always lucky.

Perhaps 150 political prisoners have been lying in the cells of police stations up and down the country for ten years or more, forgotten by all but their families and an occasional priest.

The ruling party is the Colorado and the Colorado is General Stroessner. The army and the political party, as in a Communist state, are closely integrated, and on the party's annual celebration I could have believed I was in a Communist state, for red was everywhere. The peasantry wore red scarves, the bourgeoisie more shyly bore a red handkerchief in the breast-pocket or sometimes a handkerchief carried in the hand like a passport. There was no blue (the sign of the Liberal party) to be seen anywhere.

Peasants poured noisily into town on horseback and in buses with their red favours – it was like a note of warning to the Liberals who had been allowed this year to fight an election and win a proportion of seats. If the strong man were not there, these crowds of caña-drinking peasants seemed to indicate, whose life would be safe?

If you can afford that old colonial house, with a cook, a housemaid and a gardener for forty dollars a month, it's just as well to carry a red handkerchief when you walk in the street that day and forget the trouble-makers in prison and the malnutrition you might find among the scrap-heap huts perched on the red cliffs of Asunción in the shadow of the white Shell bastions like the hovels which clung against the walls of a medieval castle.

Malnutrition rather than hunger: malnutrition from the eternal mandioca which has been the curse of Africa, too. The population as a whole is said to eat on the average half a pound of meat a day, but an average can be misleading. One evening at a barbecue I saw how my host's plate was never empty for more than the time it took to carve another steak. He ate with elbows thrust out and head well down, and I was reminded of the scene in *The City of Mahoganny* when Mr Jacob Schmitt eats his way to death.

> *Brothers, I ask you, watch me;*
> *watch me how I eat.*
> *When all is gone, then I have peace,*
> *because then I forget it, because*
> *then I forget it.*
> *Brothers, give me more,*
> *Brothers, give me more.*

'This is nothing,' my host said, raising his head for a moment from his third steak, 'I eat eight kilos a day.' The better to forget – forget charity, forget curiosity, forget ambition.

A quarter of the population is said to live abroad, some of course for political reasons, like their finest writer, Roa Bastos, but most from frustration at home. I spoke to a dozen young students. Every one of them was studying law, not one medicine, though doctors are almost unknown in the interior, no one agronomy, though Paraguay depends almost entirely on agriculture.

Yet not one of the dozen really intended to practise law; with the title doctor tacked on to his name it would be easier to find a job, that was all, if it was only in a tourist agency or behind the counter of a bank, and he could study law in evening classes and work to keep himself in the meanwhile, while medicine demanded whole-time study. They were curious about the outside world; they asked questions about Fidel Castro ('We only hear one side in the newspapers') and the Pope's Encyclical – their real ambition was simply to get 'outside'.

For inside, apart from a job as a Colorado man, only one career is really open to talent – smuggling – which, after the growing of *yerba maté* and the raising of cattle, is Paraguay's chief industry. On the Paraguayan side of the border it is quite a legal occupation. Whisky and American cigarettes are flown down from Panama 'in transit' and transferred at the international airport under the eyes of the police and customs to private planes. A token transit tax having been paid, the planes, many of them Dakotas, then set off to the Argentine, landing on this or that estancia near Buenos Aires.

Sometimes they crash and scatter cigarettes over the countryside, sometimes, when the local police are dissatisfied with their rake-off, they are seized and the pilot ends in prison – there is enough excitement to attract a man of enterprise, and there are high, quick profits. A proportion of the smuggled goods always remains behind (the customs are not particular), and you can buy whisky openly in Asunción cheaper than in any other capital, while small boys sell the smuggled cigarettes on the steps of the Ministry of Defence itself – as the President wisely says, the commerce keeps them out of worse mischief.

Across all the frontiers there is trouble: serious trouble in Bolivia, student riots in Brazil, uneasiness in Argentina, general strikes and kidnappings in Uruguay. Paraguay is almost as cut off from the world outside as in the days of Doctor Francia. Not even the flying saucers which are reported daily in the newspapers and on the Saturday radio of Buenos Aires penetrate across the Paraná, and the tourists

– they spend forty-eight hours in Asunción, visit the Iguazú Falls and move on. A few Jewish agents arrive looking for war criminals in the German colonies around Encarnación, but they get no help from anyone. No one here wants to stir up trouble.

There are no political demonstrations – except for the Colorado party – no students' protest. 'It would be impossible here,' a student told me sadly. The Communist Party is illegal: no one waves the little Red Book. I spoke to some members of the new Christian-Democrat movement (they have not yet been accepted as a political party): well-meaning men and women of the left, scholars and university teachers, they are not the stuff of revolutionaries. One of them even admitted to me that the military dictatorship allied with the Colorado party was the best government they could expect at the present cultural level.

To exchange Red for Blue periodically, as in the old days, would make no difference at all.

Only the Church (and the Jesuits in particular) seems sometimes to threaten the surface of the still pool. A priest said to me: 'The new movement in the Church makes the President uneasy. He got on well with the old monsignors, but now he doesn't understand what is happening.' Stories of Camillo Torres, the priest shot with the guerrillas in Colombia, seep over the frontier – he is the Catholic equivalent of Che Guevara.

The Jesuits in Asunción have instituted what is called an Open Mass, with Guaraní music played by harp and guitar, when sermons are preached by lay members of the congregation. On one occasion a student in his sermon criticized the President for spending money on a visit to the United States while children in his own country were dying of malnutrition. The police that time arrested the wrong student, who spent two days in prison. Priests' telephones are sometimes tapped: sometimes they are followed by agents . . .

A new archbishop is soon to be elected and, for the first time under the new constitution, the hierarchy has been allowed to send the proposed names direct to Rome. A secret meeting was held to choose the candidates. Twenty-five copies only of the minutes were Roneoed for private distribution, but forty-eight hours later a priest, calling on the Minister of the Interior, saw a copy on his desk. One bishop is unlikely to be chosen; a few years ago, when there were guerrilla forays by exiles from Argentina across the Paraná, this bishop, from his private helicopter, tried to guide the partisans away from the President's troops.

One mustn't be too hopeful of the new Church. This is South America, and there is another type of priest more understandable to the military mind, like the army chaplain who tried to keep his parish as well as his job, and, when the archbishop sent another priest to take over the parish, pinned down his successor with rifle fire from the presbytery all the long night. He was not a bad man, that priest, for at the end of the night he threw away his rifle and advanced with outstretched hands. 'I have nothing against you, father,' he said, 'I only wanted to show the archbishop.'

Another priest not long ago appealed to the archbishop for pardon. His faculties had been suspended because he was living openly with a woman. He appeared before the archbishop and an ecclesiastical court, and the archbishop asked him: 'How can you expect pardon, father, when you are still living with the same woman?'

'But I have a doctor's certificate,' he replied, 'to prove that I am impotent.'

These are the kind of priests the President can understand and use. They belong to his own old world, with the special charm and even the special charity of corruption. They live untroubled by the big questions of human rights which concern the Jesuit fathers.

I think again and again of the house in the sweet-scented garden in the land where oranges lie ungathered and no one pays income tax. Only 150 men in the police station cells to forget and the children dying of malnutrition – no evil comparable at all to the wholesale massacres in Biafra and Vietnam. Perhaps if one were sufficiently fond of beef . . .

Daily Telegraph Magazine
3 January 1969

The Virtue of Disloyalty

Surely if there is one supreme poet of conservatism, of what we now call the Establishment, it is Shakespeare. In his great poetic history of England, he began with Henry VI, who was almost as close to his own time as we are to the war of 1870, and then worked backwards, receding from the dangerous present, the England of plots and persecutions, into the safer past. Shakespeare's father was a Roman Catholic, who did not conform, but the only line I can recall of Shakespeare's which reflects critically on the Reformation is a metaphor in the Sonnets which could easily be explained away.

Bare ruined choirs where once the sweet birds sang.

If there is one word which chimes through Shakespeare's early plays it is the word 'peace'. In times of political trouble the Establishment always appeals to this ideal of peace.

God's gentle sleeping peace.
The troubler of the poor world's peace.

Peace as a nostalgia for a lost past: peace which Shakespeare associated like a retired colonial governor with firm administration.

> Peace it bodes, and love and quiet life,
> An awe-full rule, and right supremacy.

There are moments as he mocks at poor Jack Cade and his peasant rebels when we revolt against this bourgeois poet on his way to the house at Stratford and his coat of arms, and we sometimes tire even of the great tragedies, where the marvellous beauty of the verse takes away the sting and the last lines heal all, with right supremacy re-established by Fortinbras, Malcolm and Octavius Caesar. Then we are inclined to use against him the accusation flung at Antonio in *The Merchant of Venice*.

> You have too much respect upon the world:
> They lose it that do buy it with such care.

Of course he is the greatest of all poets, but we who live in times just as troubled as his, times full of the deaths of tyrants, a time of secret agents, assassinations and plots and torture chambers, sometimes feel ourselves more at home with the sulphurous anger of Dante, the self-disgust of Baudelaire and the blasphemies of Villon, poets who dared to reveal themselves whatever the danger, and the danger was very real. The first earned exile, the second a trial for obscenity, and the third possibly a hangman's cord. So we think in our own day of Pasternak, Daniel, Sinyavsky, Ginsberg, Solzhenitsyn in Russia: Roa Bastos a fugitive from Paraguay: George Seferis making his brave protest in Greece. On this roll of honour the name of

Shakespeare does not appear, and yet, and yet . . . I like to believe that if he had lived a little longer, his name would not have been absent. We grow a little tired of the artificial problem of the Prince of Denmark (a mother's incest and a father's murder is not an experience we can easily share) and a young suicide today is unlikely to brood so deliberately in the Wittenberg manner on the dilemma 'To be or not to be.' But in his last years Shakespeare did strike the same note of outrage as Dante and Villon in the two characters I prefer to think of as one composite character, Timon-Caliban.

> *You taught me language; and my profit on't*
> *Is, I know how to curse.*

If only he had lived a few more years, so that we could have seen the great poet of the Establishment defect to the side of the disloyal, to the side of the poet Southwell disembowelled for so-called treason, to the side of those who by the very nature of their calling will always be 'troublers of the poor world's peace' – Zola writing *J'accuse*, Dostoevsky before a firing squad, Victor Hugo following Dante into exile, the Russian writers in their labour camps. One cannot help putting a higher value on what their rulers have regarded as disloyalty than the musical sentiments of loyalty expressed by so unlikely a character as John of Gaunt:

> *This happy breed of men, this little world.*

We all learnt the lines at school.

> *This blessed plot, this earth, this realm, this England.*

These complacent lines were published in 1597. Two years before, Shakespeare's fellow poet Southwell had died on the scaffold after three years of torture. If only Shakespeare had shared his disloyalty, we could have loved him better as a man.

It has always been in the interests of the State to poison the psychological wells, to encourage cat-calls, to restrict human sympathy. It makes government easier when the people shout Galilean, Papist, Fascist, Communist. Isn't it the story-teller's task to act as the devil's advocate, to elicit sympathy and a measure of understanding for those who lie outside the boundaries of State approval? The writer is driven by his own vocation to be a Protestant in a Catholic society, a Catholic in a Protestant one, to see the virtues of the Capitalist in a Communist society, of the Communist in a Capitalist state. Thomas Paine wrote, 'We must guard even our enemies against injustice.'

If only writers could maintain that one virtue of disloyalty – so much more important than chastity – unspotted from the world. Honours, even this prize-giving, State patronage, success, the praise of their fellows all tend to sap their disloyalty. The house at Stratford must not be endangered. If they don't become loyal to a Church or a country, they are apt to become loyal to some invented ideology of their own, until they are praised for consistency, although the writer should always be ready to change sides at the drop of a hat. He stands for the victims, and the victims change. Loyalty confines you to accepted opinions: loyalty forbids you to comprehend sympathetically your dissident fellows; but disloyalty encourages you to roam through any human mind: it gives the novelist an extra dimension of understanding.

I am not advocating propaganda in any cause. Propaganda

is only concerned to elicit sympathy for one side, what the propagandist regards as the good side: he too poisons the wells. But the novelist's task is to draw his own likeness to any human being, to the guilty as much as to the innocent – There, and may God forgive me, goes myself.

If we enlarge the bounds of sympathy in our readers we succeed in making the work of the State a degree more difficult. That is a genuine duty we owe society, to be a piece of grit in the State machinery. However acceptable for the moment the Soviet State may find the great classic writers, Dostoevsky, Tolstoy, Turgenev, Gogol, Chekhov, they have surely made the regimentation of the Russian spirit an imperceptible degree more difficult or more incomplete. You cannot talk of the Karamazovs in terms of a class, and if you speak with hatred of the kulak doesn't the rich humorous memory of the hero of *Dead Souls* come back to kill your hatred? Sooner or later the strenuous bugle note of loyalty, of social responsibility, of the greatest material good of the greatest number must die in the ear, and then perhaps certain memories will come back, of long purposeless discussions in the moonlight about life and art, the click of a billiard ball, the sunny afternoons of that month in the country.

A great German theologian confronted, in the worst days of our lifetime, this issue of loyalty and disloyalty: 'Christians in Germany,' he wrote, 'will face the terrible alternative of either willing the defeat of their nation in order that Christian civilization may survive, or willing the victory of their nation and thereby destroying our civilization. I know which of those alternatives I must choose.'

Dietrich Bonhoeffer chose to be hanged like our English poet Southwell. He is a greater hero for the writer than

Shakespeare. Perhaps the deepest tragedy Shakespeare lived was his own: the blind eye exchanged for the coat of arms, the prudent tongue for the friendships at Court and the great house at Stratford.

Address given upon the award of the Shakespeare Prize by the University of Hamburg
6 June 1969

Papa Doc

No one alive (and the dead cannot speak from their unknown graves except to Papa Doc) is better qualified than Bernard Diederich to tell the horrifying story of Haiti under the rule of Dr François Duvalier. Diederich lived in Haiti for fourteen years and he had personal experience not only of the early Duvalier days but of what seems now by contrast to have been the golden period of Magloire's rule; he is married to a Haitian and after his arrest and expulsion by Papa Doc he followed the fortunes of his adopted country from across the border in Santo Domingo. What a story it is: tragic, terrifying, bizarre, even at times comic. Papa Doc sits in his bath wearing his top hat for meditating: the head of his enemy Philogènes stands on his desk: the hearse carrying another enemy's body is stolen by the Tontons Macoute at the church door: the writer Alexis is stoned to death. There is material here for a Suetonius: Diederich is not a Suetonius, but his book is better documented.

There is something peculiarly Roman in the air of Haiti: Roman in its cruelty, in its corruption and in its heroism. You will not walk far in any Haitian town without seeing the names of Brutus and Cato, perhaps over a baker's shop or a garage. The auguries are still told in the entrails of beasts, and a Senator will sometimes take his life in his hands by a declaration against tyranny, like Moreau who spoke up in the Senate against the special powers demanded by Duvalier and paid the extreme penalty (so far as anyone knows). We are nearer to the Europe of Nero and Tiberius than to the Africa of Nkrumah.

That is why Haiti is irrelevant in any discussion of black power. Haiti is the scene of a classical tragedy and not like many emerging states of a black comedy farce in the contemporary manner. We feel sometimes that we are witnessing a tragedy by Racine played by coloured actors – or at the worst moments *Titus Andronicus*.

'On the orders of the President, Lieutenant Albert Jerome cut Philogènes' head off and placed it in a pail of ice. Duvalier despatched a special airforce fighter to fetch the head. Why did Duvalier want the head delivered to him at the palace? Weird stories circulated around Port-au-Prince which told of Duvalier sitting alone with the head for hours, trying to communicate with it.'

We would not be surprised to see Lavinia enter on the same stage, 'her hands cut off, and her tongue cut out'. Or a messenger bearing two heads and a hand.

This is a very full account of Duvalier's reign which will be indispensable to future historians. I would suggest that the best way to make a track through the thick jungle of savagery, incompetence, greed and superstition is to consider Duvalier's reign in stages. During the first stage it might have been possible to hope that Papa Doc, as he chose to call himself, would not prove a much worse ruler than many others in Haiti's cruel history, but that hope was ended in the carnage of the first bizarre attempt to overthrow him made by two sheriffs of Dade County, Florida, in 1958. The two sheriffs and six men, only three of whom were Haitian, succeeded in seizing the army barracks just behind the National Palace. Not one survived, but they came within an ace of success.

The second stage, perhaps accelerated by fear and insecurity, saw the final establishment of the police state, when Duvalier, unable any longer to trust the army, built up the militia, the palace guard and the Tontons Macoute at their expense. Then began his long and clever blackmail of the United States. In the OAS and the United Nations Haiti had a vote which the United States needed, equal in importance to any other power, and Duvalier saw to it that they paid cash and credit for that vote. In the absurd world organization with which we have been saddled since the Hitler war, the unscrupulous ruler of even so tiny a state as Haiti can exact protection money like a Chicago gangster from the rich. This second stage ended with the shooting of his old hatchet man Clément Barbot. Barbot, who had been in touch with the American military mission, had attempted to kidnap Duvalier's children. If Duvalier was to be overthrown he seems to have been the American choice as Duvalier's successor, though it is doubtful whether Haiti would have benefited much from the change of tyrant.

After the attempt on Duvalier's children followed the third stage, the stage of terror unlimited and of ineffective guerrilla risings which have continued till today, when half the revenue of the country was spent on the personal security of the President, when American aid was stopped and the American Ambassador withdrawn, when Dominican troops were poised on the frontier and Duvalier threatened a blood-bath in Port-au-Prince and only a rash man would have bet a Haitian *gourde* on his survival. But the guerrillas failed, President Bosch of Santo Domingo was overthrown, and President Johnson gave in to blackmail, sending back to Haiti an Ambassador as timorous as his name, Benson Timmons III, whom Duvalier kept waiting five weeks for an audience and then lectured on how an Ambassador should behave, a lecture which he took to heart.

Now we have reached the final stage of tyranny (or so one dares to hope), the stage of megalomania marked politically by Papa Doc's 'election' as President for Life. Now Duvalier has begun to speak of himself as a great writer, he announces (in *Jours de France*) the publication of his collected works, he compares himself with Trotsky, with Mao Tse Tung and with General de Gaulle, and in one remarkable passage in *Le Catéchisme de la révolution* with one higher even than these.

'Our Doc who art in the National Palace for life, hallowed be Thy name by present and future generations. Thy will be done in Port-au-Prince and in the provinces. Give us this day our new Haiti and never forgive the trespasses of the anti-patriots.'

Surely the end cannot long be delayed. Classical tragedy demands that the pendulum shall swing when it has reached the furthest point of its arc.

When the pendulum does descend I share the author's hope that Haiti will be allowed to work out her own salvation, without interference from her great neighbour. The Marines were ready to bring Barbot to power in Haiti as they brought Trujillo to power in Santo Domingo. But after the rule of the tyrant, Haiti ought to be given the chance to be ruled by heroes. Heroes are produced by tyranny, and they have not been lacking in her recent history: the Deputy Seraphin, the Senator Moreau, Alexis the writer, the young man Riobé who kept the army and the Tontons at bay from a cave above Kenscoff and shot himself with his last bullet, the thirteen members of the organization *Jeune Haiti* who held out in the mountains of the southwest for three months and died to the last man.

Foreword to *Papa Doc: The Truth about Haiti Today* by Bernard Diederich and Al Burt
1969

Chile: The Dangerous Edge

'At the next presidential election,' I began a question to Señor Tomic, the leader of the Christian Democrats at the last election.

'If there is another election,' he corrected me.

It was not the first time I had heard that 'if' – an 'if' which does not reflect the intentions of the governing coalition, the Popular Unity, who are trusted to follow the path of legality even to a bitter end. The 'if' is the dark side of their courage. A man going up alone against a strongpoint, grenade in hand, might say to himself, 'If I arrive living at that next belt of trees . . .'

A Government which has done so much with a minority of seats in Congress – nationalizing the copper mines without compensation, taking control of the principal banks by the purchase of shares, expropriating land far in excess of the timid measures of the previous Government – must wonder sometimes where, when and how the counterattack is likely to fall. Will it take the form of an economic blockade by the United States or a disguised attack engineered by the CIA with the help of the right extremists who murdered the head of the army, General Schneider?

Bolivia, with the help of Brazil and the probable connivance of the United States, has had its right-wing coup, and an unsuccessful attempt was made last October to overthrow General Lanusse, the liberalizing President of Argentina, while preparations were in hand for his meeting at the Chilean port of Antofagasta with Doctor Allende. If the plot had succeeded, two out of the three land frontiers of Chile would have become vulnerable – the Andes is no more a barrier than the Himalayas have proved to the Chinese. The frontier of this strange, narrow, elongated country, extending from the tropical desert in the north to the Antarctic south, is never further from the sea than London is from Newcastle.

No wonder that the recent appointment of Mr Davis, late American Ambassador in Guatemala, the happy hunting-ground of the CIA, to be Ambassador in Santiago is felt as a hardly veiled menace. There is a sense of danger in the air: the strange thing is that a visitor for the first week or two is hardly aware of it. 'I am told by everyone,' I remarked with some flippancy to one of Mr Tomic's followers, 'that there is a lot of tension. But do *you* feel tension when you wake up in the morning?'

'Every morning,' the stout, cheerful sociologist replied, without ceasing to smile.

The sense of tension, which first affects the visitor, is conveyed by the hoardings that scream in scarlet letters for justice on the murderers of General Schneider and by the newspapers. The constant war of attrition between the political parties is oddly diluted in the complete freedom of the Press. *El siglo*, the Communist paper, and *La nación*, the Government paper, daily denounce *El Mercurio* of the right, the property of the rich Edwardes family, while *La prensa* sighs after what it considers were the good days of President Frei. The war against the *Mercurio* is even carried on to the stickers of cars: *Chileno: El Mercurio miente (Mercurio lies)*.

There are certainly plenty of stories bandied about in papers of the right (unfortunately the *Mercurio* is the best produced paper, with the greatest coverage of foreign news, so that it is read even by the supporters of *El siglo*). A dispatch, dated from Bogotá, carrying the false report that one of Doctor Allende's planes, which crashed in the Colombian forest when he was returning from his official visit, carried arms for the guerrillas, was serious enough to cause a temporary closing of the United Press news agency in Santiago. Even an unimportant visitor found himself touched by a spirit of malicious invention. The day after my arrival, so I was told, one popular paper of the right stated that in receiving me President Allende had been tricked into receiving an impostor, travelling under my name. The sense of my own reality wavered a little when I heard the story, for there does really exist one such alter ego on whom I have accumulated a large dossier. His most spectacular exploits were to be imprisoned in my name in Assam and blackmailed in Paris.

At first it is not the tension of which one is aware so much as the loaded plates in the big hotels, the well-dressed crowds, the windows full of consumer goods. At lunch with Doctor Allende I asked whether to increase the standard of living of the poor it might not be necessary to start rationing food and goods. He said he hoped not. The Minister of Economics took the point up. He said my parallel with Cuba was not a good one – Chile had industries while Cuba had none and there was no blockade. 'For the time being,' the President said.

In Santiago, small storms blow up and subside again. The

noise of shouting one morning brought me down into the central square. There was a demonstration with much noise and many banners outside La Moneda, the governmental palace, but it proved to be only the long-standing quarrel about television channels. The President had refused to extend the area of Channel 13, belonging to the Catholic University, over the whole country. Just as the temporary closing of the news agency bureau was blown up into an attack on the freedom of the Press, so the refusal to extend Channel 13 has become in the eyes of ex-President Frei's supporters an attack on the communications media. This is in spite of the fact that by a law passed by Frei himself the extension could only be made if all three non-Government channels were extended too – at the cost of how many much-needed dollars?

It must not be thought that this quarrel over television marks a deeper quarrel between the Church and the State. The Catholic Church in Chile is progressive. Eighty priests, nearly all of whom are working in the slums, have signed a declaration in support of socialism, and a new movement, the Izquierda Cristiana (Christian Left), organized by Senator Jerez, has begun to draw away support from the left wing of the Christian Democrats. This has weakened the position of ex-President Frei, who is forced more and more towards the right wing of his party. By the time of the Congressional elections next year the Christian Left will have become a political party and be able to fight the elections on the side of the Government.

On the National Day, 18 September, the Archbishop presided at an ecumenical Te Deum in the cathedral attended by the Marxist President and the representatives of all Communist States including China – a somewhat bizarre gathering. Prayers were offered by a Methodist, a Protestant, a Baptist and a Jewish Rabbi, and the address by a priest was impressive: 'It is urgent for everyone to expel the Cain inside him. Humility is necessary to recognize the homicide inside us. It is easier to declare that the aggressors are outside. No, Cain comes and goes in the depths of everyone . . .'

I was standing just behind the retiring American Ambassador, remarkable for the size and fatness of his earlobes, who symbolized perhaps the outside aggression. And the homicide within? Were the murderers of General Schneider there in the cathedral? Perhaps not. Rows of ticketed seats had remained empty, like the seats at the Gospel wedding, and were filled only after the ceremony had begun by poor people who had been waiting in the street outside. They climbed over the chairs among the diplomats – a bang, shuffle, creak of reality breaking into what might have been a ceremony stuffy with protocol.

The outside aggressor is never far from anyone's mind. The Brazilian army, equipped by the United States with more modern material than it has supplied to Chile, arranged manoeuvres for two months on the borders of Uruguay to coincide with last November's elections there. The Bolivian coup has brought a potential enemy to within a hundred miles of Chile's northern port Iquique, and it must be remembered that the great copper mine of Chuquicamata and the nitrate mines of María Elena and Victoria are all on territory acquired by conquest in the Pacific War – of which the hundredth anniversary falls in a few years.

The possibility of a war of revenge is not one of Doctor Allende's chief concerns, but the possibility can never be quite discounted. British industrialists, for the sake of the copper and the nitrate, fabricated that costly and terrible war in the desert, where men fought and died for water-holes. Copper had not until then been properly exploited by the Bolivians. (One abandoned works built by Indians with the strength of a medieval castle stands in the desert outside Antofagasta.) Is it impossible that another imperial Power might follow the British example, tempted by the greatest copper mine in the world, the former Anaconda mine, in full production?

Nevertheless, Doctor Allende told me he believed the United States was no longer a military menace in South America: the defeat in Vietnam in his opinion made another Santo Domingo highly improbable. One hopes with all one's heart that he is right. But the humiliation of a Great Power has its own danger: humiliation demands to be purged elsewhere, and the Pentagon may feel impelled to exhibit its undiminished power in what it considers its own sphere of influence – even though the power may be exercised indirectly through such allies as Brazil and Bolivia. A lot depends on the future of Argentina. There are those who believe in a master plot, of which the Bolivian coup was the first stage.

In Chile itself a right-wing army coup is regarded as psychologically impossible. The army – you hear it from everyone except the Communists – is traditionally neutral; the army is pledged to legality. It is a very fine army – with the possible exception of the Cuban, the best in South America. The goose-step remains the symbol of its German upbringing.

But a special parachute force is now trained in Panama by American officers. Doctor Allende told me there was evidence enough that the Americans had tried to indoctrinate the men, and I asked why he allowed the training to continue. He said such attempts to indoctrinate were double-edged, and in any case he was determined not to provoke the American Government by any unnecessary change. The gamble of legality is played with high stakes. At the very moment when Doctor Allende announced that no compensation would be paid to the copper companies, joint manoeuvres were in progress with an American naval force off Valparaiso.

I suppose pessimism is the doubtful privilege of an outsider with a return ticket. Optimism is a vital necessity for the man who makes the decisions. As an outsider I could indulge in pessimism, which is allied to timidity. I could say to Doctor Allende that the undoubted popularity of the army might have its dangerous side – if the army broke with its traditions, the people's trust might ensure the success of a coup. I could even question the genuineness of the tradition – hadn't Ibáñez come to power in the 1920s with the help of the army, and wasn't General Viaux in prison now after first an attempted mutiny and then his implication in the murder of Schneider? Once a new English public school called Stowe was founded and one day on the notice-board appeared the following announcement, 'From next Monday the tradition of the School will be . . .'

In Chile Doctor Allende is making a revolution under more difficult circumstances than Fidel Castro in his assault from the Sierra Maestre. This revolution requires from its leader less a heroic charisma than extreme political prudence, a sense of humour, and an unspectacular courage. And optimism of course, always optimism. Six parties are represented in the Popular Unity and the Ministries are so divided between the parties that no Minister has a second-in-command of his own party. Inevitably this causes some friction.

The end is agreed, but not always the means. The answer a critic of the system receives is that the image of unity at the moment is more important than the speed of the operations, and can one fairly complain of undue tardiness when one remembers how much has been done during one year of minority government?

The sense of unity between the six parties strikes even a pessimistic outsider as remarkable. This is not the kind of popular front, formed in an emergency against a common enemy, containing great fissures of dissent which widen when the emergency is over. In Europe the parties of the left fear Communism more than Conservatism. Here Communists and Socialists are working together without suspicion, perhaps because both parties are Marxist.

All the Communists whom I met seemed to belong to that new class of Communist who appeared so briefly and prematurely during the Czechoslovakian spring, open and experimental, with dogma as the ground of argument and not as an article of faith, men who have studied Trotsky as well as Marx and Lenin. Is the Popular Unity strong enough to exercise a magnetic appeal on waverers in the Christian Democratic party when the Congressional elections are held next year? All depends on that.

The priest had reason when in the Te Deum service he drew attention to 'the Cain within us'. The left extremists of MIR are an irritation – they will become a danger if the Government loses votes in 1973. The workers too may well demand more than the Government can offer. The sense of equality is a middle-class virtue.

The miners of Chuquicamata do not feel equality with

other workers – they feel themselves aristocrats. Anaconda has given them living conditions far ahead of other industrial workers – 100 escudos a day is a minimum wage compared with 11 escudos a day (doubled now by the Government) in the nitrate mines, and it was a shock to arrive at Chuqui after visiting the coal mines of Lota in the south.

Lota lives under a perpetual torrent of rain: every street crossing has to be forded like a river – and this is for nine months of the year. The solitary cinema looks like a flea-pit preserved in a museum. The women and children stand under the eaves staring at the rain. There is nothing to do after work but drink and wine is cheap – there were 500 absentees after the National Day, and while I was underground a man, drunk and in tears, came to the office begging to be allowed to work. He couldn't afford to lay-off, nor could the mine afford the risk he represented.

It was worse than the world of D. H. Lawrence's child-hood: it was the world of nineteenth-century industrial England, more depressing even than the slums of Santiago. It is easier to clear a slum.

But Chuqui lies in the year-long sun of the desert. Rain doesn't exist in Chuqui. The houses are well built and brightly painted. There are cinemas and churches and shops full of goods and a band playing in the dry cool air of evening, and above the town is one of the best hospitals in Latin America. There was a small strike in Chuqui the day I arrived, and looking round the smelting works with a man from the management one could feel the hate and the pride of the workers blazing as fiercely as the furnaces. They were unapproachable, unlike the men in the textile works of Yurur to whom I had been able to talk easily enough ('Do you know Agatha Christie?' one asked me).

When I inquired of a passing worker there what difference he had felt after nationalization he answered without hesitation and not in terms of money. He said, 'There is no fear now. We can speak to each other while we work. Before the brother of the owner used to walk among us like a devil.' (At the door of the factory they have shrouded from view the statue of the founder, who used to make delinquent workmen kneel and swear loyalty before a voodoo assembly of a skull, a crucifix and a statuette of Justice.)

But at Chuqui it was only money and privilege that counted. The men feel threatened by the very notion of equality.

An old Communist worker said to me one night as we sat at dinner, 'Do you think we have a chance?' and I thought of the generals in Brazil and Bolivia and of Mr Davis and the CIA, of the rain and the desolation of Lota and the slums of Santiago, and then of the proud, moneyed miners of Chuqui and ex-President Frei waiting in the wings. Two lines of Shelley came to my mind:

> to hope till Hope creates
> From its own wreck the thing it contemplates.

'I think you have a sporting chance,' I said, and he nodded in agreement – that was about the measure of it.

Observer Magazine
2 January 1972

Second-hand Bookshops

I don't know how Freud would have interpreted them, but for more than thirty years my happiest dreams have been of second-hand bookshops: shops previously unknown to me or old familiar shops which I am revisiting. It is the familiar shops which have certainly never existed; I have come reluctantly to that conclusion. Somewhere not far from the Gare du Nord in Paris I have vivid memories of a shop at the end of a long street running uphill, a deep shop with high shelves (I had to use a ladder to reach the top of them). On at least two occasions I hunted through the shelves (there I thought I bought Apollinaire's translation of *Fanny Hill*), but when the war was over I searched for the shop in vain. Of course the shop could have disappeared, but the street itself was not there. Then there was a shop in London which occurred very frequently in my dreams; I can remember clearly its façade but not its interior. It stood somewhere in the region behind Charlotte Street before you come to the Euston Road. I never went inside, and I am sure now that there never was such a shop. I would always wake from such dreams with a sense of happiness and expectation.

At various periods of my life I have kept a diary of my dreams, and my diary for this year (1972) contains in the first seven months six dreams of second-hand bookshops. Curiously enough, for the first time, they are not happy dreams; perhaps because a loved companion with whom I used to hunt books and with whom I began to form, just after the war, a collection of Victorian detective stories died at the end of 1971. So in this year's dreams an old railway book which I am planning to give to my friend John Sutro for Christmas (he had founded the Railway Club at Oxford), when I draw it from the shelf, has lost half its cover: even the old red Nelson sevenpennies (so unaccountably maligned by George Orwell, but which I love to possess when the first editions are too expensive) prove to be all mutilated copies. Nothing in all these dreams seems good enough to buy.

My friend David Low's recollections as a bookseller have set my thoughts rambling, not only through dreams but through the small adventures and friendships of fifty years of book-hunting. (At seventeen I became a wanderer in Charing Cross Road which alas! now I seldom bother to visit.)

Second-hand booksellers are among the most friendly and the most eccentric of all the characters I have known. If I had not been a writer, theirs would have been the profession I would most happily have chosen. There is the musty smell of books, and there is the sense of the treasure-hunt. For this reason I prefer the badly organized bookshop where Topography is mixed up with Astronomy and Theology with Geology and stacks of unidentified books litter the staircase to a room marked Travel, which may well contain some of my favourite Conan Doyles, *The Lost World* or *The Tragedy of the Korosko*. I am frightened of entering Maggs or Quaritch because I know there will be no personal discovery to make there, no mistake on the part of the bookseller. From David Low's recollections I realize how wrong I was to be afraid of Bain's in William IV Street. It is too late to remedy that now.

To enter properly this magic world of chance and adventure one has to be either a collector or a bookseller. I would have preferred to be a bookseller, but the opportunity escaped me in the war. During the blitz I happened to be a part-time warden attached to the same post as David Low (whom I already knew well) and little Cole, who was in those days a book 'runner'. My first patrol with Cole was in search of a parachute bomb which was said to have become entangled in the trees of one of the Bloomsbury squares. We never found it, rather to our relief. Cole took me once to see his room: I remember the shabby books stacked everywhere, even under the bed, and we agreed that one day, if we both survived the war, we would set up business together. I went off to West Africa on a different job and we lost touch. I had lost my only chance of becoming a second-hand bookseller.

To become a collector is easier. It doesn't matter what you collect, you have a key to the door. The collection is not important. It is the fun of the hunt, the characters whom you meet, the friends you make. When I was a teenager I got my first taste of collecting by buying works on Antarctic exploration; the Arctic didn't interest me. Those books have all gone. They would have a certain value now, but who cares? Before the war I collected Restoration literature because I was working on a life of Rochester only to be published more than thirty years later. They were not first editions (I couldn't afford them); they have gone too: some of them in the blitz and some I regretfully abandoned when I left England.

I am still collecting Victorian detective stories: how many I used to find in the forties at Foyle's at half-a-crown a time even though John Carter had ten years before produced his famous Scribner's catalogue which should have aroused collectors everywhere.

The value of a collection to the collector lies less in its importance, surely, than in the excitement of the hunt, and the strange places to which the hunt sometimes leads. Quite recently, with my brother Hugh, whose collection of detective stories extends from Victorian times to 1914, so that we usually hunt as a couple, I walked in pouring rain through the dismal outskirts of Leeds in a ruined area that could have been part of a Grierson documentary of the depression. The shop we sought had been included in a reliable directory, but we believed in it less and less as we got wetter and wetter between the abandoned factories. Yet when we arrived the shop *had* certainly once existed, there was a sign '. . . kseller' above a door which was no longer in place, all the windows were broken, and the floor was mysteriously littered with children's boots and shoes, good shoes too. Some meeting place of a childish Mafia? Scenes like that, and the discovery of new pubs and beers one has not previously tasted are some of the rewards of the book-hunter.

This isn't the same world as the old-established bookshop in Piccadilly, with its antiquarian section, where I went recently to pass the time, and asked if by chance they had any of the works of Wilfrid Scawen Blunt. 'What did he write, sir? Fiction?'

I think David Low is a little too kind to these expensive shops, but I suppose if one is in the trade one has to make a friendly gesture towards the well-dressed devil in his top hat and tails. The new university shops I avoid, all red brick and glass, full of second-hand academic books which were dull even when they first appeared. Alas, for Miss Dillon's shop, which survived all the bombs around Store Street, it has not the same charm today. Sometimes David Low goes too far in politeness: 'canny' is a charitable adjective to apply to the famous Mr Wilson of Bumpus. I would have preferred 'cunning'.

No, the West End is not my hunting ground now any more than Charing Cross Road, but thank God! Cecil Court remains Cecil Court, even though David Low has moved to Oxfordshire.

From David one happy day I bought a strange eighteenth-century manuscript bound in white vellum with a handwritten title 'Hultoniana'. It cost me five guineas, a lot of money in the thirties, but I got the price back, after a little research, by writing an article in the *Spectator* on this bizarre story of a series of cruel hoaxes inflicted on an unpopular tradesman called Hulton, apparently written by one of his enemies. I have the manuscript still, 'grangerized' with an interesting letter on the eighteenth-century London shop names mentioned in it, written to me by Sir Ambrose Heal. It pleases me that in that way 'Hultoniana' cost me nothing but a little work.

Perhaps the find I value most is *The Office of the Holy Week*, translated by Walter Kirkham Blount, published in 1687 with seven engravings of Hollar and bound in tooled contemporary red morocco. It is dedicated to the Queen of England. 'The Queens of England are Saints again,' Blount writes, 'and the Fruit infinitely great, when People find the way to Heaven is the way to be well at Court.' He couldn't have written that a year later, with the arrival of Dutch

William. He would have had to publish the book abroad, or without a publisher's imprint at all, not openly at Matthew Turner's at the Lamb in High Holborn. This beautiful book cost me half-a-crown at Mr Gallup's shop on Clapham Common where I bought my Anthony Woods. Mr Gallup's shop was one of the casualties of the war; it 'went up' on the same day as my house two hundred yards away.

I wish David Low had included an obituary of deaths by bombs or builders. Gone for example is the second-hand bookshop I loved in Westbourne Grove and gone the little bookshop on the triangular site opposite King's Cross Station where I bought *The Adventures* and *The Memoirs of Sherlock Holmes* in their first editions for what seemed then the exorbitant price of £5. That is the sad side of book-hunting; far more shops disappear than new shops open. Even Brighton is not what it was.

Introduction to *With All Faults* by David Low
1973

The Sign of Four

It is something of a private quest for me to rediscover *The Sign of Four*, which I read first at the age of ten and have never forgotten. Better stories of Sherlock Holmes have come and gone; I can remember nothing of *The Musgrave Ritual* or *The Man with the Twisted Lip*, and yet the dark night in Pondicherry Lodge, Norwood, has never faded from my memory.

The Sign of Four was the second of the Sherlock Holmes series. It was published in 1890, and it is a distinct improvement on *A Study in Scarlet*, which appeared in *Beeton's Christmas Annual* in 1887. Doyle was never as happy with his full-length Holmes novels as he was with the short stories. With the exception of *The Hound of the Baskervilles*, they were all padded out with subplots in distant regions which lack the total reality of Baker Street and Norwood. With little difficulty it would be possible to lift the whole subplot of Mormon tyranny out of *A Study in Scarlet*; the subplot of *The Sign of Four* is too easily identifiable with *The Moonstone*: jewels stolen from India, discovery of an empty box, murderer's entrance by a trap-door in the ceiling, even flight by way of Lower Thames Street and Tower Wharf. And yet . . . and yet . . . why is it that of all the Holmes stories it is *The Sign of Four* which

338

remains persistently in my memory after nearly sixty years?

Of course there are disappointments; one detects signs of carelessness which seem to indicate that Doyle's imagination had not yet been fully committed (perhaps it was never fully committed before he found his ideal illustrator in Sidney Paget). To take one example, a letter received 'the next day' by Miss Morstan and dated 7 July is brought hot-foot to Holmes – in September. Surely there is more than mere carelessness in the fact that the author never bothered to make a correction in succeeding editions. It is as if he were determined to treat his own story with cavalier indifference. Why care if two characters die of heart-attacks in very similar circumstances? And he abandons Doctor Watson to marriage with Miss Morstan in a perfunctory love scene as though he were dropping a page of discarded manuscript into the waste-paper basket. He could not possibly have realized that in Doctor Watson he had created a character – and a bachelor character at that – who was to become as memorable as the great Holmes himself.

Perhaps the reason why *The Sign of Four* has stayed indelibly in the memory is that in this book the great detective for the first time comes completely to life in all his complexity. In *A Study in Scarlet* the first meeting of Holmes and Watson in a hospital laboratory is quite unmemorable. In *The Sign of Four* the whole future is there in the first chapter. In *A Study in Scarlet* there is only the barest hint at Holmes's drug-addiction, but now in the opening paragraph of the second novel the great detective drives firmly home the needle of the hypodermic syringe.

' "Which is it today," I asked, "morphine or cocaine?"

'He raised his eyes languidly from the old black-letter volume which he had opened.

' "It is cocaine," he said, "a seven-per-cent solution. Would you care to try it?" '

What popular author today could so abruptly introduce his hero as a drug addict without protest from his public? It is only in one direction that we have become a permissive society.

In the same opening chapter (perhaps the richest Doyle ever wrote) we are given some of the best examples of Holmes's deductions – from the mud outside the Wigmore Street post office and from the scratches on Watson's watch; we notice for the first time in his character the strain of *fin de siècle* melancholy (and in the same sentences we are given the characteristic picture of Holmes's London which is as quickly identified by foreigners as the Eiffel Tower):

' "I cannot live without brain-work. What else is there to live for? Stand at the window here. Was there ever such a dreary, dismal, unprofitable world? See how the yellow fog swirls down the street and drifts across the dun-coloured houses." '

A scene and a character are simultaneously expressed. This is real writing from which we can all draw a lesson.

Even his housekeeper, Mrs Hudson, makes her first appearance in these opening pages, bearing the first of so many cards upon her brass salver. Perhaps she had been engaged after *A Study in Scarlet*, in which too many characters burst unannounced into the detective's chambers.

There are other indications that in *The Sign of Four,* however unwillingly, Doyle's imagination had begun its long commitment. Here he already shows his mastery of names, perhaps equalled only by Dickens: Pondicherry Lodge, Thaddeus and Bartholomew Sholto, the detective Athelney Jones, names which contrast so admirably with plain Doctor Watson and Mrs Hudson. The humour which was almost absent from *A Study in Scarlet* sparkles here: 'Men of character always differentiate their long letters, however illegibly they may write. There is vacillation in his *k*'s and self-esteem in his capitals.'

Here too is the genuine spine-creeping melodrama which appeared again in *The Speckled Band* and *The Hound of the Baskervilles:*

' "All day I have waited to hear from him, for he often likes to be alone; but an hour ago I feared that something was amiss, so I went up and peeped through the keyhole. You must go up, Mr Thaddeus – you must go up and look for yourself. I have seen Mr Bartholomew Sholto in joy and in sorrow for ten long years, but I never saw him with such a face on him as that." '

The passage calls to be read aloud as much as any passage in *Anna Livia Plurabelle.* In *The Sign of Four* one can hear the clock of destiny striking for the author of *Micah Clarke.* Doyle couldn't escape simply by marrying off Doctor Watson.

Introduction to *The Sign of Four* by Sir Arthur Conan Doyle 1974

Advice to a Friend

Pavilions by the Sea is, as far as I know, the first book to describe the real inner life of a great hotel. Arnold Bennett was an assiduous collector of facts who spoilt them with fiction, – an outsider's view: Fothergill wrote amusingly about a country inn. Here we have the creative adventure of hotel keeping.

I must declare my personal interest in this book. Tom Laughton is a friend of mine. I share his love for the old town of Antibes, though he knows its corners and characters far better than I do, and I have listened many times to his analytical study of a certain small butcher in the rue de Sade, and his method of cutting a veal kidney. 'This,' I thought, 'is the great hotelier saluting another artist of the good life.' Rashly on one of these occasions I encouraged him to write a book, rashly because the hackneyed phrase 'everyone has one book inside him' is deceptive and totally untrue. Everyone has the material in his memories for many books, but that's not the same thing at all.

> *Between the idea*
> *And the reality*
> *Between the motion*

> *And the act*
> *Falls the Shadow.*
>   T. S. Eliot

I hope he will forgive me for disclosing some details of this book's history. When I saw the first draft I was worried – the beginning was finely rendered, his family started alive from the page, his apprenticeship to farming was the best such account since Adrian Bell's *Corduroy,* a book which nearly turned me into a countryman, but . . . but . . . I tried to wrap my criticisms up like a gift package but Laughton without hesitation untied the tinsel string. When after two years had passed I read the third draft of his book, I began to realize I was not dealing with an amateur but a professional. To an amateur his words are Holy Writ – the professional knows how far they will always fall short of what he wants to say. I became used to the letters from Yorkshire written to the signature tune, 'I think I see what's wrong. I have started again.' To what an inferno, I thought, has my unthinking encouragement condemned him. Why should a man who loves good painting, good wine and good food, living in a happy and well-deserved retirement, suffer in the evening of life what all writers must suffer – in Masefield's phrase 'The long despair of doing nothing well'?

I am glad now to have been the judge who condemned him. The first paragraph of his book has the proud, confident, professional ring which the book never loses.

Foreword to *Pavilions by the Sea* by Tom Laughton
1977

Son of the Rice Paddies

One other memory of the four winters I spent in Vietnam is that of Colonel Leroy who, in his autobiography, wrote perhaps the most perceptive book on the French war in Indo-China. Half Vietnamese and half French, a peasant soldier, the child of peasants, he became at thirty the youngest colonel in the French army, a man who belonged to two worlds.

I met Colonel Leroy first in 1951 when he was the uncrowned 'King of Bentré' – an area of river, marsh and jungle in the Mekong delta which he had known from childhood. He had returned home, after imprisonment and torture by the Japanese, to his own people, to fight among friends against former friends – a boy with whom he had played football was now a Viet Minh general. On my first visit to Bentré we made a tour of his kingdom in an armoured boat with machine-guns trained on either bank: a year later we made the same tour but this time instead of guns and guards our boat carried musicians and dancing girls; the pagoda where we dined had been built on a lake in imitation of Hanoi; he had made a zoo to entertain the children of his kingdom, and works by Montesquieu and de Tocqueville lay on his table. Leroy had pacified his territory as General de Lattre had never succeeded in doing in the north – one was safe in Bentré, but not behind the so-called lines of Hanoi.

But Leroy's success made him worse enemies than the Viet Minh. He had formed a Catholic brigade who fought more effectively than the Foreign Legionaries, the Senegalese and Moroccans who formed the French army. Catholic patriots faced Communist patriots: Leroy represented a kind of Vietnam the French authorities regarded with suspicion and the South Vietnamese Government feared, because it would have meant the end of easy money and the old corruption which fitted so easily from the past like a well-made glove.

When I returned for my third winter in Vietnam Colonel Leroy was no longer in Bentré, and Bentré was no longer a haven of safety in the delta. The Colonel, I learnt, had been sent to Paris to L'École de Guerre to learn those conventional arts of war which led to the disaster of Dien Bien Phu – an honour, needless to say, that the Colonel did not appreciate. He had been guilty of a grave error of judgement: he had not merely purged Bentré of the Viet Minh, he had purged it of corruption; he had instituted agrarian reforms; worst of all he had held elections, free elections, which were not at all to the taste of the Vietnam authorities to whom a peasant was a peasant without rights, and who were growing rich with the spoils of collaboration and a bogus independence. President Tran Van Huu acted with inhabitual speed and announced that the elections of Bentré would be ignored by the Government since they were 'organized by the head of the province on his own initiative'. As Leroy remarked: 'If we elected a provincial assembly, why not a national one?' He had exposed the genuine lack of independence, though each year the independence of the country was 'finally' declared, with a new little concession, by the French Government. On this occasion General de Lattre sent orders from the United States that three battalions of Senegalese or North Africans should be dispatched to Bentré to restore the authority of Saigon out of the hands of this Colonel of the French army. In the end the affair was settled diplomatically with the promotion of Colonel Leroy to L'École de Guerre.

I have often wondered what would have happened if Leroy had been given his head and transferred to Tongking to take over command of the Vietnamese forces there. He had proved what he could do with the docile Catholics of the south; isn't it conceivable that he might have repeated his success with the much tougher Catholics of the north? The elements were already there in the partisan troops recruited, but hardly sustained, by the two bishops of Bui-Chu and Phat Diem. These men only needed real training and proper weapons. Enthusiasm the men of Bui-Chu certainly had. I remember one armoured village where the last defences had been erected inside the church itself. With no support, except a lofty condescension from the French and a blessing from the Bishop, they needed a leader of their own blood. Leroy had proved himself a revolutionary leader of the same quality in his own small area as General Giap, and he had an ideology which should have been acceptable to the French authorities; but they paid it the worst service of all – the service of the lips; Leroy believed it with his heart.

'I was thirty-one at the time. I felt myself pushed to the fore by powerful forces; I believed myself to be in harmony with a whole people who, in accepting me, would accept more than a man: would accept a true union with France built on equality and communion.

'The only people in the world who can blend completely with Asia are the French who are sometimes narrow-minded and meddling, but have no real racial prejudice. Behind all their shortcomings, you can always feel their desperate need for love, and there is no one in the world more influenced by love than my brother the peasant.'

Leroy adds with characteristic humour: 'I was never much of a politician. I was never calculating enough, and when I've had a drink too many, I often say what I think, even in front of very important people.'

One of the chief merits of his book which at one level is a great adventure story, almost a child's myth, of a peasant boy who became a king and was betrayed by his friends, is that it was certainly written with the frankness of a drink too many.

Introduction to *Life of Colonel Leroy* by Colonel Jean Leroy 1977

The Country with Five Frontiers

The American worked in the Canal Zone, but he lived in Panamá, so he was generally regarded as an agent of the CIA, but nobody now seems much afraid of the CIA. When he heard that I was moving around, he asked my friend Chuchu, 'What's the old goat doing here?' – a fair enough question, I often asked it myself, for since the thirties I had wanted to visit Panamá – perhaps because of a romantic French novel I had read which was set in dangerous, ramshackle, poverty-ridden Colón, perhaps because even then I felt a premonition of Panamá's importance. Panamá's importance is not in fact the importance of the Canal, which becomes less and less with every year – a smaller tonnage passing, a smaller revenue, a channel too shallow and locks too narrow for the great tankers of the seventies and the aircraft carriers. The Canal is now only important as a symbol of colonialism, a narrow splinter of colonialism cutting the country in two. The situation is watched with sympathy by Venezuela, Colombia, and Peru. Panamá doesn't stand alone.

The hurried, dishonest treaty of 1904, which was signed on behalf of Panamá only by a French engineer, granted the United States all the rights, power, and authority within the Zone 'which the United States would possess and exercise if it were the sovereign of the territory . . . to the entire exclusion of the exercise by the Republic of Panamá of any such sovereign rights, power or authority.' Imagine yourself a Panamanian suspected of a crime in the Zone; you can under the law of the United States be hauled off for trial in New Orleans even though your home is on the other side of the street in which you were arrested, beyond a boundary line less visible than a traffic line.

After the riots of 1964 when eighteen Panamanians lost their lives and millions of dollars of property were burned, President Johnson promised the abrogation of the old treaty: a new one would be signed which would integrate the Zone with the Republic and recognize Panamá's sovereignty. That was twelve years ago. The Arias oligarchy which had ruled Panamá since 1903 were in no hurry – their fortunes rested in the United States. In 1968 the young colonel Omar Torrijos, with a right-wing colleague, Colonel Boris Martinez, made a military coup d'état which rid the country of the oligarchy; a year later Martinez followed old Arias to Miami, and four years ago General Torrijos, the chief of state, held conversations with Kissinger, which led like so many of Kissinger's conversations only to more conversations. Once again last December a delegation arrived for talks, as usual led by Mr Ellsworth Bunker, the former ambassador in South Vietnam: they stayed for the inside of a week on the pleasant tourist island of Contadura where it had become a habit to hold such parleys, then they went home.

The diplomats, of course, are always reassuring: to Mr Aquino Boyd, the foreign minister, Mr Bunker is an 'old acquaintance' (old indeed, he is well over eighty). Gloria Emerson in her admirable book on Vietnam, *Winners and Losers*, writes less reassuringly of Mr Bunker. 'For seven years he had never faltered in supporting and augmenting American policy in Vietnam. He was thought of – in the kindest terms – as a fierce, brilliant, cold, stubborn man.' To the Vietnamese he was known as 'The Refrigerator'.

The appointment of Mr Vance, the new secretary of state, has been welcomed too for a rather odd reason – he was in Panamá when the 1964 riots raged. He was hidden for his own safety and smuggled out a very frightened man. He had seen what could happen suddenly in Panamá.

Kissinger in his talks recognized in his tactical way the principal points for discussion (the mere fact of any talks at all worried the inhabitants of the Zone). Here are the most important:

Complete Panamanian sovereignty over the Canal by the year 2000.

Reduction of American bases from fourteen to three.

An increasing share by Panamá in the running and the defense of the Canal.

Panamanian law to be introduced as soon as possible into the Zone.

Neutralization of the Canal to be mutually agreed in time of war.

The question now, after twelve years of talks, is how much longer they will go on. 1965 to 1977 is a long time. General Torrijos said to me, 'The year 1977 will exhaust our patience and their excuses.' After the mild student riots last October he announced, 'If the students break into the Zone again I have only the alternative of crushing them or leading them. I will not crush them.' He has also said, 'I don't want to enter history. I want to enter the Canal Zone.'

Panamá is not an insignificant banana republic with politicians and presidents up for sale, nor is General Torrijos in any way a typical military dictator. Panamá is dangerous and so is Torrijos, a man fighting to exercise prudence as Fidel Castro advised him, but a man bored with prudence – you can see it in the lines of weariness around the eyes, the sudden wicked smile which greets a phrase that pleases him ('You can choose your enemies, but you can't choose your friends'). There are many in Panamá who say that no treaty signed with the United States can be a good treaty. Chuchu, a professor of mathematics and yet a sergeant in the special guerrilla force, the Machos de Monte (The Wild Pigs), and one of the general's security guard, burst out rashly in the general's presence, 'I want a confrontation, not a treaty,' then looked nervously across at the general, where he lay resting in his hammock. The general said, 'I am of your opinion.'

The first time I met General Torrijos was in the house of one of his friends, my first day in Panamá. He was in his dressing gown and his underpants, and he regarded me with some suspicion. I was a writer and, therefore, I must be an intellectual. The son of a teacher, he had left home at the age of seventeen and gone to a military academy in Salvador. He likes romantic poetry and the novels of Marquez. Sometimes a touch of poetry appears unexpectedly and unnoticed by himself when he speaks. 'Intellectuals,' he said, 'are like fine glass, crystal glass, which can be cracked by a sound. Panamá is rock and earth.'

I found myself telling him of my great-uncle dead in St Kitt's at the age of nineteen, leaving thirteen children behind him, and he relaxed and we spent the day together after flying out to Contadura where Mr Bunker is so much at home. If the French had built the Canal, the general said, there would have been no problem, de Gaulle would have returned it. He began to describe the grass-roots democracy which he had substituted for the rule of the oligarchy, but broke off, 'You will understand it better if you see it in action.' He spoke of a village he had visited where he had found the grass uncut in the cemetery. Then he knew it was a bad village. 'If you don't look after the dead you won't look after the living.'

Death I was to find lies very close to him. Although he has a wife, to whom he has been married for twenty-five years, and women please him ('When one is young,' he said, 'one eats anything. Now,' he added sadly, 'one distinguishes'), he suffers from loneliness. He hates to eat alone. Once I sat with him while he ate (I had already had my lunch); it was as though he were performing a duty as rapidly as possible – a man in a hurry. He said he had premonitions of death, violent death. He seldom dreamed, but when he did, his dreams were bad. 'I see my father across the street. There is a lot of traffic between us and I am afraid he will try to join me. I call out to him. I ask him, "What is death like?" but I never hear his answer. I wake up.' Always when night comes he feels depression, but the sunrise cures it.

Death for him is not something to be avoided, so that he is a problem to his security guard. Once flying with me in his small plane to a meeting of peasant farmers he told me with satisfaction, 'You can tell today we have a young pilot – inexperienced – because he is flying over the sea. The older ones hug the land because it's safer in a small plane. Sometimes when I know that my pilot will refuse to take me by some route because of the weather, I ask for a young one who won't know better.' All the week the general drinks nothing but water and then on Saturday nights he gives himself up to serious drinking – Black Label, then water again all the long week. On one occasion he said to me, 'Like you I am self-destructive,' but I am not sure what he meant.

There is a charisma of rhetoric – Castro and Churchill are obvious examples. Torrijos is totally unaware of his different charisma – the charisma of desperation. To be only forty-eight and yet to feel time running out – not in action but in prudence: to be establishing a new system of government, edging slowly towards socialism, which requires of him almost infinite patience (and yet on his travels he hasn't the patience to take a canoe or wait for a bridge over a river – he swims across): to live day by day with the Canal problem, dreaming, as a soldier, of the simple confrontation of violence and yet acting all the same with the damnable long-drawn-out prudence Fidel advised. . . . He said to me once, 'And I thought when I had the power I would be free.'

Will he have the time to establish this popular democracy? In England I think, more than ever before, we are prepared to recognize other forms of democracy, even under a military chief of state, than the Parliamentary, which worked satisfactorily for about a hundred years in the special circumstances of those hundred years. In the Assembly of the Panamá Republic there are 505 representatives elected by regional votes. In order to stand for election a candidate must have at least twenty-five letters of support. The representatives meet only once a year for a month in the capital to report on their regions and to vote on legislation. The rest of the time they have to live with their electors and their problems. (No weekend 'surgery' in the English fashion for them. I have an impression there is a bigger turn-over of representatives than of MPs.) A Legislative Council of about fifteen members tours the regions during the year and discusses legislation on which the Assembly will vote.

Ministers are appointed by the chief of state – this was why Torrijos smiled when I said a man could choose his enemies but not his friends, for there are reactionaries among his ministers chosen for tactical reasons. The general, like his Legislative Council, is constantly on the move, listening to the complaints, carrying with him the ministers concerned who have to reply to the people. The system may well work in Panamá, a small country. It is closer to the democracy of the Agora than to the democracy of the House of Commons – not for that reason to be despised.

I went to one such meeting in El Chorillo, one of the poorest parts of Panamá City. The representative spoke at inordinate length – complaints reached down even to the slack behavior of the man in charge of the local swimming baths. You could see how bored the general was by the way he twisted the cigar in his mouth – one of the good Havanas provided for him by Castro with his name on the band. One thought of all the hours of meetings like this he must suffer as he moved around the country. Propaganda posters hung on the walls – 'Omar has his ideal – total liberation. They have not yet launched a projectile which can kill an ideal.' 'The country with a fifth frontier.' 'El Chorillo – the Avenue of the Martyrs.' (It was in Chorillo, which abuts on the Canal Zone, that many students lost their lives in 1964.)

Everyone in the crowded hall was glad when the representative left the podium. The meeting sprang to life. A colored girl, dragging an old quiet woman in her wake, shrieked like a Voodoo dancer and flung her arms around her head – the old lady was seventy-six and still working for the government and she had no pension. The points of the speeches now were underlined by the drums of supporters and that made the scene even more Haitian. A Negro speaker talked with great dignity and confidence and fire. 'We have the moral authority of those who work for low wages.' Again and again the Zone cropped up in his speech – 'We are waiting to go in, we are with you, you only have to give the order,' and all the drums rolled. The general no longer twisted his cigar.

An important complaint emerged. A number of high-rise flats had been built with the inevitable sabotage of lifts and windows that we have experienced in England and in France. High-rise flats are for the rich who can escape their isolation, not for the poor. Moreover the charge for these flats was beyond their means, so that they were in debt. There was a deposit of 500 dollars and a rent of 250 dollars a month when the average wage was 150 dollars. The general told his minister of housing to reply and a very bad job he made of it. The general asked for more information. A girl spoke up with anger, a woman had hysterics, the drums beat. There were complaints about the health service – the minister of health indignantly defended his doctors. He made a better impression than the minister of housing. A young magistrate demanded better security in the streets. The hours passed. The general was balanced on the giddy edge of the platform, a glass of water in his hand, a swim of faces close below him – not much security there. The chief of staff sat immobile on the platform, chewing gum like an American colonel.

It was the general's first meeting in the slums of Chorillo, and Chorillo was going to have its say. The faces might appear fierce and fanatical and angry, but they were friendly. 'We know you very well here, general. We see you driving by every week to buy your lottery tickets.' Laughter and the drums laughed too.

Afterward, a rumor was spread by one who had attended the meeting and knew it was a lie that the general had been drunk with vodka and fallen off the platform. One chooses one's enemies . . . .

Another meeting – this time in the country without his ministers. There was no platform. We sat and stood in a circle. The general began with an interruption. 'No, let's leave the most difficult thing to the last and deal first with the easy ones.' A new bridge to be built, a new road, the position of a new lime plant to be decided. The last item was the most important. The yucca farmers were claiming a higher price for their yucca, and the general had told me on the way, 'I'm going to grant it. This yucca center was a mistake – our mistake. Anyway I want to redistribute money – more to the country and less to the towns. All the same I'll keep them guessing.'

The banana workers are strongly behind the government ever since the successful 'banana war' against United Brands waged by Panamá in isolation – her allies had been bought off one by one, but the peasants are another matter. Their eyes are fanatic and amused as though they are thinking. 'We know what we want and we can see through you.' At the meeting they were all wearing the same round straw hats balanced on their protuberant ears; they follow the same drinking habits as the general except that they are inclined to begin after early Mass on Sunday. When drunk they bark like dogs.

On the road in the country one Sunday evening Chuchu had bought enough leather in a village store for two pairs of sandals, and the leather was being soaked and cut to fit our feet by a family we had found along the road. Suddenly we heard the barking. You would have taken it for two angry dogs if you had not been warned. Two peasants just able to stand came staggering into the yard. One adopted me and knelt beside me, clasping my hand – he said he wanted to talk about 'Religión'. He said it was the only subject he wanted to talk about – he was a Catholic, but he didn't much care for the priest who was too materialist. Religión was the only thing he was interested in. Was I a gringo? No, I wasn't a gringo. I was English. Was I católico? Yes, I was católico. Then we must talk about Religión. The other one, after a spell of barking, preferred to sing – he wanted our names so that he could introduce them into his improvised songs. The sandals took an hour and a half to make, so there was plenty of time for songs and religión – and politics. I wanted to know how they regarded the general.

'Half good and half bad.'

'What is the bad half?'

'He doesn't like the gringos.'

'What do you think about the Zone?'

'We are not interested in the Zone.'

'Why do you like the gringos?'

The Peace Corps had been expelled by the general, but at least in this poor area near Las Minas one of them had made converts. 'He was a good man. He taught us many things. And he drank with us.'

357

I told the general as we went to the meeting. He said, 'They are afraid for their land. They think Panamá is going to belong either to the States or to Russia and they prefer the States.'

At the meeting the same fanatical knowing faces formed a background. One of the faces smiled and winked at me. Was it one of the barkers?

A comedy was played on both sides, the peasants fierce and persistent, the general apparently stubborn. Who was going to provide the money? It would have to come out of the pocket of others. The rise they were demanding was too much. The general began to haggle, and the farmers began to see what he was at – now they argued with half-smiles and disputed with cracks of humor. Suddenly he gave way. There was laughter and claps. They had got what they wanted. Perhaps above all they had had fun.

Certainly Panamá is not the Canal, and the Zone is a whole world away from Panamá. You can tell the moment you enter the Zone from the well-built houses and the trim lawns. You feel the jungle has been held back by a battalion of lawn mowers. There are golf courses in plenty.

And the wind shall say: Here were decent godless people:
Their only monument the asphalt road
And a thousand lost golf balls.

Cross the street from the Colón side (Panamá) to the Cristóbal side (the Zone) and you are in another world – no wooden houses with balconies, dating from the days of the French canal, picturesque to those of us who don't live in them, and no horrifying poverty. I was told a story, perhaps exaggerated but nearly believable in Colón, of a child taken to the hospital after he had begun to eat his own fingers from hunger. Crime in Cristóbal is well under control. In Colón a friend and I were walking up the long and almost empty street leading toward the old elegant Washington Hotel when we were stopped by a Panamá police patrol and bundled into a police van for the last two hundred yards. 'This street is dangerous,' they said. 'You are carrying cameras. We've already shot two men this week who were knifing tourists.' We had been directed on our way by a photographic store in the same street – perhaps later they hoped to get our cameras cheap.

Another contrast. I went to a demonstration in a stadium in the Canal Zone only a few hundred yards away from the meeting in Chorillo. A police officer, Mr Drummond, was meant to be the star. He had issued a writ on constitutional grounds against Ford and Kissinger for holding talks on a new treaty without first getting the approval of Congress. Then his car had been destroyed by a bomb in mysterious circumstances. This gave an impression that he was a dangerous man whose life was in danger, an impression not borne out by the demonstration. Mr Drummond had the thinnest legs, bandaged in tight brown trousers, of any man I have ever seen. When he stood up to speak – very uninspiringly – one leg seemed to lean against the other for support, or perhaps to make music like a grasshopper.

Isolated by the arc lights in the middle of the stadium he was supported by a little group of men and women who looked like a committee elected to arrange Christmas entertainments. They spoke in turn, throwing back at Chorillo *their* slogans, but unaided by drum beats they seemed to get lost in the night air before they reached the audience. Only one blue-haired old lady, like a Universal Aunt, got some energy into 'God and Country' . . . 'Eighth Wonder of the World' . . . 'We left our country and our home life' . . . 'No desire to live under a repressive form of government' . . . 'The Canal can't be worked without a US Zone and US laws' . . . 'The Zone's got to be incorporated into the Union like the Virgin Islands.' The audience cheered sometimes but not often, usually when the speakers attacked their fellow countrymen.

They used Christian names like pejoratives. 'Jerry' was a traitor, 'Henry' was a traitor – they could find no term bad enough to describe the State Department, perhaps because it hadn't got a Christian name. They looked very lost and lonely in the vast stadium in the hot and humid night, and one felt a little sorry for them. God and Country would probably let them down just as Jerry and Henry had. A young woman asked the audience to send letters and 'clippings' to congressmen. 'I can supply you with their telephone numbers.' She wasn't as impressive as the Negro in Chorillo.

They too looked on 1977 as a critical year, but confrontation in their eyes was a simple affair of flying in reinforcements from Fort Bragg. Perhaps they had been encouraged by the mildness of the riots last October which had been intended to prove that Panamá was ungovernable. They didn't know that the general had fifteen days' warning of what was planned through a CIA agent who squealed under pressure. (Forty students were lodged for the day in prison and lectured on political problems.)

A confrontation means war – a war between the tiny Republic and the United States, but the smaller the country the greater the shame and the humiliation of even a temporary reverse. Is the Canal Zone worth the shame?

The Panamanians are not romantic. There is a hard cynical streak which you can find in their popular songs – 'Your love is a yesterday's newspaper', and the slogans on the beautifully painted buses – 'Don't get dressed because you are not going'. They estimate their chances in an armed confrontation realistically: they believe they could hold the city of Panamá for two or three days and temporarily close both ends of the Canal. After that it would be guerrilla war for which Panamá is peculiarly suited: the Central Cordilleras rise to 3,000 meters and extend to the Costa Rican frontier on one size of the Zone and the dense Darién jungle, almost as unknown as in the days of Balboa, crossed only by smugglers' paths, stretches on the other side to the Colombian border. Here they believe they could hold out for two years – long enough to rouse the conscience of the world and American public opinion. For the first time since the Civil War American civilians will be in the firing line – there are 40,000 of them in the Zone.

There are areas of jungle inside the Zone itself where the Americans train their own special troops, as well as troops from other Latin American states, in guerrilla warfare. The Panamanians, rightly or wrongly, regard this training school with some contempt. The general goes out on training patrols himself twice a month, and the special brigade, the Machos de Monte, believe themselves second to none. Recently when the Americans were holding jungle maneuvers inside the Zone they were surprised to encounter a Panamanian patrol who had penetrated the Zone unobserved because as they explained with courtesy something had gone wrong with their compass.

Morale is high. There is a song I have heard the recruits singing at the run. No one wrote the song: it is improvised a little by every squad to go with the beat of the feet. The theme is this:

I remember that January 9 when they massacred my people, students armed only with stones and sticks, but I am a man now and I carry a gun. Give the order, my general, and we will go into the Zone, we will push them into the water, where the sharks can eat *mucho Yanqui, mucho Yanqui.*

> *Los bottaron*
> *De Vietnam*
> *Los tenemos*
> *Ahora en Cuba*
> *Dales, Cuba*
> *Dales duro*
> *Panamá*
> *Dales duro*
> *Venezuela*
> *Dales duro*
> *Puerto Rico*
> *Dales duro*

It is not a nationalist song, it is a revolutionary song for Latin America. That is the strength of Panamá's position. She represents more than the Isthmus.

And the weakness? The old man Arias, exiled and intriguing in Miami, hardly counts, nor do the Cuban refugees and their car bombs. The Communist party supports the general in his moderate approach to socialism. The danger comes as it did in Chile from two directions – the impatience of the extreme left, who will sup even with the devil to gain their ends, and corruption in the higher ranks of the army. Junior officers are mainly promoted from the ranks and can be relied on. It is accepted that some senior officers have their privileges and their pickings. Otherwise they would turn to the CIA.

Negotiations were symbolically re-opened for a few days before Christmas when Mr Bunker arrived with his troupe. Let us hope they were genuine. My personal fear is that the ball may be kept in the air with a purpose – a little concession here, a little concession there – while underground money passes, promises are made. General Torrijos in seven years has given Panamá a national pride. It would be a tragedy for Latin America if he fell a victim to the impatience of the left or the chicanery of the right. A guerrilla war is less to be feared than the sudden limited violence which kills one man and solves nothing. As Chuchu said, as he regretfully laid the revolver, which he always carried in his pocket on our travels, down on his bedside table, 'A revolver is no defense.'

New York Review
17 February 1977

Narayan's India Revisited

There are writers – Tolstoy and Henry James to name two – whom we hold in awe, writers – Turgenev and Chekhov – for whom we feel a personal affection, other writers whom we respect – Conrad for example – but who hold us at a long arm's length with their 'courtly foreign grace'. Narayan (whom I don't hesitate to name in such a context) more than any of them wakes in me a spring of gratitude, for he has offered me a second home. Without him I could never have known what it is like to be Indian. Kipling's India is the romantic playground of the Raj. I am touched nearly to tears by his best story, *Without Benefit of Clergy,* and yet the tears don't actually fall – I cannot believe in his Indian characters and even Kim leaves me sceptical. Kipling romanticizes the Indian as much as he romanticizes the administrators of Empire. E. M. Forster was funny and tender about his friend the Maharajah of Dewas and severely ironic about the English in India, but India escaped him all the same. He wrote of *A Passage to India*: 'I tried to show that India is an unexplainable muddle by introducing an unexplainable muddle.' No one could find a second home in Kipling's India or Forster's India.

Perhaps no one can write in depth about a foreign country – he can only write about the effect of that country on his own fellow countrymen, living as exiles, or government servants, or visitors. He can only 'touch in' the background of the foreign land. In Kipling and Forster the English are always posturing nobly and absurdly in the foreground; in Narayan's novels, though the Raj still existed during the first dozen years of his literary career, the English characters are peripheral. They are amiable enough (Narayan, unlike Mulk Raj Anand, is hardly touched by politics), but hopelessly unimportant like Professor Brown in *The Bachelor of Arts*. How Kipling would have detested Narayan's books, even that Indian 'twang' which lends so much charm to his style.

> ' "Excuse me. I made a vow never to touch alcohol in my life, before my mother," said Chandran. This affected Kailas profoundly. He remained solemn for a moment and said: "Then don't. Mother is a sacred object. It is a commodity whose value we don't realize as long as it is with us. One must lose it to know what a precious possession it is. If I had had my mother I should have studied in a college and become a respectable person. You wouldn't find me here. After this where do you think I'm going?" "I don't know."
>
> ' "To the house of a prostitute." He remained reflective for a moment and said with a sigh: "As long as my mother lived she said every minute 'Do this don't do that'. And I remained a good son to her. The moment she died I changed. It is a rare commodity, sir. Mother is a rare commodity."'

The town of Malgudi came into my life some time in the early thirties. I knew nothing then of the author who had recently, I learned later from his autobiography, thrown up a teaching job in a distant town and taken the bus back to his home in Mysore – back to the world of Malgudi – where without premeditation he began his first novel, *Swami and Friends,* without knowing from one day to another what was to happen to his characters next. I too was working, in a flat in Oxford, on a novel called *It's a Battlefield* which I felt already doomed to unpopularity.

'Soon after morning coffee and bath' – it is Narayan in Laxmipuram – 'I took my umbrella and started out for a walk. I needed the umbrella to protect my head from the sun. Sometimes I carried a pen and pad and sat down under the shade of a tree at the foot of Chanundi Hill and wrote. Some days I took out a cycle and rode ten miles along the Karapur Forest Road, sat on a wayside culvert, and wrote or brooded over life and literature, watching some peasant ploughing his field, with a canal flowing glitteringly in the sun.'

I was struggling at the same time to follow the movements of my characters through the streets of Battersea and Bloomsbury and along the reach of Euston Road. We had both been born under the sign of Libra, so if one believes in astrology, as Narayan, who once supplied me with my horoscope, certainly does, we were destined by the stars to know each other. One day an Indian friend of mine called Purna brought me a rather travelled and weary typescript – a novel written by a friend of his – and I let it lie on my desk for weeks unread until one rainy day . . . I didn't know that it had been rejected by half-a-dozen publishers and that Purna had been told by the author not to return it to Mysore but to weight it with a stone and drop it into the Thames. Anyway Narayan and I had been brought together (I half believe myself in the stars that ruled over an Indian and an English Libra birth). I was able to find a publisher for *Swami*, and Malgudi was born, the Mempe Forest and Nallappa's Grove, the Albert Mission School, Market Road, the River Sarayu – all that region of the imagination which seems to me now more familiar than Battersea or the Euston Road.

In the eleven novels which extend from *Swami and Friends* to *The Painter of Signs* Narayan has never, I think, strayed far from Malgudi, though a character may sometimes disappear for ever into India, like Rajam, friend of the schoolboy Swami, simply by taking a train. Year by year Narayan has peopled Malgudi with characters we never forget. In his second novel – a very funny and happy book – there is Chandran, little more than a schoolboy, whom we leave at the end of *The Bachelor of Arts* in a bubble of excitement at a marriage which has been arranged with the help of a dubious, even dishonest, horoscope. In his third book, *The English Teacher,* the marriage ends in death and Narayan shows how far he has grown as a writer to encompass the sadness and loss. In *The Dark Room* the screw of unhappiness is twisted further, the killing of love more tragic than the death of love.

Narayan himself had known the death of love, and *The English Teacher* is dedicated to his dead wife. It took some years before a degree of serenity and humour returned to Malgudi with *The Financial Expert* and his 'office' under a banyan tree, with Mr Sampath, the over-optimistic film producer, the sweet vendor's son Mali and his novel writing machine, Raman, the sign painter who was lured by love of Daisy from his proper work to make propaganda in the countryside for birth control and sterilization, the bullying taxidermist, Vasu, in *The Man-eater of Malgudi*, perhaps Narayan's best comic character.

Something had permanently changed in Narayan after *The Bachelor of Arts*, the writer's personal tragedy has been our gain. Sadness and humour in the later books go hand in hand like twins, inseparable, as they do in the stories of Chekhov. Perhaps if we had read more closely we should have seen that the shadow had been there from the beginning. A writer in some strange way knows his own future – his end is in his beginning, as it is in the pages of a horoscope, and the schoolboy Swami, watching the friend with whom he had needlessly quarrelled, vanish into the vast unknown spaces of India, had already experienced a little of what Krishna came to feel as he watched his beloved wife die of typhoid. One is tempted to exclaim: Isn't the imaginative experience enough? Why should the author have had to suffer in himself the agony of his characters?

A new introduction to *The Bachelor of Arts* by R. K. Narayan 1978

The Great Spectacular

The Great Spectacular – the signing of the Panama Treaty – is over and there will be no general distribution. I had seen nothing like it since *Around the World in Eighty Days*. All the familiar actors from how many television screens and newspaper photographs seemed to be there – all except Elizabeth Taylor. Kissinger, before the delegations settled into their seats, could be seen buttonholing his way around the hall of the Organization of American States with his world-wide grin: five rows in front of me I could see Nelson Rockefeller being strenuously amiable to Lady Bird, as though the two of them were sitting out a dance together, ex-President Ford more blond than I had imagined him from the screen – or had he been to the barber? There too were Mr and Mrs Mondale, Mrs Carter. Two rows in front of me sat Andy Young, bright and boyish. All of them looked strikingly unimportant, like the stars in *Around the World*. They were not there to act, only to be noticed, party-goers having a night out together, pleased to feel at home with friendly faces – 'What, *you* here?'

The real character actors were all up on the platform – an unpleasant sight but more impressive than the stars below: General Stroessner of Paraguay, whom I had last seen in uniform one National Day in Asuncion saluting the cripples of the Bolivian war as they wheeled by and the colonels stood stiffly upright in their cars like ninepins in a bowling alley (he had reminded me then of some flushed owner of a German *Bierstube*, and in civilian clothes he looked more than ever the part); General Videla of Argentina with a face squashed so flat there was hardly room for his two foxy eyes; General Banzer of Bolivia, a little frightened man with a small agitated mustache – he would have looked more like a dictator if he had worn a uniform, he had been miscast and misdressed; there too was the greatest character actor of them all – General Pinochet himself, the man you love to hate. Like Boris Karloff he had really attained the status of instant recognition, he was the one who could look down with amused contempt at the highly paid frivolous Hollywood types below him. His chin was so deeply sunk in his collar he seemed to have no neck at all; he had clever, humorous, falsely good-fellow eyes which seemed to tell us all not to take too seriously all those stories of murder and torture. (A week before I had listened in Panamá to an Argentine refugee. She broke down as she described how a bayonet had been thrust into her vagina.)

Pinochet, I feel sure, knew that he dominated the scene – he was the only one people were protesting about with banners in the streets of Washington – perhaps they couldn't spell Stroessner's name and they couldn't remember Banzer's. Pinochet was tactful, he didn't wave to his ally Kissinger down below, and Kissinger never looked up at him. Then we all stood for the national anthems as Carter and General Torrijos entered to sign the treaty, a bit shop-soiled since it had been fingered and corrected for thirteen years, ever since negotiations began after the riots of 1964, when Torrijos was an unknown young officer in the Guardia Nacional and Lyndon Johnson was alive and nobody dreamt of Nixon, Ford, or Carter. Yet I feel sure I was not the only one who continued to watch Pinochet. Like Karloff he didn't need to have a speaking part – he didn't even need to grunt.

Carter looked miserably unhappy. He made a banal little speech and was almost inaudible from five rows back in spite of all the microphones. I happened by a quirk of fate to be a member of the Panamanian delegation (we were a mixed bag including, as well as ministers and negotiators, a student leader and the mother of a student killed by American troops in the riot of '64, as well as the Colombian novelist Gabriel García Márquez, author of *A Hundred Years of Solitude*). Remembering how once I was deported from Puerto Rico I savored a gentle revenge when I arrived in Washington with a Panamanian passport. I felt proud too as a temporary Panamanian of General Torrijos who spoke in a voice with a cutting edge very unlike Carter's. He began abruptly (no conventional 'Mr President, Your Excellencies, etc.') so that even the stars began to listen – it sounded for a moment as though he were attacking the very treaty he was about to sign. 'The treaty is very satisfactory, vastly advantageous to the United States, and we must confess not so advantageous to Panamá.' A pause and Torrijos added, 'Secretary of State Hay. 1903.'

It was a good joke to play on the senators, who were there in force, but it was a good deal more than a joke. Torrijos was signing the new treaty with reluctance; he had said himself it was only 'to save the lives of 40,000 young Panamanians'. Two clauses of the treaty particularly stuck in his gullet; the delay till the year 2000 for Panamanian control of the Canal and the clause which would allow the United

States to intervene even after that date if the Canal's neutrality were endangered. He will not, I think, be entirely unhappy if the Senate refuses to ratify the treaty; he will be left then with the simple solution of violence which has often been in his mind, with desire and apprehension balanced as in a sexual encounter. I asked him before he left for Washington if the long-drawn negotiations had affected his dreams. He told me that on the last night of the negotiations he had dreamt that guerrilla war had begun and he found himself in the jungle without his boots. There was nothing to be done without boots, and he felt a horrible humiliation because he would be captured in the first hours of the war.

The United States is lucky to be dealing with Torrijos, a patriot and an idealist without a formal ideology, except a general preference for left over right and a scorn for bureaucrats. His position is a difficult one; for he is a lonely man without the base of a political party, and the old parties continue to exist in the shadow – the Christian Democrats consisting of the bourgeoisie who hate him, the Communists who give him at the moment a reluctant tactical support, the extreme left groups who are all against the treaty (ironically for much the same reason as the General). Some opponents have been exiled to Miami, which is known in Panama as the Valley of the Fallen, but there are no political prisoners, and unobtrusively Torrijos gives aid to many political refugees from Chile and Argentina.

The General is popular in the countryside (especially with the children), he can trust the younger officers of the Guardia Nacional, and he can depend on the elite of the army, the Wild Pigs, trained in guerrilla fighting, with whom he goes on strenuous maneuvers twice a month. About some senior officers of the Guardia one must speak with more caution. If the treaty is not ratified Panamá will need the General, and his position and his popularity will be secure. If the treaty is ratified, the General's future and Panamá's future are more dubious.

With ratification more than three hundred square miles of valuable real estate will be returned immediately to Panama – and a great deal of cash. Plenty of pockets are ready to be lined. Their owners are not interested in the General's plans for free school meals and free milk for all children (the General's father was a schoolteacher), for the elimination of the slums of Colón and Panamá City, and pleasure parks for the poor who are now condemned to spend their free hours in such horrifying districts as the one in the city ironically known as Hollywood where for safety a visitor needs a resident to guide him.

Addressing the banana workers on a plantation Torrijos told them, 'I have no intention of exchanging coffee-colored landlords for white landlords,' but the landlords of Panamá City – and they include some high army officers – are likely to have other ideas. The General's life if the treaty is ratified will be a poor risk for an insurance company, for he is not a man who can be flown, like a politician, to Miami. No wonder he dreams a good deal of death, and his dreams are reflected in his eyes.

There were eight other generals of the hemisphere on the platform to watch Torrijos sign this treaty which he didn't like, and I think many demonstrators in Washington confused them together – they were all generals, they were all in some way dictators, a protest against Pinochet was a protest against the whole lot. Torrijos was well aware of that danger.

He had wanted only the more reputable leaders to be present, the presidents of Colombia, Venezuela, and Peru, who had given him active support. Carter insisted on inviting all the members of the OAS, so that Fidel Castro became perforce a notable absentee (as we flew from Panama over Cuba the General radioed him a friendly message).

Carter's insistence was a triumph for Pinochet, and an embarrassment for Torrijos. After the signing of the treaty Carter and Torrijos set off down the platform in opposite directions to greet the heads of state. An embrace is the usual greeting in the southern hemisphere, and I noticed how Torrijos embraced the leaders of Colombia, Venezuela, and Peru and confined himself to a formal handshake with Bolivia and Argentina as he worked down the row toward Pinochet. But Pinochet had noticed that, and his eyes gleamed with amusement. When his turn came he grasped the hand of Torrijos and flung his arm around his shoulder. If any journalist's camera had clicked at that moment it would be thought that Torrijos had embraced Pinochet.

New York Review
26 January 1978

Freedom of Thought

Before I speak of this prize with which you are honouring me, I want to express my joy of finding myself again in Jerusalem after nearly fourteen years. I came first in 1967, a few months after your Six Day War and I was very aware of the physical and spiritual scars. Today I find almost unbelievable changes in Jerusalem. New buildings in Arab and Jewish sections, which conform to the beauty of the city, unlike the new high-rise buildings which rise in European cities and diminish their character. I have heard in an Arab school from the masters themselves of the great growth in Arab education and certainly the school I visited would have been the pride of any European town. Where in 1967 I was aware too often of a latent hatred, I have felt nothing of the kind in 1981 among the few Palestinians I have had the pleasure of meeting. They have been frank and outspoken without rancour.

But surely, if anyone deserves this prize for the defence of the individual in society it is the Mayor of Jerusalem, Teddy Kollek. He has defended the individual irrespective of race. He is constructing a better world in terms of stone and trees and even sewage. More endurable than a writer's words.

That is one thing which embarrasses me about the honour

I have been given. Another, the names of my predecessors, a number of whom I have known and admired. They have spoken up in situations far more dangerous than I have had to encounter. Ignazio Silone against the Fascists, Borges against the Peronists. You probably know the story of how a telephone rang in Borges' apartment in Buenos Aires after the return of Peron. His old mother answered. A voice said, 'We are coming to kill you and your son.' She replied, 'It will be easy for you to kill my son because he is blind, but for me you will have to come quickly for I am 90 years old.' Like mother, like son.

But perhaps what strikes me more than anything about this honour is the generosity of spirit it shows in the judges. The tortuous history of English relations with Israel during the period of the Mandate, a muddle and a timidity which can be as cruel as any tyranny, is not one of which an Englishman can be proud. Nor is the history of the Roman Catholic Church in relation to Jewry one of which a Roman Catholic can be proud. Robert Browning wrote a scathing poem called 'Holy Cross Day' about a ceremony which Jews were forced to attend in Rome – an annual Christian sermon. It was left to Pius XII in our twentieth-century to make a claim which I would have thought obvious enough that Christians were spiritual Semites; for isn't our whole religion founded on what we call the Old Testament, even if in Jewish eyes we are heretics? Yet you have the generosity to award this prize to one who is both an Englishman and a Roman Catholic.

There is only one other prize which I value nearly as highly as the one you are giving me today. That prize takes the form of a collection of essays written in French and English printed in Haiti, in 1968, by Doctor Duvalier under the title *Graham Greene démasqué, Graham Greene finally exposed*, and I will quote from it if only to show the kind of man you are honouring: 'A timid personality . . . an unbalanced perverted writer . . . a negrophobe . . . a drug addict . . . the spy of an Imperialist power . . . the shame of proud and noble England . . . a torturer'. I would have thought that as a torturer I would have been certainly disqualified from receiving this prize.

Why do I feel honoured as a writer by this exposure? Because it shows that writers, even novelists, bear arms. They have their own weapon, a silver bullet which they can use on behalf of individuals against men in power – and power as we know tends to corrupt. The prize which you are giving me has inevitably political connotations, for the men in power are as a rule politicians though not always – they can be criminals and they can be religious leaders. The Pope, whatever Stalin thought, has his divisions, but in our defence of the individual we should not forget a theologian like Father Hans Kung when we find him at odds with the Roman Curia. He is not in danger of death or a labour camp or a psychiatric hospital, but all the same . . . A defence of the individual includes a defence of his family rights, and that may well put us in opposition to Papal rulings on contraception. We must remember when we listen to the Pope's pronouncements on the subject that the Papal Commission on Contraception in 1966 came to this conclusion – nine Cardinals and Bishops found that contraception was not a moral question and only two voted the other way. With all respect the price of liberty in a Church as much as in a State is eternal vigilance.

Perhaps history will find that we have been over-preoccupied with the two great national powers – the interminable conflict between Russia and the United States, West against East, the gulags of Russia measured against the death squads in El Salvador, Guatemala and Argentina, death squads which now seem to be winning the support of the United States. In the long run political dogmas and religious dogmas are not perhaps the worst danger to the individual. In politics and religion doubt and disillusion eventually set in. The ideas of Marx wear out. Papal pronouncements are subtly modified. Even the international terrorist movement has its dissidents, Gaddafi will not live forever. We are saved by a kind of agnosticism. I have a number of Communist friends in Russia, Poland, Hungary, and I have found in many of them a silent but quite visible reaction, as though I had touched a hidden nerve, when I quote some lines of the great Victorian poet of agnosticism, Clough:

> *Of all the people under heaven's high scope,*
> *They are most hopeless who had once most hope,*
> *And the most wretched who had most believed.*

We must not with honesty be too self-righteous about the Communist society. There is injustice too in Western Europe, in our democracies which is not dependent on dogma, against which the silver bullet of the writer is almost, though not altogether, powerless. Those responsible go under different names – in the United States and Italy the Mafia, in France the Milieu – in England we haven't yet found a name. This kind of injustice involves corruption in the police, even among lawyers, corruption not for an ideology which sometimes still has something of an ideal about it, but corruption by money – an oppression which means perhaps only a bribed witness, a bought lawyer, a menace of death by telephone which cannot be proved, a beaten-up woman, an appeal to the police that results in nothing, because as an honest French commissaire told a friend of mine 'Sont les grands poissons' – 'they are the great fish'. I live in the South of France and for two years I have been immersed in the same atmosphere as my own early book, *Brighton Rock*, which dealt with a city noted for its corruption. The victims have no Solzhenitsyn to describe their oppression: there is no Amnesty to take up their cause. It is left to the individual to fight alone for himself. In the words of Robert Louis Stevenson: 'With half of a broken hope for a pillow at night. That somehow the Right is the Right'. Well, I suppose thousands suffer from governments of the right and the left and only hundreds from the Mafia and the Milieu, but suffering cannot be judged in terms of quantity. The suffering of one individual is as deep as the suffering of a thousand.

One day we may be freed from the conflict of dogmas: we shall never be free from conflict with those who will do anything for money.

In the nineteen-thirties there was a general feeling among writers in favour of what was called commitment. That was because the struggle between the rights of the State and the rights of the individual was over-simplified to a commitment, natural enough, for Communism against Nazism and Fascism. Many writers joined the Communist Party, but few of them stayed the course. Today it is not a question of a simple alternative – not even the alternative between socialism and capitalism. There are degrees of socialism and degrees of capitalism and I hope and believe there are degrees of Communism. It is now more than ever necessary for the writer (of course I am thinking mainly of the novelist) to be un–committed to all except the one principle of the socialist Thomas Paine: 'We must guard even our enemies against injustice'. As a Roman Catholic I thank God for the heretics. Heresy is only another word for freedom of thought.

Address given upon the award of the Jerusalem Prize in Israel
Spectator
18 April 1981

Freedom of Information

One idle moment it occurred to me that I might find some
amusement and even a little instruction by applying through
a lawyer in the United States for the release of documents
concerning me under the Freedom of Information Act. I
certainly found some amusement, but very little instruction.
In about forty-five pages of material which were sent me,
nearly sixteen were blacked out in heavy ink. So much for
'freedom of information'.

A great many of the legible entries deal with my cousin,
Felix Greene, well known to be a friend of China. Guilt
by relationship? The press-cuttings section of the FBI had
produced a large number of pages. Five pages are given up
to a *Washington News* interview with Miss Rebecca West
on 'The Meaning of Treason'. I am honoured to find my
photograph in the company of André Gide, François
Mauriac and Evelyn Waugh: less honoured by the other
photographs of John Amery, William Joyce and Klaus Fuchs.
The last sentence of the article has been underlined: 'This
is the most devastating exposure of treachery yet made.'
Poor muddled Miss Rebecca West.

Two whole pages are devoted to a gossip column by
Walter Winchell, all for the sake of one sentence: 'Hollywood
newspapers are not happy about America's most decorated

soldier (Audie Murphy) taking the lead role in the film version of *The Quiet American* which libels Americans. The author of the book admits being an ex-Commy.' I was equally unhappy. I would have preferred a good actor. A mysterious paper called *Counter Attack: Facts to Combat Communism* honours me with a headline, 'Graham Greene and Ho Chi Chips', and in another article they quote some words I spoke in Hollywood in 1952 about the black list under the heading, 'Who is Graham Greene's informer?'

Another more intriguing memo from the FBI in 1965 to the Special Assistant to the President notes that 'Mrs Mildred Stegall has forwarded material being distributed by the Massachusetts Political Action for Peace . . . which deals with the war in Vietnam. With respect to the question whether or not the persons mentioned in the material are Communists, FBI files contain no information of a derogatory nature relative to the following individuals [blacked out]. In connection with the remainder of the individuals identified in this names check request, attached are memoranda concerning these persons, as follows: Graham Greene' – but alas, a complete blackout follows.

The authorities seem to have missed my attempt to organize a mass resignation of the foreign members of the Academy of Art and Letters as a protest against the Vietnam war, an attempt which failed. My only supporters proved to be Herbert Read and Bertrand Russell.

One press cutting from the *Miami News* of 26 July 1963 certainly interests me. It tells how a Herbert Muhammed, son of the Black Muslim leader, 'flew from Mexico City yesterday with eighty-six persons, most of them Latin-American Communists, to take part in the celebrations in Havana. One name on the passenger list was Graham Greene.

It cannot be immediately determined whether it was the English writer of that name.' It was. I wish I had known that Muhammed was on board. It would have interested me to talk with him about his father.

I am glad to find in these documents an account of my being 'placed under guard' in San Juan, Puerto Rico, and my deportation from there by Delta Airlines to Haiti, an incident which I have described in *Ways of Escape*. But they missed the fact that I refused to leave the plane when it reached Haiti and flew on free of charge to Havana, this in spite of 'local intelligence services being advised'. They print two telegrams I sent from the airport cancelling engagements, one to my friend and agent, Mary Pritchett, in New York, and one to Peter Brook in Kingston, but they have missed the third which I addressed to Reuters in London telling them of my deportation.

I am glad to see that my weight is given correctly as 180 pounds (they listed my date of birth wrong), for I had felt rather distressed reading that SAC (Special Agent in Charge) Honolulu, reporting on 26 January 1960 that I had arrived in Sydney via Fiji on the way to San Francisco, gave my weight as between 192 and 200 pounds, a considerable exaggeration. I am certain that I have never gone above 180.

Well, I can comfort myself, my watchers do make mistakes. The same report continues: 'Greene possibly identical with subject Honolulu radiogram February 13 1952 to Bureau, Los Angeles and New York, entitled Thomas Graham Greene, security matter.' Perhaps it was T. G. Greene who weighed 200 pounds. Was T.G. that Other Graham Greene who haunted my life for two decades in the fifties and sixties and whom I always failed to track down? But 'Thomas' all the same does ring a bell in my memory, for it was the extra Christian name which I chose when I was baptized a Catholic in 1927 (I explained to the priest that I was taking the name of Saint Thomas the Doubter and not of Saint Thomas Aquinas). But after looking through all these documents I doubt whether, even in the blacked-out sections, the security service of the United States were really capable of discovering my secret name.

Spectator
7 April 1984

In Memory of Borges

I would like to recount the occasion on which I met Borges. I was invited with him to lunch by my friend Victoria Ocampo, and I was dispatched to the National Library to lead him to her flat because of his blindness. Almost as soon as the door had shut behind us at the National Library, we began to talk about literature. Borges talked about the influence G. K. Chesterton had had on him and the influence Robert Louis Stevenson had had on his later stories. He spoke of the prose of Stevenson as a great influence. I then interjected a remark. Robert Louis Stevenson did write at least one good poem. A poem about his ancestors. His ancestors had built the great lighthouses on the coast of Scotland, and I knew that ancestors were an interest of Borges'. The poem began,

> Say not of me that weakly I declined
> The labours of my sires, and fled the sea,
> The towers we founded and the lamps we lit,
> To play at home with paper like a child.

It was a very noisy, crowded Buenos Aires street. Borges stopped on the edge of the pavement and recited the whole poem to me, word perfect. After an agreeable lunch, he sat on a sofa and quoted large chunks of Anglo-Saxon.

That, I'm afraid, I was not able to follow. But I looked at his eyes as he recited and I was amazed at the expression in those blind eyes. They did not look blind at all. They looked as if they were looking into themselves in some curious way, and they had great nobility.

Borges too, of course, had this feeling for ancestors, for the gauchos of the past. His later tales are full of stories of the gauchos, and in one of them he wrote, 'Just as men of certain countries worship and feel the call of the sea, we Argentines in turn yearn for the boundless plains that ring under a horse's hooves.'

He was a man of great courage. At one time, during the second period of Perón, when he was living with his old mother, there was a mysterious phone call. A male voice said, 'We're coming to kill you and your mother.' Borges' mother replied, 'I'm ninety years old, so you'd better come quickly. And as for my son, it will be easy for you, since he is blind.' This, I think, gives a picture of what the family was like.

To me, Borges speaks for all writers. Over and over again in his books, I find phrases which are my experience as a writer. He calls writing 'a guided dream', and on one occasion he wrote,

'I do not write for a select minority, which means nothing to me, nor for that adulated platonic entity known as "The Masses". Both abstractions, so dear to the demagogue, I disbelieve in. I write for myself and for my friends, and I write to ease the passing of time.'

That, I think, will make every writer feel close to him.

A talk given at the Anglo-Argentine Society, London, 1984. Extracted from *In Memory of Borges*, Edited by Norman Thomas di Giovanni.

Musings at Eighty

Being a writer is a sort of sickness, an obsession. But the writer's disease is also its own best medicine. After reworking and rewriting so much that I can scarcely decipher my own manuscript, the moment finally comes when I say, 'I have done my best.'

At its most splendid, writing can be compared to the process of sculpting. It begins with shaping, and then there is much reshaping, and at some point the manuscript reaches the stage at which I can dictate it into a tape recorder. Some authors type their works, but I cannot do that. Writing is tied up with the hand, almost with a special nerve.

There are certain rules for the writer's craft. Something that gave me trouble at the beginning was depicting action, the tempo of events. Reading Robert Louis Stevenson helped me with that. Once I read a passage in *Kidnapped* in which the action is turbulent, and I discovered that Stevenson had not used a single adjective or adverb. Swords did not gleam; knives were not drawn like lightning; faces did not glow. Action was in the forefront.

Another problem is dialogue. For me it is a form of action or of narrative movement. A discursive dialogue has,

I believe, no place in a book. Every conversation must either increase our understanding of a character or propel the action forward.

I read very few critics. Friendly but ignorant reviews of my books tell me nothing. Hostile reviews can, for a brief time, irritate me. Favorable reviews by authors I treasure make me happy for a while. But if they are by people who mean nothing to me, they depress me.

When I was young harsh criticism of my work made me unhappy, but there have been some exceptions. One very negative review of my third book, an especially bad novel – *Rumour at Nightfall* – helped me greatly. It came from Frank Swinnerton, a writer who must be 100 years old now. He wrote a devastating review, but he made it clear that I was on my way.

As I view my works, I like *The Honorary Consul* more than, for example, *The Power and the Glory*. In *The Honorary Consul* the characters change; in *The Power and the Glory* the priest is the same person at the end as he was in the beginning. Among the characters I have created, my favorites are people with contradictions – divided loyalties, hopes, and desires. They are never totally for or against anything.

I do not care much for 'literature of engagement', insofar as it divides the world into good and evil. I am not contemptuous of it, but it is alien to me. And I do not believe that a writer can influence politics. We should leave politics to the politicians.

Anyone who joins a political party stops being a writer. He expresses himself as a person. That may be necessary, but it has nothing to do with literature. The rules of literature call for an author to avoid strong sympathies, abandon scruples, and keep a distance.

That is why I have never represented a political conviction. Every person has political beliefs, and religious ones, too, and they inevitably will influence his work. But I would never write a book to bring a political or religious conviction to people's attention.

In *The Comedians* there is a character, Dr Magiot, modeled after someone I met during a visit to Haiti. That person was not a Communist, but the character in the novel developed in that direction. When I began the book I did not have that in mind, but it happened because left-of-center stirrings were in the air. I do not catergorize people or events as good and evil, black and white, but as shades of gray – where we can find hope, if it exists.

Politically I am for Socialism with a human face. So far our efforts in that direction have always fallen short, but I continue to hope. It is not possible to create a New Man, so all we can hope for is a change in conditions so that the poor are less poor and the rich less rich. I am for more humanity, not for a new concept of humanity.

I have never had any sympathy for Communism, but I have had sympathy for individual Communists. My disappointment in Communism came early – in the 1930s, with the Moscow trials and the Spanish Civil War. I was against Franco, but I could not accept what happened on the Republican side.

People have said that I am a friend of Fidel Castro's. That is not true; I have spent only a few hours with him. I was impressed, because I had experienced Cuba under Batista. I still believe that in the early 1960s Castro did a lot for his country, but I do not know what I would think of him if I were to go back.

In Castro's speeches there was as much self-criticism as

enthusiasm. I heard him speak in 1966 at a union rally, and although I understand little Spanish it was overwhelming. After the serious part he joked and invited questions. His answers were quickwitted and clever. At the end there were a few hardhitting remarks about values.

It was a fascinating mixture of idealism and rhetorical power. But I know that one must always be mistrustful when a romantic idealist is in command. Romantic politics is dangerous and tends to be inhumane. I would prefer to live under Mr Gladstone.

I came to Roman Catholicism to find out what my future wife believed, not to become a Catholic. I thought it might make us happier if I understood her faith. I was twenty-three years old, and an atheist or agnostic. The arguments that were made to me convinced me that Catholicism perhaps came closer to the truth than did my lack of belief.

I felt no emotional attraction to Catholicism until I went to Mexico in 1938. There the Church was prohibited and believers had long been persecuted. I saw the Indians come down from the mountains and go into the churches, where they tried to remember the old rites. I found that very moving. But I must say, my faith is declining as I get nearer to death.

It has always angered me when people call me a 'Catholic writer'. I am a writer who is Catholic, and my conversion to Roman Catholicism gave my books an additional dimension. Before that I believed in nothing, and I think that a person who believes in nothing has a limited interest in people.

Although I am not especially interested in myself, I have written two autobiographies – *A Sort of Life*, mostly about my childhood, and *Ways of Escape*, a collection of essays and reportage about my life and work. People have asked me why my escapism has not made me choose all fictitious situations or historical themes. My answer is that you do not flee from what happens to you, but from yourself. From days that are always the same. From routine. From boredom.

In the long run, however, you cannot escape boredom. Sooner or later the terrible moment will arrive: You deliver the manuscript and go home, wake up the next morning, there is no longer a book to work on, and the shadows fall. How long will it be until you can manage to work again? That is the crucial question.

I used to have manic-depressive tendencies. I played Russian roulette in my younger years. I had a desire to play for high stakes, and the highest stake of all was life itself. The desire to flee from boredom was at work. The remarkable thing is that even fear and danger can become boring.

I remember two situations in my life in which that happened. One was during the London Blitz. In the beginning I was afraid, but after a while I wanted it to be over more because of my boredom than because it was so terrifying. The other time was at the Suez Canal, when we were under heavy fire. At first I was afraid, but then the old feelings of weariness returned: 'I have had enough of this. It was good for a rush of adrenalin; now let's be done.'

Boredom drove me to writing, and injustice has provided my themes. The injustices that I perceive do not make me angry; they improve my powers of observation. Distance is one of the prerequisites of good literature.

I am almost eighty years old. I have been nominated for the Nobel Prize many times, but I have never received it.

However, I became bored with the whole subject a long time ago.

Extract from an interview by Joachim Fest for *Frankfurter Allgemeine Zeitung* (29 September 1984)
World Press News
December 1984

A Weed among the Flowers

I little knew the turbulent time which lay ahead of me when on the telephone my friend Margaret Lane invited me, subject to the consent of the Chinese authorities, to join a little party including herself and her husband for a month's visit to China in April 1957. It was during that deceptively hopeful season of the Hundred Flowers and I accepted the idea with enthusiasm. When I visited the Chinese Embassy I gathered that all was in order.

At London airport I was a little disappointed when I found myself without my friends, who were apparently leaving some weeks later in another group. So here we were on the tarmac, four of us, all strangers to each other: myself, Lord Chorley, who was a distinguished socialist lawyer, a Mrs Smith, a Communist lady from Hampstead, and a professor whose name I didn't at first catch. His subject, Comparative Education, was something then quite unknown to me and I shall continue to call him the Professor since as it turned out I was to behave quite abominably to him. I was even to behave abominably to the innocent Lord Chorley, but Lord Chorley is dead and he will not be hurt by anything I may write.

The trouble didn't start at the first stage, which brought us to Moscow where we changed planes, nor during the forty-eight hours which followed, in those distant days before the jet, to Pekin, so perhaps the Mou-Tai which we learnt to appreciate after we arrived in China, may have contributed a little to the trouble I caused. We saw little of each other between planes in Moscow and were still a friendly party when we changed to a Chinese plane in Mongolia at Ulan Bator. It was a very rough descent to Pekin and I asked the air hostess why we didn't wear safety belts. 'Oh,' she said, 'of course we had safety belts at first, but now our pilots are so reliable.'

I think it may have been my deeply rooted preference to travelling by myself which began the trouble. To misquote Kipling, 'He travels better who travels alone.' When we arrived at Pekin airport we were entertained at once with tea, sitting on the uncomfortable classical Chinese chairs, and we were asked where we wanted to go. Here was my opportunity, I thought, to be alone, so before anybody else could speak I said: 'I want to go to your ancient capital Sian, then I want to go to Chungking, and then I want to take a boat down the Yangtse-kiang to Hangkow and then return to Pekin by train.' There was a pause for someone else to speak, but then, to my dismay, my three companions agreed with my plan. We were doomed to be together. So what?

No trouble at first. We were told that we must wait for the second party before we visited all the right tourist attractions – and how marvellous they are – the Forbidden City, the Great Wall, the Ming Tombs – nothing in the West can compare with them. A few days had to pass before we flew to Sian and my companions got involved with serious visits to factories and educational establishments and scientific institutes, but I was able to excuse myself, as I had made friends with a gigantic tricycle driver who was ready to take me shopping in the back lanes of the old city. He was probably a police informer, but what did I care? I was innocent of any espionage intentions, I was happy to be alone, buying a case of inks here and an attractive padded jacket there for a friend at home. He even spoke a bit of English which made it even more probable that he was an informer, and I liked him better for wasting his time with me. Perhaps my desire to be alone justified a certain suspicion.

We had now been allotted two guides, a young man and a girl (the girl I suppose to chaperon Mrs Smith). Both were kind, patient and charming. At some point in our travels we visited a collective farm and I questioned our male guide about contraception. 'Of course,' he told me, 'it is encouraged and widely practised.'

'In this village, for example, there would be a chemist shop?'

'Yes. Yes. In all places.'

'Where a man can buy a sheath?'

'Yes, yes, of course.'

'Would you mind going and buying one for me?'

He hesitated a long while before he found his reply. 'That I cannot do. You see I do not know your size.'

It was at Sian that I began my addiction to that dangerous drink, Mou-Tai, which has an alcoholic content of between 50° and 60°. I had been told by an expert that outside the great cities one should choose the dirtiest restaurants to eat in and this proved to be true in Sian where the Mou-Tai was also of first-class quality, which perhaps explains gaps in my memory. I only half remember in Sian watching a Pekin opera modern style where girls sold refreshments during the performance like the orange girls in Stuart London, but they sold not oranges but pickled garlic.

Perhaps already I was feeling a certain irritation with the Professor who seemed to me, I am sure quite unjustly, to speak in paragraphs even when replying to such a simple statement as: 'It looks like being a good day.'

'Yes,' he would reply, 'when I went to bed last night I noticed that there was a slight breeze coming from the west and I believe . . .'

Anyway Mou-Tai, even without the Professor, would probably have been my downfall. I bought a small bottle to take with me on the very small plane in which we flew to Chungking where the real troubles began. On the plane, as it descended, the Mou-Tai blew out its inadequate cork and the fumes filled the cabin.

The airport is on the top of the hill which dominates Chungking. A group of our hosts were waiting for us with cars to take us down into the city. We all smelt of Mou-Tai. But I was avariciously guarding what was left in the bottle, having made an even more inadequate cork with a spool of paper.

A young man ushered me into a taxi. He spoke excellent English and he began to tell me how timely our visit was, for a festival was being held in Chungking for that great English poet, Robert Burns, and the guest of honour was another great English poet who had written an ode to Lenin, Hugh Mac . . . Mac . . .

'Diarmid?' I suggested correctly.

'I am a little poet myself,' he went on, 'and I admire much the poetry of Robert . . .'

He broke off abruptly. I looked at him. The colour of his face was a strange shade of green. He gestured wildly with his hand. I realized that he was trying to indicate the bottle of Mou-Tai — such a small bottle to cause so much distress. With regret I threw it out of the window and my companion was reproachfully silent as we made the long circular drive down into Chungking. (I met MacDiarmid a few days later at the festival. I think he was a little annoyed at the presence of an English writer at a Burns festival, but when I spoke to him about the blends of Scotch which I preferred he became friendly.)

We were lodged in a very comfortable hotel architecturally based on the Temple of Heaven in Pekin and we won golden opinions, when we were asked whether we preferred European or Chinese food, by giving the right answer. Our Russian fellow guests (it was still the period of *entente*) had chosen European, and there were large crates of food from Moscow outside the back door. As a reward we were taken into the kitchen and introduced to the chef who was secretary of the local Communist Party.

The golden opinions cannot have lasted long. The Mayor of Chungking invited us to dinner at the hotel, and the chef surpassed himself. The food was Szechuan which is justly regarded as the best in China. The Mou-Tai too was excellent. The trouble which had so long been brewing between me and the Professor switched suddenly and unexpectedly and Lord Chorley was the victim.

I had been asked in London to inquire into the fate of an imprisoned writer called, I seem to remember, Mr Hu Feng. As we relaxed over the Mou-Tai at the end of our magnificent meal I asked the Mayor if he happened to know anything about the case of Mr Hu Feng. 'Oh, of course, yes,' he replied. 'Mr Hu Feng is a citizen of Chungking.'

'Then I suppose,' I went on with a certain lack of tact,

'you will be relieved when he is at last brought to trial and you will learn whether he is guilty or innocent.'

'He must be guilty,' the Mayor replied, 'or he would never have been arrested.'

There was what seemed a long moment of silence. I think all four of us were a little stunned, even Mrs Smith, by the frankness of his reply. Then Lord Chorley spoke up to ease the embarrassment and only made it worse. He even rose to his feet to emphasize the serious intent of his words.

'All of us here,' he said, 'realize the special difficulties you suffer from in the People's Republic, overrun as you are by spies from Taiwan.'

The image of the *Times* map flashed before my eyes – the huge white patch of China extending from Canton in the south to the wastes of Sinkiang and in the far north to Mongolia and off-set, like a little green ear drop, Taiwan. China 'overrun' by spies? Excited as I was no doubt by the Mou-Tai I too scrambled to my feet. I was deeply shocked, I said, to hear an English lawyer speak in such outrageous terms. Was a man considered in his eyes to be guilty without being tried? In that case I must refuse to travel any further in Lord Chorley's company. The dinner party broke up.

Next day was Easter Day. I attended a crowded Mass in the Catholic cathedral and when I returned to the hotel I felt a sense of guilt, which was increased when Lord Chorley met me and held out his hand and apologized for his conduct. The apology of course should have been mine. However, we shook hands and forgave each other and next day found us quite amicably sharing a cabin on the boat to Hangkow.

The only irritant in the party was now the Professor who continued to talk in paragraphs. He shared a cabin with our male guide, and Mrs Smith, who remained in a kind motherly way superior to our quarrels, shared a cabin with the young woman guide. She was always quite beautifully calm and a credit, I felt, to her Communist faith. Half the boat was given over to soldiers for whom patriotic music was played throughout the day. The four of us were partitioned off from them in a sort of first-class of which we were the only members.

I do not remember whether it was the first night or the second night on board, after dinner on deck and of course some glasses of that insidious Mou-Tai, that I could bear the Professor's paragraphs no longer. Our voices were raised. I forget what terms I used, they must have been severe, for the Professor threatened to throw me into the Yangtze-kiang. I expect it was Mrs Smith who calmed things down and we went to bed.

In the middle of the night I was woken by extraordinary noises, as though somebody was being strangled. They seemed to come from next door and I thought at once of the dangerous Professor. He too had drunk a lot of Mou-Tai. Was he assaulting his cabin companion, our young and friendly guide? The choking sounds continued. I looked across the cabin at Lord Chorley. He was sleeping peacefully. Something had to be done. I got up and went into the corridor and banged furiously on the Professor's door. 'Stop that fucking noise, you bugger,' I shouted. There was silence and I went back to bed.

I fell asleep, but when I woke again it was to the same strangled cries of strangulation, only this time they seemed to come from the deck above. Had our guide escaped there and been pursued by the murderous Professor? Would he, as a substitute for me, be flung into the Yangtze-kiang?

After a look at Lord Chorley, who slept peacefully on, I left the cabin to go on deck, but then I realized the true origin of the strange sounds. It was just the Chinese language. The cooks were talking to each other in the kitchen.

Next morning when we were all together Mrs Smith remarked with motherly disapproval: 'Mr Greene, why were you shouting those bad words in the passage last night?'

I explained how I had feared that the Professor was strangling our guide. I don't know what the Professor thought, but I had the feeling that then and there I gained the guide's trust and friendship.

I had quarrelled with Lord Chorley, I had quarrelled with the Professor. There was no one else left to quarrel with, for no one, I believed, could possibly quarrel with Mrs Smith. Our short stay in Hangkow was peaceful and so was our train journey back to Pekin (I appreciated the Chinese thoughtfulness in providing fly-flippers in the restaurant car), and it was a relief to me to learn in the hotel that the Margaret Lane group had arrived.

Only one thing went wrong. Both parties were expected to take tea with the Minister of Culture, but we were nearly an hour late in joining him because Miss Beryl de Zoete, the dancer and companion of Arthur Waley, had got locked in her lavatory and nobody seemed able to open the door.

Together we did the tourists' sights and then the Lane party left on the route they had chosen and we four were entertained at a farewell dinner outside Pekin. I am sure that the occasion would have gone off splendidly if I hadn't been there.

Lord Chorley made an impeccably brief speech of thanks, but then to my dismay the Professor found it necessary to make another speech which threatened to be as long as the longest of his paragraphs and which gave me time to drink another glass of Mou-Tai. The Professor began: 'I want to join my thanks to those of Lord Chorley so admirably expressed by him, and I want to add only one thing: that we have paid our Chinese hosts – not to speak of our two friendly and efficient guides – perhaps the greatest compliment in our power by behaving with such complete naturalness in their presence, and moreover I feel . . .'

I could bear no more of it. I rose in a rage to my feet. 'We have done nothing of the sort,' I said. 'We have behaved abominably and we owe our hosts a very deep apology.' The Professor sat down and the party ended, but before we left the Professor took me on one side. He was not angry. He was only hurt. 'I do wish you hadn't interrupted my speech, Greene,' he said. 'You cannot have realized the circumstances which made it so necessary. You see this afternoon Lord Chorley quarrelled with Mrs Smith.'

The Times
27 May 1985

Thoughts on Nicaragua

On my third visit to Nicaragua, in December 1985, I was impressed by the enormous enthusiasm and piety of the crowds at the Catholic feast of the Immaculate Conception and the fact that it was celebrated at all. You would not have been able to celebrate like that in Romania or Czechoslovakia or Russia.

It's true that the leadership of the Catholic Church in Nicaragua opposes the Sandinistas. Archbishop Obando certainly does. But the Church consists not only of the hierarchy. It consists of priests and people. I can't help remembering Archbishop Hélder Câmara of Brazil, who is a very popular Archbishop in the northern part of the country. He was subject to a good deal of pressure from the government and he said: 'When I give food to the poor they call me a saint. When I ask why they are poor they call me a communist.' I think that rather describes the situation.

It's also true that in December the Nicaraguan government shut down the Catholic radio but you must remember there is a war on. In England we had censorship during the war. And I saw very little suppression of civil rights or the right to dissent when I was in Nicaragua.

I'm very interested in the Sandinista government because it's not a fully Marxist government. I have no reason to believe that the two Jesuits are Marxists. Father Ernesto Cardenal, who is a very old man and a minister of culture is a Marxist. But I don't believe for a moment the two Jesuits who look after health and education and foreign affairs are Marxists. And in any case, I find it interesting to see a different Marxism. One has always hoped that Leninism might be dropped. I would describe the government as Marxist but not Leninist.

The difference is that the new constitution, which has been made with the help of the opposing parties, includes political pluralism and also a mixed economy. I think it's an interesting experiment which should be encouraged to see whether Marxism can alter its shape, as it were, can get away from the dogmatic Marxism-Leninism and become much more inclined toward social democracy. I don't know why social democracy now seems to have got a bad name. The churches are all open. You have celebrations of that like the Immaculate Conception in all the towns and villages of Nicaragua. You have separate parties, including a communist party, in opposition to the government, and you have a mixed economy guaranteed in the new constitution.

So Nicaragua interests me very much but I won't write a book about it because I haven't been there enough and I'm getting old. I don't want to spend six months or more in Nicaragua. I dealt a good deal with Central America in my time but I don't feel able to go for a long enough period to Nicaragua. And anyway, I never go to a place in search of a novel. A novel finds me.

Interview by WETA Radio, Washington
Georgetown University Library
Unpublished
1986

The Meeting in the Kremlin

Mr General Secretary I admit I came to this forum with a certain degree of scepticism. I belong to section number two – Culture.

Talk is so often an escape from action – instead of a prelude to action – and big abstract words have to flow too far and too fast. I feel incapable, really, of summarizing some of the excellent and long essays which were read in my section. It would do injustice to the authors, and my memory as an old man is getting weak.

What I have found, if I may be personal, is that I have been attacked several times by Western correspondents, whom I try to avoid, and they all say, 'Why are you here?' This is because for over a hundred years there has been a certain suspicion, an enmity even, between the Roman Catholic Church and Communism. This is not true Marxism, for Marx condemned Henry VIII for closing the monasteries. But this is a suspicion which has remained. For the last fifteen years or so, I have been spending a great deal of time in Latin America, and there, I am happy to say, that suspicion is dead and buried, except for a few individual Catholics, nearly as old as I am. It no longer exists. We are fighting – Roman Catholics are fighting – together with the Communists, and working together with the Communists.

We are fighting together against the Death Squads in El Salvador. We are fighting together against the Contras in Nicaragua. We are fighting together against General Pinochet in Chile.

There is no division in our thoughts between Catholics – Roman Catholics – and Communists. In the Sandinista Government my friend Tomàs Borge, the Marxist Minister of the Interior, works in close friendship with Father Cardinal, the Minister of Culture, the Jesuit Father Cardinal, who is in charge of health and education, with Father D'Escoto, who is Minister for Foreign Affairs. There is no longer a barrier between Roman Catholics and Communism.

The dream I have, which, I am afraid, I should have spoken to the Commission here about, but somehow it did not seem to come under the heading of 'Culture', the dream I have is that this co-operation between Roman Catholics and Communists will spread and prolong itself in Europe, West and East. And I even have a dream, Mr General Secretary, that perhaps one day before I die, I shall know that there is an Ambassador of the Soviet Union giving good advice at the Vatican.

Address given in Moscow
16 February 1987

My Worst Film

In January 1940, in my last months as a film critic of the *Spectator*, I wrote of a film which had caused me some disappointment, but a good deal of amusement in retrospect: 'Perhaps I may be forgiven for noticing a picture in which I had some hand, for I have no good word to say of it. The brilliant acting of Mr Hay Petrie as a decayed and outcast curate cannot conquer the overpowering flavour of cooked ham. Galsworthy's story, *The First and the Last*, was peculiarly unsuited for film adaptation, as its whole point lay in a double suicide (forbidden by the censor), a burned confession and an innocent man's conviction for murder (forbidden by the great public). For the rather dubious merits of the original the adaptors have substituted incredible coincidences and banal situations. Slow, wordy, unbearably sentimental, the picture reels awkwardly towards the only suicide the censorship allowed – and that, I find with some astonishment, has been cut out. I wish I could tell the extraordinary story that lies behind this shelved and resurrected picture, a story involving a theme song, and a bottle of whiskey, and camels in Wales . . . Meanwhile, let one guilty man, at any rate, stand in the dock, swearing never, never to do it again . . .'

I'm afraid, when the war was over, I broke my oath by

writing two screenplays, *The Fallen Idol* and *The Third Man,* which were made, like the deplorable *21 Days,* for my friend Alexander Korda.

The mysterious mention of camels, whiskey and a theme song in my criticism puzzled some readers. Now when most of the protagonists are dead, the reference can be safely explained – as well as the incident of the coffee sugar which I might have included.

The director of *21 Days* was Basil Dean, not one of the easiest men for whom to work; he was inclined like Preminger to bully his actors, and he was a stickler over trifles. I worked on the script with a man older and more experienced than myself and I remember vividly one unhappy day during the shooting at Denham Studios. I had added to Galsworthy's short story a scene, during the course of the innocent man's trial, in which the Lord Chief Justice gave a bachelor dinner. All seemed to be going well (there had been two or three takes – crane shots from above the round dinner table) when Dean let out a cry of anguish. The dinner had reached the coffee stage and Dean pointed with horror at the sugar bowl. 'That's not coffee sugar,' he cried. No coffee sugar was available at the Denham Film Studios, so a car had to be sent to London to Fortnum's and the shooting of the film was suspended at I don't know what cost until it returned with the coffee sugar.

This scene may have been an unfortunate side-effect caused by the loss of our assistant producer who had suddenly been removed by Korda. Korda needed him to accompany a train of camels to Wales where a far better film was about to be shot based on one of Kipling's stories. So much for the camels.

There remains to be explained the business of the whiskey bottle and the theme song.

It was the last night of writing. My collaborator and I were engaged against time in finishing the script. Basil Dean before going out to dinner had made us promise to deliver it next morning to Lajos Biro, Korda's fellow Hungarian, for final approval. We had no time to eat, but at least we had a bottle of whiskey. There was only one sequence left to write – we had laid it in the fun-fair at Southend where Laurence Olivier, tormented in his conscience, for it was he and not the man on trial who was guilty of murder, tries to forget things with Vivien Leigh on a switchback. Unfortunately their real-life love affair at that time had reached a climax and in spite of Basil Dean's efforts their carefree laughter on the screen was a little out of place.

It was that scene we were finishing and also the whiskey bottle. I said, 'At this point we ought to have a theme song.' (I was just as carefree as Olivier but with less excuse – not love of a beautiful woman but the whiskey bottle.) My friend agreed, and we wrote alternate lines of the theme song, which I cannot remember now. Off the script went to Lajos Biro and we to bed. I must admit that the next day we were a little surprised to learn that our script had been approved without comment or criticism.

The weeks passed and Basil Dean asked me to accompany him and his camera man to Southend to plan the shooting. We took a river-boat from Westminster, travelling second-class because Dean said he wanted to see how 'the other half' lived. We then began to walk around the fun-fair. Suddenly the moment which I had long feared arrived. Dean said, 'I didn't quite understand, Graham, about that song . . .' but before he could finish or I could reply the camera man called to him from beside the switchback, 'Mr Dean, please come over here. I think I've found an angle . . .' and when Dean returned he had forgotten all about the song.

But when I saw the film on the screen I was not surprised, though a little disappointed, that the song had disappeared. I have always wondered whether before Dean abandoned it they had reached the point of setting it to music.

Unpublished
March 1987

A Constant Question Mark

While I was reading with great interest Brian Inglis's new book *The Unknown Guest* and his account of what he calls 'the mystery of intuition' my own experiences came to mind.

I can well believe in telepathy for it has been part of my life since childhood. My mother had the gift of picking up thoughts from my elder sister. The two used to play it as a game at parties and I can still see no way in which they could have cheated.

My mother would leave the room and the guests would decide between them with no intervention from my sister some action for my mother to perform when she was summoned back into the room. My mother would gaze closely for a moment at my sister and then would make the action we had chosen, moving a cushion or a chair perhaps or taking the lid off a box. I never saw her fail.

My own first experience of what could be a kind of telepathy I would have put down to mere coincidence if it had not been repeated twice under roughly the same circumstances, each involving a tragedy at sea and a heavy loss of life. The first occasion was during an Easter seaside holiday at Littlehampton when I was seven years old. I dreamt of a shipwreck and I can still see clearly one image of the dream. A man is scrambling up the staircase of a ship and a great wave is coming down to swamp him. Next morning we heard the news of the *Titanic* sunk that night.

Of the second dream of a wreck about ten years later I can recall no details and I have long lost the dream diary which I was keeping at the time during a course of psycho-analysis in London. Perhaps writing down the dream cancelled the memory of it. Again my dream coincided with a real wreck, this time in the Irish Sea when I seem to remember that a whole orchestra lost their lives.

Always the sea, always lives lost. But the third occasion was not a dream. I was in my flat in Antibes one morning some six or seven years ago with nothing to worry me when around breakfast time I was overcome by a deep depression, and an anxiety agonizing in its acuteness. I have a witness, for a friend came to lunch with me and I told her what I feared, that something terrible had happened to one of my family. To distract me she turned on the radio for the one o'clock news. A plane coming from Corsica had crashed that morning into the sea off Cap d'Antibes a few miles away and there were no survivors. On board was General Cogny whom I had known and liked in Vietnam.

Why is it always deaths at sea that concern me? I have no particular fear of the sea, whether I am in a boat or a plane, and my two dreams were not nightmares, just records of an experience. Brian Inglis writes of telepathic cases which 'strongly suggest that there is a mechanism by which alarm can be transmitted and picked up by somebody "tuned in". There are plenty of examples of effective action being taken as a result. In a few cases, it is as if a distress signal had been directed successfully at the person who is best placed to come to the rescue.'

But why should a child be tuned into the *Titanic* or a boy to a sinking ship in the Irish Sea, and why should General Cogny send a signal of distress to a writer he had probably long forgotten? It was I who had good reason to remember him, for he had arranged for me, a man General de Lattre had accused of being a spy, to spend a day and a night in the besieged camp at Dien Bien Phu.

Here is a postscript of a very different kind which might well come under the same heading, 'the mystery of intuition'. In 1984 I wished to find an epigraph for my book *Getting to Know the General*. My favourite poet Browning failed me and unwillingly I turned to Tennyson and opened a volume of his collected poems at random. Under my eyes was a long poem *Audley Court* which I had never read and had no intention of reading now, yet my eye went straight to two lines which were exactly what I needed.

> '*I go, but I return: I would I were*
> *The pilot of the darkness and the dream.*'

Georgetown University Library
Unpublished
1987

Out of the Dustbin

1

All novelists, I suppose, have a box of rejected ideas. As the years pass I sometimes in an idle moment turn over the bits and pieces like an old photograph album before throwing them into the dustbin. Here are three examples. In the first one to my surprise I find a name which I have been using in quite another story. The name is Quigly — I first heard it ten years ago in Panama. It cast a mysterious spell and it will appear in my next novel if the book is ever finished.

The following fragment is obviously meant to be the start of a novel not a short story, for it is headed Part 1 Chapter 1, and this ghostly Quigly certainly bears no resemblance to the Quigly I am dealing with now. On whom was he based? Could it possibly have been . . .?

Charles Painter was not in the true sense of the word a diarist, but during certain periods of his life when he was suffering from writers' block, he would, for want of anything better, begin to record the events of each day. The entries were never intended for publication. They were like the exercises of an athlete or a ballet dancer — they kept the muscles of the mind in train. No one saw them except himself – not even his wife, from whom for thirty years he could claim to have had no important secret. These were not secrets; they were simply a remedy against despair – they encouraged him to think that one day an idea might come to him and he would begin to write again. On 10 December he noted: 'Saw Quigly today in Hatchards. He asked me when he could expect my next book. He meant it kindly I think. On the fiction counter there was a pile of his last novel. No cause for him to be jealous of me. So I am sure he meant it kindly. I said "God knows." There wasn't anything else to say. I walked out of the shop – I wish I had found a few more words, but somehow I've never really cared for Quigly nor his books, though there must surely be something good in them because my wife likes them. Perhaps better than my own. Perhaps she's right.'

That day Charles Painter twisted his ankle on the way up the stairs to his flat in Kensington. He said jokingly to his wife, 'I think Quigly pushed me.'

'What do you mean?'

'Perhaps the spirit of Quigly.'

'I thought you were friends.'

'Yes. In a way. I suppose so.'

'What was he doing on the stairs?'

'It was a joke, darling. I said his spirit . . .'

'He's a very religious man.'

'So you believe, darling, I know.'

'I saw him called Holy Quigly in a newspaper.'

'Not once, darling, many times, and it was Holy Quig. That was a joke too.'

'Holiness is not something to joke about.'

Veronica had a habit of making statements too true to be contradicted. It made conversation difficult.

'He would never push you on the stairs.'
'No, I am sure he wouldn't.'

2

The next fragment may be a novel or a short story, I think a novel. The title is

A Position in Life

For the first time I was really satisfied with my position in life when I became Public Relations Officer for one of the largest crematoriums in Europe, if not in the world. I was only forty – I had twenty years of service to the community ahead of me, and my position was becoming noticeably more important with every year. There was a time when I had represented Ford cars, but it was always possible that Ford cars might one day go out of business – there are fashions in cars, there are take-overs and always a threat of strikes.

The great thing about a crematorium company is that people go on dying, there is little danger from strikes, and as land becomes more and more valuable with the growth of population, graveyards are in danger of disappearing. As matters stand a grave is sometimes to be rented only for a period of years. Afterwards the bones are disposed of and a new occupant takes over the site, and the cost of the site rises steeply with the price of land, while the cost of cremation is relatively stable. Quite a small increase will cover a rise in the cost of fuel, and I knew that my company was actively researching to find an alternative to the present fuel. They believed it would be possible in a few years to destroy a corpse more completely and economically with acids and relieve the relatives of the embarrassment of what to do with the ashes. A lot of valuable building land is still wasted by making Gardens of Repose for urns which the relatives are unwilling to take home with them.

It was an ideal situation, except that I was sometimes nagged by the thought how sooner or later cremation might well become compulsory and a government service, so that a Public Relations Officer would have no more opportunity for personal initiatives than a PRO in the post office.

3

The next fragment was obviously intended to begin a short story. It is called

Five Little Girls

I remember nothing about this idea except that by the end of the flight all five were noisily drunk. It was intended as a comedy, not a story of sexual perversion.

The five little girls sat in a row at the back of the Air France plane. They each wore a plastic pouch round the neck containing a card with name and address. They were very well behaved. One was serious-minded and turned over a large pack of picture postcards, pictures of the Alps and the castle of Chillon and cows in a meadow and the Château Gruyère and the bears in the zoo at Berne and kindred Swiss subjects. The flight was a short one – forty minutes from Geneva to Nice.

'They'll be no trouble at all,' the air hostess said to the steward. This was a good thing because the plane was full and lunch had to be served and cleared very quickly. Two little girls by the window looked at the clouds, one in the middle seat was busy with her cards, two just sat and stared. The man who occupied one of the gangway seats said to the little girl beside him, 'What is your name?', and she giggled, but made no reply. She had been taught not to speak to strangers.

The Caravelle climbed above the Alps into the sunlight and the steward and the hostess began briskly to serve lunch. On each platter was a smoked salmon sandwich, a cheese sandwich, some salad with mayonnaise, a tinned peach on a piece of pastry, Evian water in a plastic container closed with plastic and sitting in another plastic container, and a quarter of a bottle of red wine. There was no time to discriminate among passengers: the bottles of wine lay unopened on the little girls' trays. They had some difficulty in opening the water.

The man in the gangway seat was obviously fond of children and explained how it was done to his two neighbours and the stewardess who happened to be passing gave him a grateful smile. He said to the little girl beside him, 'Wouldn't you prefer grape juice?'

'Is there grape juice?'

He poured himself a glass from the bottle which described itself on the label as Bordeaux. 'This is grape juice,' he said and he showed her how to open the bottle on her tray.

Foreign Press News
1988

Judith Adamson has written several books, including *Graham Greene and Cinema*, *The Dangerous Edge*, a political biography of Graham Greene, *Charlotte Haldane*, a biography of JBS Haldane's first wife, and *Max Reinhardt: A Life in Publishing*. She edited and introduced *Love Letters*, the thirty year correspondance between Leonard Woolf and Trekkie Ritchies Parsons. She lives in Montreal.

THE HISTORY OF VINTAGE

The famous American publisher Alfred A. Knopf (1892–1984) founded Vintage Books in the United States in 1954 as a paperback home for the authors published by his company. Vintage was launched in the United Kingdom in 1990 and works independently from the American imprint although both are part of the international publishing group, Random House.

Vintage in the United Kingdom was initially created to publish paperback editions of books acquired by the prestigious hardback imprints in the Random House Group such as Jonathan Cape, Chatto & Windus, Hutchinson and later William Heinemann, Secker & Warburg and The Harvill Press. There are many Booker and Nobel Prize-winning authors on the Vintage list and the imprint publishes a huge variety of fiction and non-fiction. Over the years Vintage has expanded and the list now includes both great authors of the past – who are published under the Vintage Classics imprint – as well as many of the most influential authors of the present.

For a full list of the books Vintage publishes, please visit our website
www.vintage-books.co.uk

For book details and other information about the classic authors we publish, please visit the Vintage Classics website
www.vintage-classics.info

www.vintage-classics.info